WALKING THE NILE

WALKING THE NILE

LEVISON WOOD

SIMON & SCHUSTER

London · New York · Sydney · Toronto · New Delhi

A CBS COMPANY

First published in Great Britain by Simon & Schuster UK Ltd, 2014
A CBS COMPANY

1 3 5 7 9 10 8 6 4 2

Simon & Schuster UK Ltd
1st Floor
222 Gray's Inn Road
London WC1X 8HB

www.simonandschuster.co.uk

Simon & Schuster Australia, Sydney
Simon & Schuster India, New Delhi

A CIP catalogue record for this book
is available from the British Library

ISBN: 978-1-47115-104-0
ISBN: 978-1-47113-564-4 (Trade Paperback)
ISBN: 978-1-47113-566-8 (ebook)

Typeset in the UK by M Rules
Printed and bound by CPI Group (UK) Ltd, Croydon, CR0 4YY

For the people of the Nile.

In memory of Matthew Power.

CONTENTS

BOR, SOUTH SUDAN

April 2014

The moment we entered the compound, I knew things were bad. The South Sudan Hotel had been opened in the run-up to independence in 2011, promoted widely as a safe place for foreign dignitaries to stay while visiting Bor, but as we approached I saw the hotel minibus sitting gutted on the edge of the road, riddled with bullet holes.

Through the gates, the scene was no different. The reception hall had been devastated. Fire had charred the walls and the desks had been trashed. We waited in the ravaged compound for some time before the manager appeared from one of the missing doorways and welcomed us.

'What happened here?'

The manager smiled. 'Come,' he said, 'we still have rooms.'

He led us across the hotel forecourt. Along the verandas most of the doors had been kicked in, the rooms torn apart. The floor was dusted with broken glass from the smashed lights overhead. When we finally reached our rooms, the metal door hanging off its hinges and a footprint lay where the handle used to be. 'Fifty dollars,' the manager began. I looked inside the obliterated room. No water, no electricity, but it was still the best option we had. 'We'll take it,' I said.

Before the manager left, he tried to explain. The 'small protest' we had heard about was actually a large-scale demonstration by the Dinka, the semi-pastoral people who make up almost a fifth of South Sudan's population, against the Nuer, another of South Sudan's ethnic groups. The Nuer and Dinka have a long and complicated history of attack and counter-attack along this part of the Nile. Today, the Nuer had barricaded themselves into a United Nations compound, but the Dinka had stormed the building and opened fire. In the ensuing chaos, forty-eight Nuer were killed, while seven Dinka lay dead. Now, the whole of Bor sat under a stalemate of sorts, waiting for the next eruption. All foreigners, the manager explained as he walked away, were valid targets as far as the Dinka were concerned.

There was no food at the hotel, so after some time we ventured back into the town centre – fully aware of the risk, with real trepidation. Soldiers, policemen and hundreds of armed civilians still flocked the city's filthy streets. The market place stood empty – burnt to the ground by rebels in January – and all of the banks had been looted. An ATM machine hung like an eyeball out of its socket on an outside wall. Inside, credit cards, cheque books and filed accounts were strewn across the floor. Rebels and government soldiers alike had used the bank's date stamps to plaster the walls with evidence of their pillage. The pillars around us were covered in graffiti. 'Fuck you Nuer!' cried one, and 'Dinkas Defeated!' claimed another. Bor, it seemed, had changed hands three or four times since the hostilities began only a few months ago. What was happening today was just another episode in the ongoing fight.

We ate at a small Ethiopian restaurant but we didn't stay long.

The looks we got from fellow diners – all armed to the teeth – were enough to drive us back to the relative safety of the hotel.

In a hotel without power, night seemed to come suddenly. After dark, I lay staring at the ceiling, wondering what tomorrow had in store. I had crossed the border into South Sudan from Uganda only one month previously. In that time, I'd come two-hundred-and-forty miles north through a country described by the UN as the most fragile in the world – refugees on the roads, armed gangs roving and raping through the countryside, a government on the verge of collapse – but there were still four hundred miles to go. From here on, the hostilities were only going to grow fiercer – and, as if that wasn't enough, between here and the border lay the vast sprawl of the Sudd, the biggest swampland in the world. It had been the Sudd that stopped the Romans venturing further south in their conquest of Africa, the Sudd that held back Livingstone and Speke and the other Victorian explorers whose journeys I had hoped to emulate in their exploration of the Nile. For a second, in the hotel room, the lights flickered on and then off again, and I was left wondering: was it worth it?

In that moment, the night came alive. Gunshots punctured the silence, machine-gun fire rattling perilously close to the hotel. I sat up. Through the shuttered windows, I saw the darkness illuminated in flashes of brilliant red, tracers lighting up the skies above Bor.

I scrambled out of bed, stumbling onto the veranda. In the room alongside me, Siraje, my Ugandan porter, was already awake. As the thud of heavy weapons played in bursts outside the hotel, we hurried to pack our rucksacks. 'Where to?' Siraje asked. Outside the room, I looked across the courtyard. Soldiers and armed civilians were already gathering among the shadows. Who were they?

There was only one way to go. 'Up,' I said, and started to run.

Across the courtyard, close to the river's edge, a half-finished five-storey building stood as a reminder of better times. We burst through the shattered door and swept away the hanging wires that blocked the stairwell. Running up the concrete stairs, we didn't stop until reaching the open rooftop. If the hotel was to be stormed again, I judged this would be the safest place.

From here, we could see the street fight being played out in snatches of light, machine-gun fire in the thoroughfares, fires erupting in buildings a few streets away. The night was warm, and the sounds and smells put me in mind of my tour in Afghanistan, which seemed such a long time ago.

The fire-fight lasted for forty-five minutes, finally slowing down to a succession of sporadic bursts. As the worst abated, I looked to the north. All that I could see, by the light of the waning moon reflected in the shimmering waters of the Nile, were the rooftops of Bor, stretching on into an indistinguishable horizon. But I knew what was waiting for me up there. Beyond the boundaries of the town, the marshes seemed to go on forever. Miles away to the north, the key towns of Bentiu, Malakal and Renk were being contested by rebels. Escaping villagers were following the river south, searching for sanctuary in hastily erected camps – and, always, there was the spectre of the impenetrable Sudd.

In that moment, it seemed I had a decision to make. Four hundred miles of war-torn swampland lay ahead of me on my journey, but the question was – was this stretch of the Nile going to deny me, as it had so many others?

BEGINNING AT THE END: THE SOURCE OF THE NILE

December 2013

I don't know where the idea to walk the entire length of the Nile came from. It was a question I'd been asked a hundred times or more, by well-meaning family, friends, and the occasional journalist, in the weeks before I set out on the expedition. I'd given each of them a different answer – but all of them were true. When George Mallory was asked by a reporter from the *New York Times* why he wanted to climb Mt Everest, he retorted with perhaps the three most famous words in mountaineering history: 'Because it's there.' In the end, I could think of no better way to express the singular urge that drove me to Africa. I wanted to follow in a great tradition, to achieve something unusual and inspire in others the thirst to do the same. Much of my motivation was selfish, of course – to go on the greatest adventure of my life, to see what people can only dream about and test myself to the limits. But, ultimately, it came down to one thing. The Nile was there, and I wanted to walk it.

I sat in a truck, rising high through the Rwandan hills. Even now, that same question was buzzing in my ear. The man sitting beside me was staring out of the window, looking smart in a green polo shirt, his hair closely cropped. He smiled as the banana plantations passed us by.

I liked Boston because he hadn't asked why. Boston was different; he instinctively knew that those who have to ask 'why' would never understand. Ndoole Boston, descendant of Ngumbirwa, King of the Nyanga, was to be my guide for the first leg of this journey, and he was more interested in the practicalities of our mission.

'How far is it?' he said, as the green expanse of the Nyungwe rainforest came into view.

'Four thousand miles.'

Four thousand, two hundred and fifty miles, to be precise – and that didn't even include the diversions we were bound to have to make in trying to cross the river's most inhospitable domains.

We had driven all day yesterday and camped in these rain-drenched hills, but this morning the wait was almost at an end. Mist seeped through the forest as we rose, but occasionally we'd burst through one of the reefs and I could see the forest dropping steeply away beneath us. It was, I knew, almost time.

At last, the car came to a halt on the very edge of the Nyungwe Forest. It was known locally as the 'buffer zone', an expanse of planted pines and eucalyptus, trees alien to Africa but introduced in colonial times to meet the growing need for firewood. Stepping out of the truck, I got to thinking how very English it all looked, like a tiny piece of Staffordshire plucked up and planted on top of the indigenous tropical forest. Under other circumstances, it might have been disappointing – but not for me, not today.

Our local guide was waiting for us under the trees. Amani was a representative of the National Tourist Board of Rwanda, a Tutsi by ancestry. There was no mistaking him against the backdrop of dense foliage: he was wearing a fluorescent red plastic raincoat and carried a tattered child's rucksack over his shoulder. No sooner had I set foot outside the truck than he was shaking my hand earnestly. 'Come, it's this way!' he declared, taking off into the bushes before the introductions were even concluded.

Setting off to follow, Boston muttered into my ear, 'Don't trust this man. He is a government agent.' I looked sidelong at him; Boston was deadly serious – but, up ahead, Amani was waving us on with the vigour of a young man who genuinely loved his job.

'Government tourist agent,' I said, and started to follow.

Amani was a government guide by profession but, as we entered the forest, I got to thinking he was probably far more at home taking corpulent Russian businessmen around the night spots of Kigali than he was hacking through the jungle. Before long, it seemed he had lost his bearings, and I doubted he could find his way back to the trail where we had begun. Still, his efforts at pretending he knew where the river flowed were second to none and soon, whether by accident or design, we had joined a path that screamed out 'tourist trail'. I could tell this path was well-trodden because its edges were crisp and clear, the encroaching foliage beaten back. Spanking new signs and litter bins reinforced my impression that this was as tame as England's own woodlands.

As we went, Amani gave us a spiel I knew must have been given to a thousand other visitors. 'Most people think the source of the Nile is in Uganda at Lake Victoria,' he began, 'but most people are wrong. What you're about to see is the true source of the river – it's furthest tributary.'

Once again, Boston wasn't impressed. I heard him tut beside me. Boston, it seemed, had his own beliefs about where the true source of the Nile was, but people have been fighting over the origins of this magnificent river since before recorded history began, and perhaps this was not the right moment to try to settle it once and for all.

'Here,' said Amani, 'I hope you are not disappointed . . .'

At Amani's side, we stopped. Despite the tourist trail, the tiny spring below us was every bit as insignificant and natural as I had hoped. A hole in the rock sprouted a trickle of water so pure it glistened in the mist. Dropping to my knees, I took an army-issue metal mug from my rucksack and dipped it into the water. It tasted cold and sweet, and would live forever afterwards on the tip of my tongue.

'Not disappointed at all,' I said, and offered the mug to Boston.

This was the Nile. More than four thousand miles to the north, the waters trickling through my fingers would meet the spectacular coast of the Mediterranean Sea. I was going to follow them, walking every step of the way.

What we were standing beside was only one of many contenders for the true source of the river. What we think of as the Nile is actually the confluence of two great rivers, the Blue Nile, whose waters rise in the highlands of Ethiopia, and the longer White Nile, whose tributaries stretch further south, through Uganda, past Lake Victoria and Tanzania, until they turn into the faint trickle whose waters I was now tasting. Even this is contested. White Nile purists are fervent in their belief that the Nile only truly begins at Jinja on the northernmost shore of Lake Victoria, but those with a less conservative approach argue that the river actually flows into Lake Victoria from the west. Here it has no name, but a few miles downstream it is known as the Mbirurumbe, and after that the Nyaborongo, and after that the Kagera; as wide as the Nile and longer than the Thames, the Kagera itself has tributaries originating in both Rwanda and Burundi. It was the longest of these, by a scant thirty miles, that Amani was showing us now.

The Nile has captured the imagination of mankind since the days of the Pharaohs, and the mystery of its source is one that held explorers at bay for millennia. The location of this little spring was a question that confounded Alexander the Great. It was a secret denied to the Roman Emperor Nero despite his expeditions upriver from the delta far to the north. In Rome, in 1651, a public fountain – the Fountain of the Four Rivers – was erected to depict the four major rivers of the known world, and the Nile was portrayed by a god with a cowled head, symbolising the fact that nobody could ever know from where the waters came. For a fascinating period in the middle of the 19th century, the urge to discover this tiny water source became a kind of grail quest for a particularly dedicated, and often idiosyncratic, group of British explorers. Piece by piece, these reckless, intrepid individuals had forced the mighty Nile to give up its secrets – by guile, pig-headedness and sheer power of will. Some of those explorers gave their lives to accomplishing this quest – others gave their legs, or their sanity itself – and in doing so, opened the world up to great swathes of the African interior.

Those Victorian explorers – David Livingstone, John Hanning Speke, Henry Morton Stanley, Samuel Baker and countless others – had lived long in my imagination, and it was faintly surreal to be standing here, having reached the apex of their quest so easily, with a big wooden sign that announced, in bold yellow letters, 'THIS IS THE FURTHEST SOURCE OF THE NILE' in the corner of my vision. My quest, however, lay in the opposite direction. The idea of recreating this fantastic voyage of discovery in reverse had first come to me in the winter of 2011, and it had taken almost two years to reach this point. For as long as I can remember, I had wanted to embark on an epic journey, one that harked back to the great expeditions of times past, a journey that would test me both physically and mentally in a way that no other could. I had done plenty of expeditions before, of course, and more or less devoted my life to travel and exploring the world. At the age of 21, I had hitch-hiked home from Cairo by way of a very troubled Middle East, including a reckless perambulation through Iraq just after the fall of Baghdad in 2003. A year later, I continued my roadside-thumbing career with a four-month voyage overland to India, following the fabled Silk Road. Again, I took the road less travelled, by heading through the middle of an insurgent-infested Afghanistan and fanatical Iran. It wasn't the thrill of warzones that drew me to these hostile environments; rather, I hungered to discover the people in these places, the way humanity shines in the most troubled places of the Earth. The Nile itself had first cast its spell over me in 2010 when, as part of a charitable expedition, I had driven overland from London to Malawi to deliver ambulances to communities in need. Now, three years on, I had given in to its irresistible spell. I wanted to see the places Livingstone, Speke, Stanley and the rest had discovered as they cut their path into the heart of this most challenging continent. And, as in my expeditions in the past, I wanted to learn more about the people who lived along this mighty river, people whose lives were dictated by its ebb and flow. In a continent in which borders are always in flux, the Nile is a constant. I wanted to see how it shaped lives from the ground, day by day and mile by mile.

'So,' said Amani. 'Now you begin, no?'

I stood and put the metal mug back in my rucksack. 'Let's start walking.'

The spring that fed into the puddle that, in turn, disappeared under the dense foliage soon faded into memory. As the day wore on, the excitement of having left the source of the Nile turned into something new: the promise of movement itself. Just as the Nile begins with a tiny trickle of water, this year-long voyage was beginning with a few tiny steps. No more planes, buses or Land Cruisers; no more anticipation and worry; now, only forward motion. On foot.

In the space of a few hundred metres, the forest seemed to alter immeasurably. Coming down the forested escarpment, we left behind the pines and eucalyptus. As we walked, the jungle grew more tropical, thick with oversized ferns and vines that wrapped around teak and mahogany giants.

Amani had nominated himself our leader, though as we progressed I could tell that my first impression of him hadn't been far off the mark. The difficulty in following a river from a forest source is that it keeps going underground, or gets hidden by the vegetation, ferns and thorn bushes that fill the jungle floor. Above us the canopy was so thick that it was almost impossible to see the sky, and it seemed that we were walking in a perpetual twilight. On occasion, I could hear where the water trickled. It was this tiny trickle that would become the greatest river on Earth, the life's blood of civilisations that had risen and fallen since time immemorial. This elusive trickle gave life to six nations before it met the sea, but today it proved impossible to follow.

It soon became evident that Amani was not practised at blazing a trail. His occasional entreaties – 'This way!' 'Here is the river!' – soon proved themselves little better than wishful thinking.

At my side, Boston silently shook his head. 'All he does is go east,' he muttered. 'He thinks, if we get out of the forest, he will see the river then. These Rwandans, they're not jungle people like the Congolese.'

I had known Boston for less than a week, though he came highly recommended by two friends, Tom Bodkin and Pete Meredith, who had availed themselves of his services in the past. Pete in particular had spoken highly of Boston's skills; Boston had looked after the logistics of one of Pete's own expeditions, to make a film about kayaking the Nile's biggest rapids, a feat never before attempted. What they hadn't told me was that Boston wasn't really a guide at all. In fact, Boston had never had any formal training in anything, and I was quickly beginning to understand that he was a jack-of-all-trades wheeler-dealer. Whatever you wanted Boston to be, that was him.

He was also the most outspoken man I had met in all my travels, and it was evident he was not going to pull any punches where Amani was concerned.

Ndoole Boston had grown up in eastern Congo, at a time when that country had been rife with fighting and internal conflict. Boston was proud to come from a royal bloodline. 'My great-grandfather ruled a tribe in the mountains west of Lake Albert,' he had told me, before adding that, 'He ate men. It was normal then. He was the king, and would eat whoever he wanted – men, women, enemies. It was usually enemies – but, if he had a lazy servant, he'd eat him too.' Across the generations, though, savage cannibalism had given way to religion and Boston's paternal grandfather, Mwalimu Ndoole Nyanuba, had been a Pentecostal pastor with his own church in rural Machumbi. Boston's own father had rejected family tradition again, becoming first a professor of geography who passed his disgust for religion onto his son, and later an MP under Zaïre's – later, the Democratic Republic of Congo's – Mbutu regime. In 1993, as Boston told me, tragedy struck, when his father died under mysterious circumstances. 'Poison,' Boston declared as we followed Amani aimlessly through the forest. 'He was probably murdered, although I'll never know. That was the year I became a soldier.'

After Boston's father died, Boston became the head of his family. When he was only seventeen years of age, his mother encouraged him to take up arms and head out to fight the roving gangs that plagued eastern Congo and protect their family ranch. In no time at all, Boston had become head of his own militia, commanding some 300 troops, and it was with these men that he joined the then-rebel forces led by the future president, Laurent-Désiré Kabila, in 1996. Boston's unit were instrumental in taking the cities of Kisangani and Lubumbashi from government forces, and bringing about the end of the Mbutu reign.

In 2005, eight years before we met, Boston had fled the Congo. His flight followed months of targeted assassinations of former soldiers and activists like himself, and escalating violence against his family. His 'home' was now in Kampala, the capital of Uganda. Boston would accompany me on my journey that far, but there we would part ways, I on my journey ever north, Boston back to the comforts of his wife Lily and their three children.

Around us, the jungle was becoming denser, and the trickle of water seemed to be ebbing further away. With it impossible to keep the river – if this could truly be called a river – in sight, the only really effective method was to look around at the mean height of the trees and estimate which way was downhill. By following invisible contours, I hoped we would stay abreast of the water. The theory seemed to work, albeit slowly, but by the time we stopped to refuel with lunch we'd covered only five hundred metres in a straight line, despite our GPS having logged a distance of 4km walked. We hadn't completed our first day of this journey, and already I had a sign that I was actually going to walk much further than the 4,250 miles I'd planned.

'We need to cover more ground,' said Boston, with an ironic smile pointedly directed at Amani. 'It is not even hard going! It reminds me of my time in the Congo, but there it is much thicker.'

There was an element of malice in Boston's voice, and I could tell that he was trying to provoke Amani in some way. Boston, the proud fighter, didn't want to cede any authority to this skinny Tutsi who, he believed, was leading us in circles. 'You know, Lev,' he went on, 'we Congolese are jungle people. We know the forests. Rwandans, well, they just look after cows. They know nothing of trees. Do you know what they call snakes in DRC?'

I hadn't a clue.

'Go into any restaurant in Kinshasa and you can ask for two types of fish. Water fish and tree fish.'

'What's a tree fish?' This sounded like the beginning of some terrible joke.

'It is a snake. Everything is related to the trees in the Congo. Lev, I believe I should lead from now on.'

As I tried to pick my way through the logic of this particular argument, Boston unsheathed the machete I had bought for him and encouraged us to take off. It was a sturdy army-issue panga with a comfortable wooden handle, not like the flimsy machetes that are for sale all over the African bazaars. Gripping it with an iron fist, he pushed past Amani and started cutting blindly at vines and branches. I gave Amani what I hoped was a conciliatory smile and, together, we followed.

Boston's path didn't seem any better than Amani's – but his panga was making short work of the dense vegetation, and our progress was faster. With Boston blazing the trail, too, we were able to stay closer to the occasional gurgle of water that marked the Nile's first passage. In places the water didn't seem to flow at all, and the only indication that we were following the mighty Nile was the soft earth underfoot. Sometimes this bog seemed to suddenly grow deeper and more expansive, so that we had no choice but to pick a way across.

Thick and glutinous beneath the feet, it had the same effect as quicksand, and on more than one occasion I plunged into the quagmire up to my waist. As I wriggled, shouting profanities and grappling for Amani to help me, Boston seemed to float above the filth, keeping his boots as clean as the moment they came out of the box. He really was a jungle man.

As Amani hoisted me from the quagmire for the second time, I fixed my gaze on those boots. A nice pair of desert Altbergs, they were the best money can buy. I knew it – because I'd bought them for him. He looked back at me from the undergrowth ahead, beaming. He was proud of those boots, determined not to get wet feet.

With Boston hacking away, I could better take in the wonders of the Nyungwe Forest. Amani might have been a poor bushwhacker, but he was good at one thing: it was Amani who first saw the colobus monkeys leaping through the trees above us like little black ghosts. By mid-afternoon, we had dropped a couple of hundred metres in altitude, following the natural contours of the valley. In a short distance, the stream had grown from a pure, clean trickle to a bog and then, as it filtered through layers of vegetation, it finally emerged as a fully-fledged little river. At the moment it was hardly a foot's length across, but it was clean again and definitely flowing. Trailing my fingers in the stream, it felt as if the water – even more than me – wanted to be rid of its forested womb and head out into the open sunshine beyond.

The water and I both got our wish when, in the late afternoon, we emerged from the Nyungwe. The forest ended suddenly, snatching us from the close darkness under the canopy to the bright sunshine of fields and mountains. It had been silent in the forest, save for the gurgling of the river and the occasional sniping of Boston and Amani, but now there were new sounds: the lowing of cows.

After leaving the sweaty humidity of the forest, it was a relief to be welcomed by the sight of this open plain. From the trees the stream trickled down, through small waterfalls, and seemed to be revelling in its first touch of daylight. With Boston's panga back in its sheath, our feet followed the water. The first sign of life was a single large cow, wading in the long grass at the bottom of a hill. On the hillside were the first signs of human habitation. Neatly furrowed fields and a few banana trees stood before the distinctive shape of a track leading south. At the bottom of the track, still clinging to the stream, several small huts hid behind a stand of tall brown-and-white eucalyptus trees.

It dawned on me that what I was looking at was the first village that depended on the Nile.

'Come on,' said Amani, with renewed vigour. 'These are Batwa. Let's speak to them before they run away.'

Amani had already set off when I realised who he was speaking about. Outside the huts were the outlines of four diminutive people.

'Pygmies,' said Boston as he watched Amani stride ahead, shaking his head in what I thought was reproach. 'Do not believe what this man tells you. He is a government agent.'

'What's that got to do with it?'

'The Twa were in this country long before Hutu and Tutsi,' Boston told me. 'Amani will not tell you that.'

I followed Amani to the edge of the village, where he was already in conversation with the Batwa men outside their huts. Only one of them appeared particularly small, and none of them looked concerned at our approach. They simply sat on a grassy bank, looking rather nonplussed at this band of sweaty pedestrians who had emerged from their forest.

As I approached, their leader, a man a little more than five feet tall introduced himself as 'Kazungu'.

'Isn't that what you call white people?' I asked Amani.

'No,' Amani replied, 'that is Muzungu, but it means the same thing. Look at him – he is lighter than these others.'

The village was nothing more than a collection of five small huts among the banana trees. As Kazungu led us around, Amani translated his story in fits and starts. At my side, Boston occasionally snorted. I made daggers at him with my eyes. No matter what spin Amani was putting on this story at the behest of his government superiors, I still wanted to hear it.

'Kazungu's fathers lived in the Nyungwe. They were forest dwellers. They did not grow crops like they do now. They hunted and foraged. But, after 1994, things had to change. Education for all!' announced Amani. 'The Batwa came out of the forest to join the one Rwanda.'

Amani was veiled in how he spoke about it, but he was making a tacit reference to the event that still, in spite of everything else, defines Rwanda: the genocide of 1994, which had both put this beautiful country on the world map, and changed its history forever.

Since 1990, Rwanda had been engaged in a bloody civil war. The Hutu-led government was desperate to suppress the Rwandan Patriotic Front, a rebel organisation largely made up of refugee Tutsis based across the border in Uganda. Some of these refugees had been settled in neighbouring countries for a generation, but still considered themselves to have fled from the country that was rightfully theirs. For three years a war was waged between the two, until a ceasefire in 1993 seemed to bring an end to hostilities. It was not to last long. A plan was being prepared that would eventually see a power-sharing government in place in Kigali, but to many Hutus this felt like a concession too far. Tension was high, and a delicate balancing act would need to be performed to ensure peace.

It didn't come. All that was needed to trigger something devastating was a smoking gun, and it came in early 1994. On 6 April, a plane carrying the Hutu premier of Rwanda was shot down on its approach to Kigali, killing all on board. To prominent Hutus in the armed forces, this was nothing more than a political assassination. On the very next day, the genocide began in Kigali and spread rapidly outwards to consume the whole of Rwanda. Soldiers and police quickly executed prominent Tutsis in the capital and, within hours, roadblocks had been established to contain refugees. Systematically, the Hutu police and militias swept Kigali and, checking the documentation of every citizen to ensure ethnicity, began a genocide that would go on to claim an estimated one million lives.

Perhaps the most terrifying thing was that Hutu civilians were later pressurised to take up their own guns and machetes and join in the slaughter. So it was that Hutus turned on Tutsis across the country, and Rwanda was defined forever as a place of genocide. The killings lasted a hundred days, brought to an end only by the mobilisation of the RPF across the border and a military campaign that moved south, from Uganda, capturing first the north of the country and, finally, Kigali itself. We would reach Kigali in about a week's time, if the walking was good, crossing the killing fields to reach the centre of the tragedy itself.

I looked at Amani. He was still talking, but I was thinking less about the Batwa and their village than Amani himself. He was, I knew, a Tutsi by ancestry. I wondered what his experience of those hundred days had been like, how many friends and family members he had lost, what it now felt like to be living in a country carrying those fresh scars. Those were all questions Rwanda itself was trying to answer every day.

'Since 1994, we do not have ethnicity. All Rwandans have the same language, the same history, the same culture. There is only one ethnic group – the Banyarwanda. We are all the same, and we are all Rwandans. It includes Kazungu and his village here. That is why they came out of the forest.'

'So they were forced out?'

Boston felt it was time to interject. 'In Rwanda, you cannot even *remember*. You cannot say my father came from here, or my grandfather came from here. Talking about those kind of things – it is not allowed.'

It sounded draconian to me, but when I asked Kazungu – through Amani – if he and his people missed the forest, he just shrugged. 'In the village,' he said, 'we can grow bananas, eat potatoes, eat beans. We can even own a cow, or a mobile phone – if we are rich enough.'

'There are Batwa in Uganda also,' said Boston. 'They lived in the Bwindi Impenetrable Forest. But the government forced them to leave. Do you know why?'

'Why?'

'Because the forest was needed for gorillas. Can you believe?'

'It makes all Rwandans feel like Rwandans,' said Amani. We had reached the middle of the village, and one of Kazungu's headmen was approaching with a plastic bucket. When he set it down, I saw that it was filled with honey and pieces of comb.

Kazungu said something to Amani. 'It is for us,' he began, 'to give us strength for our walk. It is wild honey. They sell it on the roadside for fifteen dollars a kilogram.'

Reaching into the bucket, I took a spoonful of the hard yellow substance. No sooner was it in my lips than I regretted it.

Picking bits from my teeth, I looked round to find Kazungu's face open with laughter.

'Lev,' began Amani, not unkindly. 'You have to get rid of the wax first . . .'

*

The stream grew wider as, renewed by our taste of wild honey, we walked into the afternoon. Downstream, the valley broadened and the perfectly clear water ran between manicured fields of sweet potato and maize, small tea plantations and – higher up – pine forests that disappeared into high cloud. Amani was keen to point out how almost all of Rwanda's land was put to use to feed its people. Agriculture was one of the ways society held itself together since the dark days of the genocide. 'Rwanda,' he kept saying, much to Boston's chagrin, 'is about co-operation and setting differences aside. This above all else.'

The constant reminders of how the disparate peoples of Rwanda were compelled to unite were beginning to grate. Boston's silence was telling. Yet, as evening approached and thoughts turned to making the expedition's very first camp, another stark reminder of the past was about to appear.

We had come fifteen kilometres out of the forest and, by the time dusk drew near, we'd reached the plantations outside the village of Gisovu. On the hillside above, overlooking the vibrant greens of the riverside, stood a high-walled compound, with crumbling watchtowers in each of its four corners and an intimidating metal gate against its south-west walls. As Boston, Amani and I set up our small, blue tents, my eye was constantly drawn to this imposing fortress. Even at a distance I could tell that its walls were pockmarked, not just with natural decay but with the unmistakable marks of bullet holes – vicious reminders of the past.

As we finished setting up camp and brought together kindling for a fire, a crowd was appearing out of the village. 'Hutus,' said Boston as the chief made himself apparent.

'What is this place?'

In the shadow of the fortress, the village chairman was approaching.

A fat man in his fifties, he wore a tattered blue shirt and a face bearing a benevolent grin. As Amani stood to greet him, they shook hands warmly.

'It was a prison,' Amani explained. 'Gisovu Prison, for genociders.'

I looked across the riverbank, to where the crowd was growing. Boston gave a firm nod. 'Yes, Lev,' he said. '*These* genociders.'

Amani returned with the village chairman. 'Do you want to see the prison?' he asked. 'They are happy for us to do so. It is . . . full of cows now. The government gave it to the community after the prisoners were all released.'

Part of me didn't want to see this place, but another part wanted to understand. With Boston and Amani, I followed the chief up the steep hillside to the great iron gate. When he pushed it open, I expected him to show us around but, instead, he simply waved us on. The prison, to them, was a thing of the past, to be forgotten – but to me it felt very real.

Inside, the prison was in a state of disrepair. Walls had crumbled, long grasses had grown up. Piece by piece, the stone was returning to the earth. Another twenty years, I thought, and it would be gone, not even the bullet holes in the walls to remind us what had happened here. The smell of cow manure was strong as we crossed the open yard and into the cells that remained. Shards of the day's last sun filtered in through shattered windows and holes in the roof. Spiders had built empires of webs in the corridors and, as Boston and I clawed through, I saw that the cells were daubed in faded graffiti in a language I didn't understand.

'What does it say?' I asked Amani, but Amani only shook his head. 'I do not know.' By the way his eyes were lingering on the words, I knew that he was lying. Whatever the prisoners had scrawled on these walls cut into his own memories of that terrible year. Amani, I knew, was thirty-one years old. It made him eleven in the year of the genocide.

'What happened here, Amani?'

He stared for a while. 'This was a prison for genociders. Eventually, it wasn't needed any more. Prisoners who confessed could halve their sentences and go and work in the fields or the city instead. We did not keep them locked up. We set them to work, rebuilding Rwanda. You have already seen some of them, in the village out there. Probably every man in that village killed a Tutsi. A friend, a neighbour, somebody they'd known since they were children.'

'There's more,' I said, tracing the bullet holes scored into the cell wall. 'There was fighting here.'

'When the genocide began, hundreds of Tutsi were rounded up and brought here. The Hutus crammed them, eighty into a cell, before they opened fire.'

I was standing in the scene of a massacre, in a place that had later been used to imprison those responsible. Twenty years had passed, but the feeling of dread in the air was still palpable.

'Amani,' I ventured, not knowing if it was the right thing to ask, 'what happened to you in 1994?'

But Amani only shook his head and brushed past Boston as he made to leave the cell. 'I will tell you stories about Rwanda, Lev, but not my own. It is too painful.'

That night, in our camp beneath the prison, there was quiet. As the red African sun descended into a horizon clad with pines, the river turned the colour of copper. I trailed my hand in the water. I was thinking, again, of how this same water would one day reach the coast. But I was thinking, as well, about the thousands of Tutsi corpses that had been thrown into this same river as a kind of symbolic gesture, the Hutus sending the Tutsis back home to North Africa, from whence they believed they had come. The prison looked down on us, the mellow sound of the river filling my ears, and I knew for certain then that this was going to be a journey through the past as well as the future.

KIGALI, NEW HISTORY AND OLD TERRORS

December 2013

The journey from the source of the Nile to Kigali, the capital of Rwanda, lasted more than a week. From Gisovu Prison the hills had been tough, but we found friends in the villages along the way and, when we didn't make camp at the banks of the Nile – now more recognisably a real river – we found places to stay with the local people. It had not always been easy and, for the first time, Amani's presence on the journey had felt like a real boon; it was Amani who negotiated the stables for us to sleep in on the final night before we reached the city, while Boston lurked just out of my field of vision, muttering murderously that the village chief was a backward, illiterate brute.

Sometimes children from the villages followed us on our walk and, though we knew they were there, they managed to remain totally unseen, concealed in the banana fields that often flanked the river's brown torrents. 'Muzungu!' they goaded us. It was colder than I had anticipated, and the rain, when it came, came in wild, concentrated bursts, flurrying down from the steep escarpments and mountainsides all around. On the fifth night it stayed for hours and, in the darkness, Boston, Amani and I had to abandon our camp at the edge of the river and scramble for higher ground.

On the day we arrived in Kigali we had walked more than 53km – an epic march, and completed entirely in flip-flops; after ten days of travelling, my feet were so blistered and swollen they no longer even fitted in my boots. The day had been spent wading through the stagnant water of the paddy fields, an early reminder of how people across Africa depend on the Nile for agriculture. Boston, wearied by the day – not to mention his constant bickering with Amani – was arguing vehemently that we should give up and spend the night in a village, but the thought of an actual bed in a Kigali hotel spurred me on. Finally, limping, we left the paddy fields behind and entered the western suburb of Nzade just as darkness was falling.

When we reached it, central Kigali was throbbing; this small, hilly city had an air of the tropics and, in stark contrast to the rest of Rwanda, it never seemed to sleep. I had flown into the city only ten days before, but that felt like a lifetime ago. Though we found a place to stay, the only room we could find was a dormitory at a youth hostel, Discover Rwanda, in the heart of town. As we carried our packs into the bare room, to be faced with rows of naked bunks, the look on Boston's face was implacable. I got the feeling he would have preferred the cow sheds and swamped riverbank that had been our bed for the past week. Still, I was grateful for a few home comforts. Ten days walking the riverbank had taught me some stiff lessons about my body, and a hot shower, cold beer and a decent meal were the restoratives I needed.

In the morning, I set out to explore the city. I'd promised myself two days of rest here, while my body recuperated. I was going to need it. Much of the time I'd have to spend provisioning for the journey ahead – new boots were a must, and I intended to find somebody who could stitch new pockets to my rucksack as well – but Kigali has a unique part to play in the history of the Nile, and I wanted to explore that while I was here.

Kigali is the boom-town of Rwanda. Twenty years ago, this was the centre of the genocide, but today it shines like a beacon in the heart of central Africa. On the day I had first arrived, I'd been intrigued to find it clean, orderly and fresh. Its broad avenues were green and leafy, and gated mansions adorned the hilltops amidst lush trees and vegetation. A city of a million people in a country of only twelve million, life in Kigali is the polar opposite of the village life that dominates much of the nation, and it feels metropolitan in a way no other part of Rwanda could match. In two days here, I was to eat Chinese, Italian and Indian meals, and there were moments when, as the glistening sheen of glass-plated banks and shiny Land Cruisers rolled by, it would be easy to forget that this was the scene of one of the world's greatest tragedies.

It was a stark contrast to the image I first had of Rwanda, one cultivated by movies, books and news bulletins. Just the name of this country invokes images of darkness, machetes and death; it has become so synonymous with the genocide of 1994 that it was difficult to balance my preconception with this gleaming, up-and-coming capital city. But it was on my first day in Kigali, before we had set out for the source of the Nile, that I got my first inkling of the way this country has forcibly pulled itself up from that dark episode, the nadir of its history. There was an element of truth in Boston's observation that Amani towed a kind of party line; moving on from the genocide, I was to discover, required a kind of collective decision, an effort to make amends and work together – and this could only be achieved by a form of coercion.

On the day I flew into Kigali and first met Boston, the city was unusually quiet. The hustle I had expected from this capital city was non-existent. Cars didn't cram the roads, horns didn't blare at intersections; the shops were all shuttered up and the people in the streets barely whispered a word. I strode through the strangeness with Boston and whispered, 'Is it a national holiday?'

'Of a kind,' Boston snorted, and rolled his eyes towards some bushes on the edge of a small park. 'Look.'

Behind the bushes, a group of men were all holding automatic rifles.

'Police,' Boston said, 'in plain clothes. It is *umuganda*.'

Umuganda, Boston explained, was a custom particular to Kigali itself. On the last Saturday of every month, the entire population of Kigali is required to devote itself to the city's upkeep. For one day a month, business in Kigali comes to a stand-still and every man, woman and child turns out to sweep the city's streets, tend its parklands and hedges. It is a remarkable feat of civic co-operation, but as Boston directed my gaze to the police guarding over the *boda-boda* taxi drivers tending the park, I understood it as something more: here was a great leveller, Hutus and Tutsis both being forced to work for one common goal, on the streets of the city they were obliged to share. In the quest to reach some form of reconciliation, the government was using every tool at its disposal – and force has always been one of Africa's most effective methods.

'They don't have any choice,' said Boston. 'They're like prisoners.'

It was not the last time we were to see the way the government exerted its influence on the population in an attempt to find a resolution to its recent bloody history. Between Gisovu Prison and the first suburbs of Kigali the perfect paddy fields had been tilled by prisoners.

Agents of the genocide, dressed in orange and pink boiler suits, these prisoners were both the convicted and the accused – and here they were, in hard labour, twenty years after the atrocities were committed. Some had been captured, some had handed themselves in – in what was, I suppose, a mass-assuaging of guilt – but it was evident, in every corner of Rwanda, that those events of twenty years before still defined the country. In a village three days back along the river, Amani had introduced us to a local pastor. The pastor had welcomed us with a feast of cassava, bananas, beef and hot milk – a platter of delicacies compared with the provisions we were carrying – and, as we ate, he told us all about his work in peace and reconciliation. Like Amani, the pastor was a Tutsi, and had lost close friends and family members to the extermination of 1994. As he spoke, Boston grew incensed at what he saw as Amani's one-sided tour. The current policy, he exclaimed, was for the country to engage in an act of wilful amnesia, and simply forget the truth of what happened. But Amani fixed him with a look. 'How would you feel if your mother had been gang-raped and beaten to death in front of your eyes as a ten-year-old boy? That's what happened to many people.' In these circumstances, Amani suggested, forgetting was just one of many useful tools in moving on. These were the kinds of questions that Rwanda grappled with daily. How do you judge and sentence half a population? Is forgiveness a real possibility, and how can we collectively put paid to the past? In this context it was not so surprising to be watching Kigali's citizens being forced to sweep the streets. It seemed, in that moment, as much an act of collective penance as it was a scheme to force co-operation. On the surface, Rwanda has turned itself from a country destroyed by hate and racial violence to a seeming paragon of virtue – but, like Amani's insistence that the country has made accommodation with what happened here, it is all a façade. The orderliness of

Kigali is the result of heavy policing and arbitrary arrests. Human rights are commonly flouted, boys regularly abducted by government officials and families torn apart. In Kigali, you can go to Chinese markets and African bazaars, stay in luxurious hotels and visit glistening modern banks – but while the country has taken several steps forward, the hearts and minds of its citizens seem yet to have caught up.

'I want to see the crocodile,' said Boston, his face breaking into a half-deranged smile.

He had been talking about it all morning, as we traipsed from one market to the next on still-swollen feet. At the back of a bazaar where cheap new imports from China were being sold alongside second-hand European goods, I had found a small tailor's shop, where a one-eyed tailor hunched over a fake Singer sewing machine and fixed two new pouches to the sides of my rucksack. For the few minutes' work he had charged the exorbitant sum of $15 – he had clearly seen me coming, but it was worth it. This was the last place in Rwanda I would be able to get them attached. That was one of my first lessons about Rwanda – outside Kigali, there is virtually nothing. It is as if the entire economy is built around creating a surreal urban veneer that bears no relation to the rural reality.

The crocodile Boston was intent on seeing was on show at the Natural History Museum of Kigali. A sixteen foot monster, it had been killed in April 2012 and the taxidermist tasked with preserving it – badly, as it turned out – had discovered a pair of shoes and a woman's hair braids inside. 'A man-eater,' Boston kept saying, clearly quite taken with the idea. It reminded me, unnervingly, of the stories he had told about his great grandfather, the cannibal king.

On this occasion, I was happy to give in to Boston's whim. There was another reason to see the Natural History Museum, one more closely aligned with my own quest – the building used to be the home of one Dr Richard Kandt.

Richard Kandt is not a name as famous in the pantheon of great African explorers as Burton, Stanley and Speke, but he holds a special place in my heart, and he felt especially important to this expedition. It was Kandt who first explored the Nyungwe Forest and, in 1898, declared it the true Source of the Nile.

Kandt was born in Posen, in latter-day Poland, in 1867. A physician by training, he had explored swathes of German East Africa around the turn of the century and, in 1908, been appointed Resident of Rwanda. Residents, of the time, were effectively government ministers asked to take up residence in another country – and their duties often amounted to a form of indirect rule. It was in this capacity that Kandt had founded Kigali itself. His name has lived long in the memory here, and he is still, more than a century later, a feted citizen.

Kandt's house sits atop a suburban hill and is one of the few original colonial era buildings in the city. As we entered the museum, to be faced with racks of toy dinosaurs in what passed for their 'Evolution Exhibit', I tried to picture it in the days when this was the official German residence. That was the thing about the early African explorers – many of them were officially appointed colonialists, traders, merchants, doctors and bureaucrats. Some had long titles and family histories, while others were misfit chancers who saw Africa as a way to make their name and, hopefully, pocket lots of cash on the way. I was saying as much to Boston, but his eye had already been drawn to the racks of bad taxidermy that surrounded the museum's prize exhibit. The crocodile certainly was huge, and its glass eyes looked as callous as its man-eater reputation deserved, but there was something almost pathetic about the way its body had been mangled in its preservation.

'Exploration's changed,' I thought, drifting through the exhibits. 'Now it's a pauper's game.'

It wasn't, of course, the only way it had changed. Before I set out on this expedition I had been asked, more times than I care to remember, about the idea of exploration. The question of what it means in the modern world isn't so easy to answer. To some, the very idea seems archaic – and, in a world of Google Maps, where every valley and hillside has already been plotted, the traditional age of exploration is certainly gone. But exploration has always been about more than pure discovery, or of being the first to do something. The famous Victorian explorers were, of course, not the first into Africa; Africa is a continent where mankind has lived for longer than any other, and when Stanley found Livingstone he was doing so in a land where civilisations had existed for millennia. In the modern era, it is more important than ever to acknowledge this fact. There is a certain romanticism attached to the Victorian explorers, but the truth is that their motivations were not really so clear-cut as we would like to think. Livingstone was, first and foremost, an evangelical missionary, Stanley an egomaniac journalist and mercenary whose talents for self-publicity knew no bounds. John Hanning Speke was a glory-hunter with no reservations about making bold and often unfounded geographical claims, while Richard Burton had more in common with a 1970s hippie than a classical adventurer; his desire to immerse himself in cultures was most often expressed in relentless fornication. Kandt himself was one of a breed of explorers working at the behest of their governments. Their missions were officially sanctioned exploits – all part of what we would come to know as the Scramble for Africa, as Europe's colonial powers sought to carve up the newly discovered parts of the world.

As I wandered through Kandt's old residence, part of me knew I was on a different kind of journey from the ones I had grown up reading about, but our journeys did have some things in common. Like them, I was here exploring *people*. Constantly in flux, constantly evolving, there is always something new to discover about people – and I was here to bring home stories of what life was like in corners of the world that do not always make it into our headlines. I had this, at least, in common with the heroes in whose footsteps I was following.

I stopped to linger over a photograph in the hotel lobby that depicted the house as it had originally been, back in Kandt's time. In the frame a grand bungalow sat alone amongst the bare hillsides, with only a few wattle huts for neighbours. The Kigali of Kandt's time, I realised, was little different from the country we had been walking through – but, whereas that country had remained in the past, Kigali had somehow contrived to join the modern world.

'Boston,' I said. 'Are you done?'

Boston was positively slavering over the thought of the crocodile, and it took some moments before he looked up. 'Let's hope we don't meet any further north.'

Kigali's Genocide Memorial Centre is not far from the place where Kandt used to live, and it is much more than a museum. When we arrived, Amani was waiting for us at the gates. Eager as ever, he took my hand in an enthusiastic hello.

The Memorial Centre stretched before us, and there was no denying its beauty. The air was heavy with the scent of eucalyptus, and the gardens of the hilltop were vivid and bright, their flower beds perfectly arranged. Colourful birds – western citrils and mustard yellow canaries – darted around in the trees. Somewhere, as Amani began to tell us of this place, I heard children playing.

'It has been open ten years,' said Amani, 'and that was ten years after the events. It is all here, everything that happened.'

He was speaking about a record of the genocide. I already knew that one of the principal aims of the Memorial Centre was to bring together the testimonies of all those who had survived, and taken part in, the atrocities – as well as taking part in the Gacaca trial process, the traditional community courts whose role had been to try those accused of involvement. But it wasn't until we reached the foot of the Memorial Centre building, a piece of modern architecture seemingly at odds with the natural surroundings, that I understood that Amani meant something different as well. Outside the building, which looked somewhat like an English crematorium, were a series of large concrete slabs inscribed with names. Trellises and decking served as a path between these great stones. We followed it in silence, finally reaching the centre's exterior wall which was dominated by a single, vast brass plaque. Here were inscribed hundreds of names written in a list that was still incomplete, petering out half-way down.

Amani was not being his usual energetic self, and now I understood: the Memorial Centre is not just a museum to memories of the genocide: it is a mass grave, a site of genocide itself.

'There are a quarter of a million victims buried here,' he explained. 'We can collect only a fraction of their names.'

Inside, the centre was black, the only lights those illuminating the laminate display boards recounting individual stories of those horrific months. Boston and I followed Amani from room to room. In one, banks of bleached skulls glared at us, each one of them wearing the wounds from bullets and machetes. In the next room, nothing but thigh bones, stacked from floor to ceiling. With only our footsteps to break the silence, I slowly understood that the graves we had seen outside were only a fraction of what the Memorial Centre could show, and even this was only a fraction of the people who lost their lives in 1994. Death on a scale like this is hard to absorb, even when you are faced with it so starkly.

In the next room thousands of portraits stared at us. These, Amani told us, were the images of those who had died: men, women, and children. Most of them were smiling. These were photographs taken at Christenings, weddings and graduations. Some were classic portraits, gazing to one side like posed Victorian sittings, while others were taken from afar, in the background an object of pride – a new car, a motorbike, a young couple in front of their first home. As I stared, I saw Boston focusing on a picture of a mother who held her new-born children, and a man in a shiny, black suit.

All of them were dead.

Beside me, Amani was unusually still. 'Just walk around,' he said. 'See it for yourselves.'

A video, which showed indescribable scenes of murder on a constant loop, masked Amani's quiet exit. It wasn't until an hour later, shell-shocked by what we had seen, that Boston and I emerged from the Memorial Centre, back into the glorious sunshine, to find him sitting on a bench beneath the eucalyptus trees. He looked emotionless, and the only noise was that of cicadas.

That night, I got to thinking about this first staging post of our journey. If ever there was a place to give life to the cliché of Africa's dark heart, it is here in Kigali. I sat in the incongruous surroundings of an Indian restaurant and, as I looked into the eyes of the waiter, the diners, and the people who passed outside, I understood in a way I hadn't before that every one of them had been there. Every one of them was a survivor or a perpetrator, locked together in uneasy accommodation. There is a sense in which Kigali and Rwanda have worked a miracle in forging a way ahead. Coercion, recounting, memorialising, and even a kind of ritualised forgetting, have all been components of that – but the scars remain fresh, twenty years on, and in some way they'll remain fresh for the twenty to come.

Across the restaurant, at the bar, Boston was propped up with a drink, engaging some locals he had just met with one of his tall tales. I caught his eye across the restaurant. 'We have an early start,' I mouthed at him – but, right in that moment, he didn't want to know.

BANDIT COUNTRY

Tanzania, December 2013 – January 2014

From Kigali the river wound south and east. Two rest days in Kigali might have helped heal the feet, but it had in other ways made me feel weaker somehow. Perhaps it was the drying up of momentum, or the sobering thought of the city we were leaving behind. As a parting gift, Amani had helped organise a local man who would walk with us to the border. We hoped to reach it by Christmas, but there was no telling if it was possible; here, the river disappeared into miles of thick, sometimes impenetrable swampland. Vianey, the porter Amani had organised, took to it without complaint – but, always, in the back of my mind there was the memory of how Amani had first described him. 'Vianey,' he had said, 'is a genocide perpetrator.' I did not know whether I believed it or not, and Vianey himself claimed to be only twenty-four years old, but occasionally, in the right light, I got the impression that he could be much older, so perhaps there was some truth in it after all. Like many Rwandans, I decided it was better to look the other way and not broach the subject. I was sure it wasn't a tactic of which Boston would approve.

Outside metropolitan Kigali the country returned to its impoverished, rural state. We built our days by trekking from village to village. Sometimes the river was kept at bay by dense papyrus marshes. These were the true Rwandan wetlands and, where the papyrus did not dominate, the villagers had turned the land into paddy fields and cultivated rice. On a diet of painkillers and rice wine bought at every village, we followed the twisting river south. The paths were virtually non-existent and we resorted instead to trampling down the reeds and walking for miles on what felt like a water bed; the reeds held our weight, but there was always the sensation that they might break at any moment, plunging us into the stagnant marsh beneath.

'Do you remember the crocodile?' Boston kept asking. I laughed in reply, but in truth I didn't feel like laughing at all.

We'd been walking now for two weeks and steadily become attuned to the environment around us. That's not to say it was easy; in fact the constant shifting from swamp to field to mountain to jungle made for tough-going. In a day we'd sometimes gain a thigh pummelling thousand feet as we crested a ridge, only to drop down again into a misty valley where we'd get lost amongst the reeds and orchards, cursing the muddy slopes as we fell over every few steps. Mentally it was tough too; although we'd started off eager to make headway, the reality hadn't even sunk in yet as to the magnitude of the distance we were undertaking. Neither of us had any clue whether our feet and minds would hold up.

The Rwandan wetlands are dominated by great lakes and, though I knew none was as great as the one we would eventually reach – Lake Victoria, the vast inland sea of southern Africa, was already looming in my mind – after a few days the river wound between shimmering expanses of grey and brown. On the west were the smaller lakes – Gashanga, Kidogo, Rumira and Miravi – while, on the east, were the bigger, more majestic Sake and Mugesera. Soon we had to give up our attempts to stay true to the riverbank itself and followed it at a distance, sticking to the higher ground above the marshes, from which we could look down on these magnificent natural reservoirs. A series of finger-like ridges pointed south to the point where the river curled east and became the borderline between Rwanda and Burundi. The trek through the hills was slow-going and, though I sometimes wondered about Vianey and his past, I was glad he was with us to help shoulder our packs. As we tramped slowly onwards, the silence was broken only by the drone of mosquitoes coming up from the swamps, and Boston's continual lament. He had somehow pulled a ligament in his left heel.

'I thought you used to be a soldier. A leader of men,' I said jokingly.

'That was a long time ago. I was a young man. I am not used to hills, not after seven years in Uganda. Kampala is completely flat.'

'You spent long enough in the Congo,' I said. 'What about Goma? It's full of mountains.'

'Yes,' said Boston, with newfound nonchalance, 'but who's stupid enough to climb them?'

Each day we gained and lost a thousand feet or more in height – and, on the eighteenth day, reached the Rusumo Falls border crossing. Back home, the festivities of Christmas would be fast approaching, but this was a different world. At 1600m above sea level, the land felt almost Mediterranean. The villages had terracotta tile roofs, and were surrounded by beautiful orchards and meadows. It was easy to get lost in daydreams as the walking found its own rhythm, and to forget the thousands of miles that lay ahead, and for a moment or two the pain in my feet, and to sink into blissful immersion in this wonderful foreign land.

At the falls, we stopped to take in the view. We were approaching the point at which three borders meet: Rwanda was behind us, Burundi to the south, and ahead, Tanzania, where the river banked north towards Lake Victoria. As Vianey set down our packs and stared into the falls, I was reminded suddenly that this was one of the Rwandan genocide's most memorable images. It had been at Rusumo Falls that the genocide had come to the attention of the world, when thousands of dead bodies that had been cast into the river further upstream floated under the bridge into Tanzania while, on the bridge above, thousands of people tried to flee the slaughter for sanctuary across the border. Many of those who fled were Hutu, fearing revenge killings as the RPF swept south in response to the genocide.

I looked at Boston, and Boston was looking at Vianey, and I knew we were both thinking the same thing: had Vianey been responsible for any of that? The idea of living among people who had systematically turned on their neighbours and friends was still difficult to comprehend, and I was finding that the longer we remained in Rwanda the more admiration I had for Amani.

The Rusumo border heralded an entry into an Africa more familiar than the Rwanda I had passed through. Between Rwanda and Tanzania there is a kilometre-long no-man's-land; Boston and I walked it together, and crossed the bridge that would forever be associated with the genocide. As we ate fried grasshoppers and *ugali* – a staple dish of the African Great Lakes, maize flour cooked with water to form a kind of thick porridge – on the other side, I had to admit I was not unhappy to leave the country behind. I had come into Rwanda with a preconception of the people built on stories of the genocide. Those preconceptions had not been shattered. Rwanda was a haunted place and I was eager to leave it for a country less consumed with guilt and barely concealed scars.

'You hear that, Lev?' Boston began as we returned to the river. At Rusumo the river banked north-east. It would lead us across the border into Uganda before it finally joined Lake Victoria, but that was still three or four days' walk away.

'What?' I replied.

'It is Swahili,' he said, and nodded sharply as if I would instinctively understand.

'So?'

'You know what kills Africa?' Boston began. I could sense another tirade coming and, without Amani here to bear the brunt of it, knew I would have to listen. 'It is all these dirty, dirty languages Africans speak. If there's one thing good about Tanzania, it's Swahili. They should impose it on everybody, like they do here and in the Congo – but your liberals would say it was destroying indigenous cultures. Well, I'll tell you what destroys indigenous cultures – war and division and starvation. On my life, it's these ridiculous languages, ones only a few hundred or thousand people even understand, that cause all of this. How can a country work when people can't even talk to each other?'

Three strides ahead of him, I stopped. 'You have a point, Boston.'

Boston beamed. 'I know it.'

The United Republic of Tanzania has a chequered history, and Boston and I began to believe we could see the results of it in the attitude of the locals we came across. Tanganyika, which formed the greater part of what would later become Tanzania, was originally part of German East Africa but, after Germany's defeat in the First World War, the country became a British mandate. Britain treated Tanganyika in the same way it did its other African territories, parcelling off much of the country to retired generals and servicemen in gratitude for the years they had devoted to consolidating the Empire, while at the same time investing in railways, roads, farming and the other infrastructure that made modern countries flourish. Wheat became important to the Tanganyikan economy, but the most important product of this era was the humble peanut; British investment in what became known as the 'Tanganyika Ground Nut Scheme' brought an influx of Western migrants to the country and, though the groundnut scheme itself was not successful, it transformed the makeup of the population.

After the Second World War, when the independence movement in the neighbouring Kenya was lurching towards violence, with the Mau Mau fiercely resisting British rule, Tanganyika somehow bucked the trend and found itself gliding towards self-government in an ordered and peaceful fashion. After the war ended, it became a United Nations trust territory and, in 1954, a schoolteacher by the name of Julius Nyerere – one of only two Tanganyikans educated to university level – founded a political party, the Tanganyika African National Union. Nyerere would go on to oversee the transition to independence when, in 1961, Tanganyika became self-governing. Two years later, the neighbouring territory of Zanzibar declared its independence from Britain and, after a bloody civil war, threw off the shackles of its own monarchy and formed a government. One year later, Tanganyika and Zanzibar were formally joined, and symbolically united their names to form the new 'Tanzania'. It was a joining of cultures as well as governments – for, though both countries had at one time been British colonies, Zanzibar had first been subsumed by the Portuguese expansion into Africa and had, latterly, become part of Islamic Africa, with the island nation being pivotal to the Arabic slave trade. This joining of different histories gives Tanzania a flavour unique among African nations.

Christmas came two days into our time in Tanzania. In that time we had slowly made our way north, along the bank of the Kagera river. The water was wide and slow-moving; there would be no rapids to speak of until we crossed the Ugandan border and came close to the great lake. Tanzania had a wilder, edgier feel to it than Rwanda, even with the ghosts of Rwanda's past. 'It's because of the Communists,' Boston declared. The banks of the river here were fed by countless little tributaries that we were forced to cross, and the best way of doing so was to enlist the help of local villagers and their small dugout canoes, made from native palms. The hostile way the local fishermen looked on as we climbed into their precarious little crafts was enough to convince me of Boston's theory: years of Communist rule had instilled in the population a certain paranoia and a constant suspicion of others. 'Every Tanzanian has the right to question someone not known to the community,' Boston explained. I could feel it too. In the villages we had passed through we faced more suspicion than we had encountered in all our time in Rwanda, where every day we shook hands and ate with possible killers.

Soon after Tanzania gained independence, the new Prime Minister, Julius Nyerere, had moved to suppress opposition in all its forms, including not just other political parties but trade unions and community groups as well. It was Nyerere's belief that, in a nation made up of hundreds of different ethnic groups – and coming from backgrounds as distinct as Tanganyika and Zanzibar – multiple political parties would destabilise the new nation. His aim was to suppress not just the parties but the cultures themselves, and he swiftly instituted a policy that banned all languages except his native Kiswahili. Everything was nationalised, private businesses destroyed, and Nyerere implemented a policy of 'Ujamaa', a kind of African Socialism that brought his government into a close relationship with

Communist China. Boston's belief was that we were seeing the relics of that as we walked: the suspicious nature of the locals was itself a direct product of those years of close, scrutinised rule. Tanzania is a democracy now – but its people seemed somehow to be defined by the suspicion and hostility of those years.

Christmas Eve came and with it the fiercest sun we had encountered. In the morning, Boston returned to camp, trailing two local Tanzanians who could act as porters for us until we reached the Ugandan border some seventy miles north. I was grateful for the help carrying our packs, but I was less than convinced by Boston's choice of men. Both were scrawny, dressed in rags and broken flip flops, and my instinct was they would be more of a hindrance than a help. 'They look like criminals,' I told Boston, who only shrugged. The taller man, whose name was Selim, had a lame eye and scars across his face. The other, shorter, had a broken nose and seemed to be permanently drunk. 'They're the best we've got,' Boston declared, and we started the day's walk.

There was no path that day. The river wound its way through national park land, the Kimisi Game Reserve, and though we were not supposed to walk here without permissions and rangers as guides, there had been no officials on duty in Rusumo and we decided to go ahead regardless. As we walked, despite the dark looks from our porters – who muttered to each other constantly in Swahili – the Africa I knew and loved stretched out in every direction. The river snaked through complete and utter wilderness – forest savannah as far as the eye could see, so thick and green that, from the escarpment above Rusumo, it looked impenetrable. Tall elephant grass and spiny acacia trees covered the hillsides. There were elephants here, hippos too. Boston took great joy in pointing out their spoor during the day.

At Rusumo we had picked up a goat, but the animal was almost as obstinate as the porters and refused to be led. Taking it in turns to carry the brute, we followed the widening river. There were a few fishermen here and, more than once, we had to pay for the use of their dugout canoes to cross tiny crocodile-infested tributaries. We were practised at this now, and managed to barter a regular price to only a few cents. Slowly, I was getting used to using the precarious craft too. Though Boston was able to slide into the narrow slit of the boat, I was much less supple and had to kneel up, making it more prone to capsize. The only moment I saw anything close to a smile grace Selim's lips was when he saw me concentrating on keeping my balance while he and his brother floated effortlessly past.

By midday on Christmas Eve, the sun was unbearably hot and we stopped to rest in the shade of a marula tree; it was eighteen metres tall, in full leaf, and it was pleasingly cool beneath the branches. Selim and his brother settled down in the roots and, almost at once, I saw their eyes begin to close. A second later, Selim was asleep. The rope by which he had been holding the goat slipped out of his hand and, sensing his opportunity for escape, the goat took one look at Boston and disappeared into the undergrowth.

When I cried out, Selim's eyes snapped open. They seemed to track the goat as its backside disappeared into the foliage. Then he looked at me. Muttering something in Swahili, he was about to close his eyes again when Boston let fire with a string of invective.

I think, if Boston had screamed at me with such vehemence, I too would have obeyed. In seconds, Selim had dragged his brother to his feet. Muttering darkly again, they took off after the goat.

'You should never have hired them, Boston. They're bone idle.'

'No,' said Boston. 'They're scared.'

'Scared of what?'

'They don't know I speak Swahili, but I've been listening to them.

They talk of bandits and robbers and Rwandan rebels. I think that's part of the reason they resent us. Because we came out of Rwanda. They're certain this place is haunted too.'

'Haunted?'

'It's because of the bodies that came down the river. Rwandan ghosts washed up all along these banks.'

I wanted to dismiss the notion as African superstition but, when I recalled the sensation of walking over Rusumo Bridge, there was something dangerously familiar in what Boston was saying. Africa is a continent that gets under your skin and never had I felt it more than that day.

Selim and his brother returned over an hour later, dragging the goat behind them. Without word, they sank back into the roots.

'Up,' I told them. Then, with my hands, I made a walking gesture. The looks I got were more withering than the one the goat had on its face.

By the evening we had reached the shores of Lake Bisongu, a remote, virtually unknown water source that borders Rwanda to the west. As Selim and his brother made camp, staking down the goat, the only other evidence of humans around was the occasional flash of torchlight from an illegal fisherman out on the water.

'Lev,' Boston began. 'They're talking again.'

Selim and his brother were kindling the fire, chattering in Swahili.

'So?'

'They're speaking about us. Lev, listen . . .' Boston's eyes seemed to open wider with every word that he heard. 'Do you know what they're saying?'

'Tell me.'

'They plot to rob us. If we don't share the goat with them, they mean to tie us to the tree and take everything.'

When I looked, Selim was still whispering to his brother, words smothered by the crackling of the fire.

'Selim!' I cried out.

His eyes darted to find me in the dark.

'You'll get some goat, don't worry. You won't starve. But I warn you – any more talk of robbing us and we'll leave you here in the forest. You have no idea where you are and the Rwandans will get you.' I stopped, fixing him with my eyes. 'Do you understand?'

He nodded, terrified.

'Happy Christmas,' I said, and patted him sternly on the shoulders.

In the dead of night, I woke with a start. From the shallows of the lake, only metres away from our guttering campfire, there came the sound of a most terrible thrashing. As I scrabbled up, wondering if it was Selim and his brother somehow making that racket, I saw that Boston was already awake. I followed his gaze to the water, where a family of five angry hippos were rolling and snapping at each other.

'We've ruined their Christmas, Lev.'

Shrinking into our tents, we waited until morning.

Christmas Day was blisteringly hot. By dawn the hippos were gone and we were able to stake out our camp again. Despite having spent much of my working life overseas, I had always managed to make it home for Christmas; this would be the first year I would not wake to a cold English morning in the familiar surroundings of childhood. Still, I was determined that this would be a celebration. Boston and I decorated the thorn bushes with pants and socks in place of baubles and, since there were no turkeys to be snared, we said goodbye to the goat and butchered him for the day's festivities. Despite their mutterings of the night before, we shared the meat with Selim and his brother. The day was long, the water of the lake inviting – but Selim was adamant that the shallows were alive with crocodiles, so the best thing we could do was sit in the shade and drink from the bottle of whisky I'd carried all this way for the occasion.

'Boston,' I began, as I passed him the whisky, 'I have something for you.'

He thought I meant the bottle and took it hastily, but I had something else as well. Until now, the jumper I had wrapped up had been serving as my pillow, and the one piece of warm clothing I was carrying. But Christmas is a time for making presents of jumpers, and I gave it to Boston with a smile.

He beamed. 'It looks like I'm going to need it, Lev. Look . . .'

Above the lake, storm clouds were gathering, brooding and black. They were coming this way.

Before the day was done, the rains had started. The way it fell in sheets across the lake was a spectacle of light and sound, the spray distorting the surface of the water so that it seemed we were staring through a constantly shifting veil. In the camp, Selim and his brother sheltered beneath a tarpaulin sheet, but there was no longer murder in their eyes – only misery. Boston and I sat out and let the storm rage all around.

The rains moved on in the night and, by morning, the sun had returned with all its ferocity. Boston and I were up at dawn, debating whether to spend another day resting by the lake or to continue our push north, when Selim and his brother made their announcement. Animatedly, they summoned Boston to the tarpaulin and ranted at him in Swahili. When Boston returned, there was murder in his own eyes. 'You were right when you said they were bone idle, Lev. Well, they were scared, but bone idle as well. They're leaving us.'

'Leaving?'

'And they'll leave us here, with all our packs, unless we take them back to the road today.'

I looked at the camp. There was too much gear for Boston and me to shoulder ourselves, and it was twenty miles to the nearest road where we could realistically hope to find new porters. Part of me wanted to scream at Selim but the better part won out and I couldn't help but smile in dismay. This was exactly the kind of thing the original Nile explorers had contended with on a daily basis: truculent aides who turned out (as I'd predicted) to be a hindrance rather than a help. There are certain clichés about African travel that always turn out to be true.

I couldn't bring myself to speak to Selim. Boston ordered them to begin packing up and we set off.

It was a silent twenty miles to the nearest road, hacking through the entangled forest. When we reached it, the road was little more than a dirt track, running parallel to the river. When we emerged from the forest to see the red earth snaking north, a large cross, choked with creepers, stood amid the bushes on the opposite side of the track. Behind the creepers there hung a tarnished brass plaque. A chill ran through me: this was a memorial to a Danish aid worker who had been killed by robbers on this very spot in 1994.

'I told you it was dangerous here,' muttered Boston, darkly.

'But that was twenty years ago,' I said, trying to convince myself as well as Boston.

We had to wait some hours before a truck rattled through. Fortunately the driver was happy to be flagged down and Selim and his brother clambered aboard the flatbed in silence. 'Be careful,' the driver told us as he gestured at the memorial. 'He wasn't the only foreigner killed round here. Bandits and rebels from Rwanda come across the national park to steal and kill. Make sure you get to Benaka tonight. Don't camp here.'

Before I could question him further, the truck's engine burst to life and they rattled off southwards. I looked at Boston, who only shrugged.

'Benaka, then,' I said.

'Uganda will be different, Lev. There are good people in Uganda. At least, in Uganda, a policeman will ask you for your name before he beats you up.'

Boston was beaming again, but I wasn't in the mood to reciprocate. It was 10km until Benaka, and another thirty until the border. Along the way we would have to ditch the more cumbersome parts of our packs and hope to re-provision, but I was eager to get every one of those kilometres behind us.

AFRICA'S GREATEST LEVELLER

Uganda, January 2014

Boston had been singing Uganda's praises for weeks, and I was anticipating the country with perhaps over-eager expectations. 'There is a guesthouse in every village,' he said as the border point of Mutukula came in sight, 'and you can't fail to find food. There are even internet cafés. Lev, you will see – Uganda is a different world to these backwaters.'

There is a small rainforest that straddles the Tanzania–Uganda border that teems with colobus monkeys. Boston and I spent two days hacking our way through the vines until, eventually, we discovered tracks made by illegal loggers and were able to make steadier progress north. At Mutukula we made the official crossing. According to Boston, now that we were in Uganda, we would see civilisation flourish – but, for the first day, there was only more impenetrable forest. It wasn't until we banked back east to re-join the course of the river that we would come across our first town and I would see if Boston's bold claims were true.

A few kilometres north of where the river meets the shore of Lake

Victoria sits the fishing village of Kasansero. The phrase has connotations of a small, idyllic community with a long-established way of life, but Kasansero was more properly known as a 'landing site', a warren of houses and industry that had sprung up for workers to take maximum advantage of the lake. Like other landing sites along the shores of the lake, Kasansero had been founded to harvest the famous Nile Perch that flourish in the lake. In the 1950s, when Uganda was still a British colony, the prevailing view had been that Lake Victoria was an under-exploited resource that could feed great swathes of East Africa – and the Nile Perch had been introduced to the lake to create a new fishing industry. Places like Kasansero appeared all along the shore, people flocked to the lake to build businesses, and a new economy began to boom. But, though Uganda's local population benefited, the introduction of the invasive fish was an environmental disaster. The Nile Perch are brutal predators. With no natural controls on their numbers, they colonised the lake with astonishing speed, condemning other species to extinction.

As the shanties closed in around us, great crowds began to throng the streets. Our arrival had been heralded by an article in the Ugandan press, written by a photographer and freelance journalist named Matthias Mugisha. The piece in *New Vision* magazine had announced to Uganda's literary classes that a white man was daring to walk the length of the Nile, and crowds of fishermen, drunk from bags of cheap waragi gin, lined the streets to welcome us. One vociferous rascal even had a microphone and announced our arrival to the eager mob. Off to the side of the first street, African rap blared out of big black speakers sitting outside a barber shop where a badly drawn sign advertised a trendy mullet cut. Half of the population seemed to be wearing red and white Arsenal football shirts, the other half whatever ill-fitting garments had come over from Europe on the last charity delivery.

'But how do they all know?' I asked, as Boston and I were subsumed by the crowd. Surely these fishermen weren't the types to read Uganda's literary magazines.

'This lot don't read,' Boston confirmed. 'Not unless it's the *Red Pepper*, full of scandal and what-not. They wouldn't be interested in our trip unless you'd been terrorising young boys like those corrupt pastors they have here.'

At that moment a man emerged from the crowd, wearing a guilty grin. I could tell instantly that he wasn't one of Kasansero's fishermen.

'How do you enjoy your welcome to Uganda, Mr Tembula?'

'Matthias,' Boston began, 'it's madness!'

I looked sidelong at Boston; despite his protestations, the fact was he seemed to be enjoying being the hero of the day.

'Tembula' means 'to walk' in the Bugandan language, and that is what Matthias had called me in his article: the white walker. Now, as we followed him deeper into Kasansero's dense streets, that was what the crowd relentlessly cheered. One of them tried to force a bag of the cheap gin into my hands, but most were keeping it for themselves. Even the workers about to depart for their night fishing were still having a few for the road.

Being a Ugandan – and, as a journalist, prone to a bit of play-acting – Matthias took my hand and led me towards the shore of the lake. Dusk was deepening and we would soon have to find somewhere to stay, but first I wanted to see the shore.

The waters of the lake appeared through the filthy streets like a light at the end of a very dark tunnel. Beyond the shacks and corrugated tin structures lay the beach, which seemed completely crammed with boats. Most of them had little coloured flags at the bow, and others, less quaint, used white plastic bags instead. Many barely looked like they could float, although they must have done judging by the size of the catches coming in. The air reeked of fish and you couldn't walk across the sand without stepping in guts or tripping over discarded bits of netting.

Seeing the shore for the first time came as an incredible relief. It was everything I had imagined, and as I stood listening to the gentle sound of the water and the insects that buzzed around its shallows, I got to thinking about what it must have felt like for John Hanning Speke, the first European to 'discover' it. Speke and his fellow explorer, Richard Burton, had been on an expedition to locate the Source of the Nile when they reached this great water's southernmost shore and named it after the reigning monarch. What they had discovered was one of the biggest freshwater lakes in the world, second only to Lake Superior in the United States, with more than 26,000 square miles of water. To me, as to them, Lake Victoria seemed a vast inland sea – and I was left in no doubt as to why, for many years, it was considered the true source of the Nile. The Nile is, in fact, the only river to drain out of the lake – all the water here would travel down that conduit, out to the sea.

John Hanning Speke was an officer in the British Indian Army, born in Devon in 1827. He was twenty-seven years old when he first came to Africa, joining an expedition into Somalia led by Burton, an explorer already famous for his African endeavours. Burton was a scant six years older than Speke but already a seasoned campaigner by the time they met. The legends about Burton were many and vast; if ever there was a true polymath it was Burton, who – as well as being a geographer and explorer – was also known for his writing, including poetry, and for his amazing capacity to absorb and retain languages. Some sources claim he was fluent in as many as twenty-nine tongues. Speke and Burton's expedition into Somalia, in 1854, was disastrous and very nearly got both of them killed; attacked by indigenous tribesmen,

Speke found himself captured and stabbed several times by spears, while Burton escaped with a javelin skewering both cheeks. But their dances with death hardly deterred the two explorers and they returned to Africa together in 1856, consumed by their desire to be the first to locate the source of the Nile. This trip was no less arduous. Both men became stricken with tropical diseases and, when Burton was too sick to carry on, Speke followed rumours of a great body of water. It was then that he first set eyes on the lake in front of me now.

Matthias asked me how it felt to be here, and the truth is I could not find the words to express what I felt. I'd arrived at the first major milestone in this journey, reaching a body of water that was vital to the explorers of old, and perhaps for the first time I felt like I was truly walking in their footsteps.

'Now, Mr Tembula,' said Matthias, 'you can begin your journey properly.'

'Properly?'

'You know, Lev, those hundred miles you've just done?'

'Five hundred,' I corrected him.

'Well, it was nice, but you could have saved your legs. Here in Uganda, we know the truth. The real source of the Nile is here, at Jinja, like your Speke used to say.'

Boston's face was set rigid. I could tell he was about to explode, but I looked at him and we let it pass. Now was not the time for yet another argument about the true source of the Nile. I would leave that to be squabbled over by the ghosts of Burton and Speke. I was only here to keep on with our walk.

In the morning we stood outside Kasansero, on a hill overlooking the small landing site, where fishermen were already bringing in their catches of the night. The graveyard we stood in was simple and unadorned. Here was another reminder that the river we had been walking along connected Africa – beneath our feet was yet another mass grave housing the remains of thousands of victims of the Rwandan genocide. There is a man still living in Kasansero who personally buried more than two thousand bodies here. In May 1994, the first bloated corpses of those Tutsis who had been cast into the river and not been eaten by crocodiles had begun to reach Lake Victoria. If ever there was any doubt that the river that emerged from the lake at Jinja was the same one that entered it just south of Kasansero, here was the most grisly evidence: when the bodies entered the lake in the south they drifted north on the current, forming a gruesome trail of some ten thousand corpses across the lake and proving that the water that begins in Rwanda is the very same that leaves the lake and becomes the mighty Nile herself.

There are other gravesites outside Kasansero, and as we tramped back into the landing site to reach the shore I was reminded of the town's most nefarious claim to fame. Kasansero, Matthias had told us, is reputed to be the place from which the AIDS virus first spread around the world.

'Perhaps it spread from here,' said Boston, keen to play devil's advocate as ever, 'but it came from the Congo. It was a trial on polio by some scientists that went wrong.' He chuckled hysterically. 'We all thought you whites were out to kill us.'

This seemed a strange moment for Boston to return to his usual theme of Congolese supremacy, but before I could chip in Matthias had other ideas.

'It came from Tanzania,' he said. 'Prostitutes. Who knows where they got it from? Either way, this is where it started spreading.'

We had come back into Kasansero now. Some estimates put the

percentage of people infected with HIV here at as high as seventy per cent, and one of the first buildings we passed was the settlement's AIDS orphanage, where children watched us from the doors. 'These fishermen just thought it was malaria,' Matthias went on, 'or flu. Pretty soon, they all got it and sent it back to their families. It wasn't long before it reached Kampala.'

Thirty years ago, the world had not heard of HIV or AIDS, but in Kasansero people had started falling ill, and nobody knew the cause. The people here called the disease 'slim' because of the shocking weight loss most sufferers experienced before dying. Hundreds died as the infection first took grip, and the deaths haven't stopped since.

As we reached the shore, Boston whispered, 'It's because they all share their wives, these dirty *Bugandans*.'

'Everyone knows it. If you marry a woman, you are entitled to her sisters – and, likewise, your brothers are entitled to your wife. No wonder they all got AIDS. Look at these people!' Matthias was watching a group of fishermen spreading out countless fish on the sand, to be salted and dried in the day's sun. 'Don't shake their hands, Lev, you'll catch it!'

Matthias was smiling, but I couldn't bring myself to smile back. There is a gallows humour among Africans who speak of AIDS, but the thought that seven in every ten of the people around me would live short lives because of this scourge didn't seem so funny to me.

'They've come to accept it,' shrugged Matthias as he showed us to a boat. 'It's no worse than malaria to them. If they die, they die. Most don't bother even getting checked.'

We spent the morning out on the water, fishing with one of the locals. As Kasansero dwindled on the shore, I found myself glad to be away from it, drawn to the purity of the lake. The water glistened pristine in the golden midday light. The stench, the filth, the AIDS and the noise seemed irrelevant out on the seemingly limitless water. It really was, as John Hanning Speke had described it, a tropical sea.

Back on the shore, the day's first catches were being landed. Crowds of ragged-looking fisherman were hauling their nets in from the water, or dragging their boats up onto the beach. The landing site hummed with the smell of newly caught fish. Great piles of tilapia, the freshwater fish common in the shallower waters of the lake, were being sorted and laid out, gills opening uselessly against the air.

Among the crowd one man in particular stood out. It was his eyes that drew me to him; they betrayed indescribable sadness. He seemed to have noticed me too, because I had not yet found my shore legs again when he made his way through the fish to find me. I got the impression he had been waiting.

'Please, sir,' he began, in English, 'come and see my children.'

Still feeling groggy from the boat, and having had quite enough attention from boisterous teenagers on the beach, I was in no mood to see more children, but the man introduced himself as Moses and there seemed to be an element of begging in his tone. 'Please,' he repeated. 'I have one hundred and twenty-three to look after.'

I looked at him dubiously. Any man with a hundred and twenty-three children is either a liar or mass fornicator on the scale of Genghis Khan – but those eyes told me differently. I gestured for Boston, and followed Moses up shore, through the ragged crowd.

Moses, it turned out, wasn't a prolific womaniser, and nor did he have any actual children of his own. He was, in fact, the overseer of Kasansero's AIDS orphanage and, as he led us past piles of plastic bottles, discarded nets and stinking fish bones that littered the narrow, muddy streets with open sewers on either side, I remembered Matthias's declarations of the day before. Palms and orchids grew wonderfully out of the heaps of shit. Goats bleated from doorways and the occasional cow would munch without care on a piece of car tyre. All the while, reggae blared out of the barber shops and all-day drinking dens. It was, I decided, like an even unhealthier version of Sodom and Gomorrah.

We reached the orphanage soon after. A collection of wooden huts with tin roofs were filled with dormitory beds, each housing three or four children apiece. A classroom consisted of a tin roof with some scaffold holding it up, and there was – to my surprise – a neat little garden where sweet potato and beans grew. As Moses showed us around, some of the children were digging. 'It's the holidays,' he said, 'so they must work. It's the only way I can feed them all.'

Moses led us into a small hut. On the walls a poster warned against sin and the evils of fornication. 'Abstinence is the way of the Lord!' declared one. 'Jesus loves those who avoid the sins of the flesh,' read another. They seemed righteous and perhaps even backward to my Western eyes, and Boston snorted at their mention of God, but they all made sense against the third poster we saw. 'HIV is Real!' it declared, simple and stark.

'There was a census done, ten years ago,' Moses began. 'Of a hundred people, only eight were reported to be HIV negative. This is where AIDs came from. The first reported case in Uganda was right here, on this very street. It was a woman called Nafakeero. She'd gone to Tanzania to trade in the markets at Kanyigo, and when she came back she fell very ill. The weight fell off her.'

'It's because of the hookers here,' Boston suddenly interjected. 'All these fishermen, they do nothing but fish and fuck, fish and fuck. All day long. No wonder they all have AIDS. I can smell it in the air.'

'Boston,' I said, with a stare that he understood to mean, 'Shut up!' In spite of his insensitivity, though, he did have a point. When landing sites like Kasansero sprang up to take advantage of the lake, the effect was of a gold rush. Fishermen flocked here, leaving their families behind, and so did businesses who could take advantage of the new populations. Traders, tinkers, barbers and restaurateurs came – and, so, too did the prostitutes. When I had asked the fishermen I was out with what they spent their money on, 'Ladies' seemed to be the general consensus.

'The fishermen I was out with on the lake, they talk about it like it's malaria or flu.'

'That is one of our biggest problems,' said Moses. 'After Nafakeero, it spread around Uganda like wildfire – and all because we dismissed it.'

I wondered if, in a continent that has faced up to and found a way to live with the constant threat of malaria and other tropical diseases, it was easier to dismiss AIDS as 'just another illness' than it was in the West. But Moses had other explanations. 'At the time,' he explained, 'people blamed it on witchcraft. They said those afflicted must be cursed. In the end, we put some of them onto islands in the lake and wouldn't let people visit them. We treated it like leprosy, something that could be contained, but we were not fast enough. By then it was already a way of life.'

'In the Congo, we did not blame witches. We all thought that the lubricant in condoms was to blame – that you could actually get AIDS from a condom!'

'It is a lack of education,' said Moses.

'We all thought you whites were out to kill us, sending condoms here!' By now Boston was roaring with uncontrolled laughter. Then, at once, he stopped, and fixed Moses with a look. 'Do you have AIDS?' he asked, quite nonchalantly.

My heart plunged at Boston's lack of tact, but Moses simply smiled benevolently and shook his head. 'I am one of the fortunate sons.

Both my parents died of AIDS when I was a boy, and I could so easily have been infected. But I was not, and this is why I wanted to help all of these children.'

We walked back into the sunlight. All around, the children were playing. Most of them had barely known their parents; Moses was all they had. He had not asked for any money, only that – through me – the world might know a little of his story. All the same, I handed him a few dollars. It was nothing more than a token, perhaps enough to feed a few of these children for a while. With Boston still shaking his head, we left Moses behind. Moved by his complete selflessness, we went back across the rubbish dumps, back to the beach, to watch those teenage fishermen laugh and joke. Soon, I imagined, some of them would have children of their own; and then, perhaps, they too would fall prey to 'slim' and disappear, leaving those children behind for Moses to look after. I wondered how many of those children would make adulthood, and how many of those would go on to fish on this lake and produce more children for the orphanage to take in. Moses was right: there was only one way the situation could change, and it was not with a few dollars pressed into his hand. It was with education, a changing of hearts and minds, the disintegration of all the myths of witchcraft, treacherous American scientists, and poisoned condoms, that thrived in places like this. But here, among people who either didn't notice or didn't seem to care, it was difficult to imagine how that could ever come to pass.

The following morning we walked north, away from Kasansero, with the glittering expanses of the lake on my right, a vast forest inland to my left, and the soft tread of sand beneath my feet.

THE ROAD TO KAMPALA

January 2014

North of Kasansero, the plan was to follow the shore for another 160km, seven days of hard trekking that would finally take us to Kampala, Uganda's boomtown and capital city. In Kasansero the fishermen warned us that the way north was a morass of tributaries and dense swamps, and if we wanted to stay close to the lake the trek was going to be laborious. Boston and I bickered about which route to take and, in the end, settled on a compromise: we would gather the services of a few locals and their boat – not to ride in, but to ferry our packs along the shore while we walked along the bank so as to make us light enough to move through the swamps, and if necessary swim around the mangroves. On the night before we departed I left Boston to source some likely guides and lay awake, thinking of the walk to come.

In the morning, Boston introduced me to the boatmen he had hired. At the shore of the lake, three policemen in uniform were lined up, with AK-47s slung over their shoulders. Beaming, Boston introduced me to the first, who told me his name was Fred. Before I could say anything, they began to load our packs into the boat.

I looked incredulously at Boston.

'It is better pay than for being a policeman, Lev,' said Boston as the three jolly officials pushed their boat out onto the lake.

We pushed north. There was something quite indulgent about walking along a beach for days on end, with palm-fringed shores, rickety fishing boats and quaint wooden villages making it feel as if we were in a clichéd image of holiday perfection. Despite warnings of 'chiggers', the voracious red mites that lived in the sand, it was too beautiful to wear boots and a nice change to walk either barefoot or in sandals, with the lapping waves to cool our feet. Most of the lake was flanked by thick forests, some of it national parkland, where colobus monkeys and waterbuck abounded. All along the shorelines birds of every variety gathered in their thousands: sacred ibis, white storks, Ugandan crested cranes and Egyptian geese. Yet, for all this perfection, for long stretches paradise turned to hell. The locals in Kasansero had not been exaggerating when they called this place a quagmire. For miles the path disappeared into impenetrable mangrove swamps, and Boston and I hacked our way on, turning in circles, until we stumbled upon a trail blazed by locals to the next settlement along the shore.

The swamp seemed to stretch forever. An hour later, lost – and with the next settlement still ten miles distant – we were wading through brown, soupy water that reached our waists. More than once, I had stumbled and become entirely submerged, having to be fished out of the stinking brine by Boston. We had backtracked in search of Boston's lost shoe, and spent ten minutes working out a way to pull him out of the soft earth that was trying to swallow him up. There was a part of me – some insane, masochistic part – that was beginning to enjoy the torment when Boston's eyes drew mine down to what appeared to be a pool of black liquid right beside my feet.

'It's a snake,' he whispered. 'Look, Lev! A python . . .'

I saw the blackness uncurl and disappear, setting the surface of the water to ripples. I froze. Then, putting on my most nonchalant face, I smiled back at the overjoyed Boston. 'It's probably just a monitor lizard.'

'I don't think so, Lev.' Boston had crouched and was already plucking a ghostly white snake skin from the reeds – by its rubbery texture, quite fresh.

'Still,' I muttered, with my eyes constantly on the water, 'at least he's quite small . . .'

An hour later, soaked to the skin, we stepped up onto dry land and, in front of us, stood three wooden huts and a crowd of villagers. Most of them were half-naked or just wearing filthy rags. By the remoteness of the place and the piles of shells lying on the sand it seemed they were shell-fish miners. We were to see more of them as we ventured north, men who collected shells to grind up and sell as chicken feed in the local markets. It is one of the worst-paid professions on the shores of Lake Victoria and, as they turned to see us, they were evidently thrilled. To them, strangers meant opportunity.

They rushed to meet us, eager to shake hands. One man cried out to congratulate us on not being constrained by such foolish things as 'paths' – and, as the crowd shifted, I saw something staked out on the beach, reflecting the cruel midday sun. Boston and I shared a look. It was another python skin – but this didn't belong to the friend we had made in the swampland. This was ten times as big, more than six metres long. Nor was it a skin that had been shed. This gleamed black and blue, a true snakeskin taken from a dead python and pegged out to dry. It was the kind you only see in movies and nightmares and I couldn't tear my eyes away.

A drunk man, deeply proud of his achievement, clawed his way to the front of the crowd.

'You want to buy it?' he slurred.

'I don't think I'd get it through customs,' I replied, but the joke was lost on him.

'Twenty dollars?'

Boston knelt at the skin to study it. By turns, he was shaking his head in what appeared disgust and grinning at the monstrosity of the beast.

The man in front of me produced an old mobile phone from his shorts and told me, with increasing pride, how just yesterday one of the villagers' goats had disappeared. Fearing the worst, they had tracked its last movements – and there, lying before them, was this enormous python, gorged and swollen with the goat inside.

'So we killed it. Watch . . .'

The cracked screen of the mobile phone came to life and I realised, with grim fascination, that he was about to show me the snake's final moments. In the picture the man appeared to be pulling on its tail as the swollen beast thrashed around. Then, from out of shot, a machete appeared. The final act was half-obscured, but at last the python was still.

When the image turned black, the man was nodding in appreciation.

'Did you eat it?' I asked, for want of anything better to say.

He looked at me with disbelief. 'Of course not!' he exclaimed, as if to say that the very idea was absurd. 'Snake meat is bad. It will become a drum.'

As we left them to their work, Boston sidled up to me and shook his head sadly. 'Savages,' he muttered.

It was the most ecologically minded thing I had ever heard Boston say. 'It's a predator,' I said. 'Perhaps they had to do it, to protect their goats.'

'I did not mean that, Lev!' Boston balked as we resumed our trek. 'I mean – why kill such a beautiful creature, just for a drum skin? They could have made so much more money if only they had sold it to a zoo . . . These Bugandans, Lev, they're too stupid to even think.'

Over the next days the shore alternated between dense swamp and pristine beaches where more landing sites like Kasansero had grown up. At times the mangrove forests were so alive with fire ants and spiders that we were forced to wade out into the lake and skip around the swamp instead.

The closer we got to his adopted home, the brighter Boston seemed to become. Passing from landing site to landing site, with the lake always glittering on the right – and, somewhere in it, the Kagera transforming to the true White Nile – he constantly chipped away. This, he told me, was a civilised country. I was humbled to admit he might have had a point. From the moment we set foot in Uganda the local attitude towards us seemed to change. Matthias's news story must have helped, but the villages we passed through were not as immediately suspicious as were in Tanzania, and the police didn't seem as eager to apprehend us for being English spies or the CIA. Uganda is a country that emerged from British rule in 1962 and it felt as if, unlike in some other corners of Africa, the colonial times were looked back on fondly. English is still the first language of Uganda, though the languages of the different tribes also proliferate, and perhaps it was this shared tongue that made it seem an easier, simpler country to navigate.

The Uganda we walked through might have felt more peaceful than Tanzania or Rwanda, but the truth is it is another piece of Africa with a violent, complex past. Unique among African nations, Uganda is a country inside which several kingdoms still exist, and perhaps it was this that meant it did not take to democracy easily after it gained independence from Britain. Uganda had been a British protectorate for sixty six years when independence came in 1962, and the first democratic elections saw an alliance between the Uganda People's Congress and the Kabaka Yekka, a monarchist party primarily comprising ethnic Bugandans, who make up more than half of the population, come to power. The alliance lasted only four years before the UPC forced out the Kabaka Yekka, forcibly changed the constitution, and formally abolished the traditional kingdoms of Uganda. This new situation couldn't last either and, in 1971, a military coup saw the UPC removed from power, and Idi Amin – a name now synonymous with East African dictatorship – begin his eight years of tyranny. This was a period marred by violence on a scale that came close to matching what we had seen in Rwanda. To maintain his military rule, Amin murdered more than 300,000 of his countrymen, drove the business-minded Indian minority out of the country – a feat which destroyed a once-flourishing economy – and led the nation to war by attempting to annex the Kagera region of Tanzania through which we had walked. Nor was Amin's deposition, prompted by a mutiny in the army during that same war, to bring peace back to Uganda; his legacy can be felt, even to this day, in the succession of civil wars the country has endured.

On 23 January, the forty-fifth day of our journey, came the first truly seminal moment in our expedition: Boston and I each took a single step and crossed from the southern to the northern hemisphere. We were straddling the equator.

Fifteen kilometres south of the small town of Buwama, still two days' trek from the suburbs of Kampala, there lies a nondescript, diagonal line in the road. At each end of the line stands a clear circular monument, with the word EQUATOR etched into the concrete. As Boston and I trudged up the Kampala road, the lake's shimmering vastness somewhere off to our right, we could tell we were near. Tourists had gathered around the monuments and there was a shop too, selling wooden shields and tacky key rings.

As we reached the line, I checked my GPS. According to the little contraption the line itself was nine metres away from the actual equator, but, looking into the eyes of the gathered journalists, I thought it prudent not to mention this. In the south, Boston and I took one look at each other and, the next step, we were in the north. There was an element of theatrics in it but, as I beamed at the journalists – 'At last,' I grinned, 'back in the north!' – I saw, in the corner of my eye, that Boston was beaming with genuine pride.

With the journalists scuttling off to fill their columns, Boston and I headed on up the road. For a time he was unusually silent. At a coffee shop we sat down to fortify ourselves for the fifteen kilometres we meant to complete that day, and watched the tourists mill. It felt strange to be in the presence of other outsiders. Until now I'd seen less than a handful of white faces in weeks – I'd been living, eating, and breathing an unseen Africa, one far away from the safari hordes and luxury lodges. The key rings being hawked from the side of the road cheapened the experience, somehow, but they also brought us down to Earth.

'Lev,' Boston began, breaking his silence. By the look in his eyes, I thought he wanted something. 'You know, we're like brothers now.'

Now I *knew* he wanted something. I put down my coffee. 'Yes, Boston . . .'

'Well, since I began this trip, I have been thinking.' He paused. 'I have been your guide. I have done a good job, have I not?'

'You have.'

'And I have been loyal and worked hard. And . . .' He seemed to be growing bolder with every statement. 'And we are brothers in arms!'

He had begun to beam, and I did not want to shatter the moment. Besides, though I wouldn't have stated it so plainly myself, there was truth in what he was saying. Boston's forthright banter had enlivened many monotonous days of hacking through jungle, or trudging through swampland – it would not have been the same without him.

'We are,' I admitted.

'And I have taught you a lot about Africa.'

'You have.'

'And you have taught me a lot about your world. And also about leading expeditions. Do you know, Lev, that is what I want to do in the future – to run my own expeditions . . .'

'It sounds like a good idea.' By now I was growing impatient. When he was not cutting straight to the heart of Africa's problems and proselytising sudden, violent solutions, Boston had a way of dancing around a subject like the most slippery politician.

'This is the biggest expedition of your life, Lev. You will be promoted in the army for this. You'll meet the Queen of England, and she'll make you a Sir. Then you'll become an MP.'

Hot coffee erupted from my lips as I tried to stifle my laughter. 'Things don't really work like that in England, Boston.'

Boston just snorted. 'You will,' he said. 'Believe me, Lev. I know.'

'Why don't you just say what you want, Boston? You're beginning to make me nervous.'

'Lev, this is the biggest expedition of my life also. It is a very important thing for me.' He gestured back at the monument to the equator, where some of the journalists still hovered. 'It makes us heroes of the people. Lev, if I walked all the way to the delta with you, I would be just as famous as Mr Levison Tembula. I could run my business and make some money . . . and then, then I could go back to the Congo with a big name. I could become an MP too!' He finished with a flourish. 'Lev, I want to come to the end. I want to see the pyramids and the sea.'

I couldn't help but feel sudden warmth for the mad Congolese sitting beside me. If it had been in my mind that my journey was barely even beginning, it had been in Boston's that his was almost at an end. Kampala was only two days' trek away, and my original proposition had been to leave Boston there, with his family, and find another guide to accompany me north, across the rest of Uganda and into South Sudan. The thing was – and perhaps I hadn't realised it until this exact moment – Boston was more than a guide to me now. It had happened while I wasn't looking, but he'd become a friend. His wild stories had been the things that kept me going through the first weeks, when my body had ached and complained at the torture I was putting it through.

'I know I'm not qualified, Lev. I don't speak Arabic, but I can learn.'

'In a few weeks?'

'I can do it.'

'But what about your family?' He had been looking forward to seeing them – and I had been looking forward to discovering what kind of woman had chosen to spend her life with Boston, and what kind of rebellious, curious children they were raising.

'Lily would understand,' he replied, with cool steel in his eyes.

For the longest time, I remained silent. I drank my coffee and thought. At last, I made my decision.

'Come to the north of Uganda with me. Help me get through South Sudan.' I couldn't promise any further than that, and I was not certain how useful Boston would be as I tried to cross South Sudan's infamous Sudd marshes. 'How does that sound?'

Boston smiled and said he was happy with the compromise – but there was a twinkle in his eye, the muted pleasure of a victory quietly won, and before we had started to walk again I already knew that it was only a matter of weeks before he raised the question again.

On the forty-seventh day of our journey, Kampala came in sight. We were up before dawn, walking through the pitch black, past lay-bys where lorries were emblazoned with banners declaring 'God is Great, God Is Good, God Is Everywhere!' and along a road where the traffic police kept demanding to know what we were doing. By the time the sun came up we had already travelled ten kilometres, and stopped to find something to eat at a dingy roadside pub. As Boston and I picked our way through plates of goat liver, a beautiful Ugandan girl in a simple flowery dress came to sit with us. It was a nice change to speak to somebody who was not Boston; I could not remember the last time I had such an involved conversation with a woman – and, as she finished her drink, she leant across the table and asked if she could take my phone number.

'Nice girl,' I said, as we watched her leave, disappointed that she hadn't got it.

Boston leaned in across the table and grinned. 'You have a way with prostitutes, Lev.'

I looked after her, bemused. 'I thought she was just on her way to Church . . .'

'Maybe she was,' Boston shrugged. 'Even prostitutes have God, Lev.'

In the hills outside Kampala, the country suddenly burst open with activity and life. Ten kilometres away from the city centre, the suburban sprawl grew up. Suddenly the dirt tracks became roads, the roads sprouted pavements, and *boda-bodas* – the bicycle and motorcycle taxis peculiar to this part of Africa – appeared everywhere.

We had come 35km already today, but entering the city limits gave me a newfound sense of determination. Boston, meanwhile, needed no such encouragement. I heard only half of what he was saying, but he was virtually frothing at the lips to tell me about the city's best restaurants and hotels, the bustling Nakasero Market, the hangouts of all the hotchpotch nationalities who made the city their home.

Walking into Kampala was like landing on the moon compared with my experience of Uganda so far. It is wrong of me to say it felt like stepping from the past back into the present, but that was what came to mind as we saw the first of the city's skyscrapers in the distance and felt the crowds thickening around us. Boston had described the place with such passion that I might have expected the streets to be paved in gold; right now, I would have given all the gold in the world for the promise of a comfortable hotel bed.

Kampala is a teenager of a city – boisterous and messy, contradictory but naïve and growing fast. As at the equator, the Ugandan press had been warned of our coming and, as we trudged up to the central Kibuye roundabout, the crowd of faces waiting for us was immense. Among them I saw Matthias again. It seemed as if half of the city had heard about the *Tembula Muzungu*, and for the final few miles we were surrounded by a horde of hacks, baying like so many hyenas, all shouting out for photographs and interviews. I suddenly felt thoroughly self-conscious and embarrassed at the attention.

At the roundabout police had cordoned off the thoroughfare, halting all traffic, and Boston and I walked into the crowds to rapturous applause. From somewhere off to the left there came a roaring of engines and, when I looked up, I could see a bank of motorcyclists turning circles around the roundabout. There must have been twenty of them, local Ugandan men dressed up like Hell's Angels from some dire '80s movie. Perhaps they had been tempted down by the promise of getting their souped-up scooters and Harley-Davidsons on national television, but their presence lent our arrival an even more carnival air.

Just as the crowd threatened to swallow us, one of the bikers wheeled around, ignoring the exclamations of a particularly agitated police officer, and gestured at his seat. Another was getting into position to offer Boston his when the police began to force the crowds back.

'Come on, Lev. We need to arrive in style!'

The biker who was offering me his seat introduced himself as Commanda. The one who was tempting Boston up to ride pillion was named Gangsta. Somehow, I doubted that these were the names their mothers had given them. Still, the crowds were only getting thicker, and somehow we had to make our way to the centre of the city. It wouldn't ruin the purity of the expedition, because we'd have to return and begin our walk here, at this same roundabout. And so, with the crowd still chanting my name, I climbed up beside Commanda and, with a whoop, he wheeled his Harley around and took off up the road. Behind me, Boston rode pillion with Gangsta while the rest of the bikers formed what I can only describe as an honour guard.

It was not, all things told, how I expected to arrive in Uganda's capital city.

Stunned by the somewhat incongruous reception, I barely noticed the way Kampala grew up around us. The police had cleared the highway and soon we were riding between two whooping columns of Ugandan Hell's Angels, right into the city's heart. Sometime later, with the tower blocks of newer Kampala giving way to the old town, where colonial buildings still lined the streets and the evidence of Uganda's British past was increasingly evident, the bikers deposited us in a square where yet more well-wishers had assembled. So much for getting to know the real Africa – this was a cavalcade of celebrity, and I wondered if it was the kind of reception of which Stanley or Speke would have approved.

I turned to say as much to Boston, but he was already swinging down from his bike and striding into the crowd. It took me a moment to register where he was going, but then I saw him put his arms around one of the ladies in the crowd, and for a second he disappeared as he was mobbed by children. These, I understood, were the family who had been waiting for him to come home. Lily, his wife, and his eldest daughter Penny, a resolute fourteen-year-old, looked as embarrassed by all the attention as we did. Clinging to Lily's shoulder was his middle child, Aurore, a beautiful, frizzy-haired girl of six who hid her face in her mother's breast.

In an ungainly fashion I clambered off the motorcycle and, in seconds, the bikers were off, riding in wild circles around the square in what I could only assume was further celebration. For a moment, I was lost. Coming out of the plodding serenity of our walk into this carnival seemed to have taken all of five seconds; I was in danger of losing my grip on reality.

Then Boston bounded back to my side. When everything around me was going crazy, there was still the – relative – normality of Boston to keep me grounded.

'You will see me later, yes, Lev?'

'Later?'

'Are you forgetting already?'

In the moment I was, but Boston had invited me to his family home for dinner the following night. He had been chattering about it all the way into the Kibuye roundabout, and I had to admit to being particularly intrigued at seeing how Boston lived a more sedate, family life.

'I'll be there, Boston,' I said, and we clasped hands in the African way – first up, and then down.

With Boston gone, it was only me and the revellers. For a moment I stood and watched them, and it was then that exhaustion truly caught up with me. We had come a long way today, and it was time to make camp.

A piece of Boston's endless chatter came to my mind and I weaved my way to a place he had recommended, the Hotel Le Bougainviller. The hotel was located in a quiet, residential area of town, away from the bustle of the market and financial area. There, among the leafy hills and white-walled embassies, I closed myself in my room and found peace and privacy for the first time I could remember.

There is a guilt that comes when you experience a moment of luxury in a country where you have seen such poverty. As I lay back on the hotel bed, I was thinking of Kasansero, Moses and the AIDS epidemic, the stragglers I had seen eking out their subsistence lives on the shores of the lake – but I was thinking of other things too: the promise of a good steak, a glass of red wine, and a long, dreamless sleep. I closed my eyes. This was all, I told myself, very surreal. I resolved to make the most of it because, in a few days' time, it would be back to the road – and, a few days after that, the luxury of Kampala would seem a very long way away.

Kampala is the pride of Uganda, a capital city that has more in common with the affluent cities of the West than it does the landing sites we had passed through on our way north. We were going to be here for seven days, the first real lull in our journey and, though I wanted to rest, I also wanted to know what made this city tick.

In this city of more than a million people there are a great number of different cultures all existing side by side. Although the Buganda, the local ethnic group, make up more than half the population, the city's ethnic mix is truly diverse. As in most modern countries, the growth of the urban economy has seen people flock to the capital – but Kampala's expansion has been driven by political factors too. During the rule of Idi Amin, and Milton Obote – who was overthrown by Amin and then restored to power following Amin's deposition – many Ugandans from the native northern tribes were brought into the city, to serve in the police and army, as well as to shore up the government's other, more shadowy, security forces. When the current President, Yoweri Museveni – who hails from the west of Uganda – came to power in 1986, many western Ugandans flocked to the city, especially those from Museveni's own tribe, the Banyankole. The way that Amin and Obote crippled the once-flourishing Ugandan economy, driving out foreign investment and curtailing the freedom of business as they pursued their Socialist ideals, meant that unemployment was rife outside the vital urban centres like Kampala – and this fuelled a mass influx of people to the city during the 1970s and early '80s. The result is a city with both the tensions that come from people with varied backgrounds and languages living in such close proximity, and the wonderful intermingling of those cultures. Many of the city's suburbs consider themselves miniature versions of the ancestral homelands of the tribes whose members live there, and many Kampala residents don't consider themselves to be 'from Kampala' at all, rather remaining true to their tribal roots. The city I was about to explore was not one I could ever hope to understand in a week – Boston still seemed to be working it out after all the years he had lived here.

I was woken, that first morning, by the sound of the call to prayer from the Ahmadiyya Central Mosque, which would have been fine had I not been kept awake, long into the night, by the sound of revellers from the Kampala Casino in a shopping centre not far from the hotel. January was the start of Uganda's short rainy season, but even early in the morning the sun was scorching overhead. I took a leisurely shower, washing away all of the grime that had worked its way deep into my skin, and then filled myself with more breakfast than I had eaten since Kigali. My body wasn't quite sure what to make of it, but once I had rested, it was time to go out into the city. It was time to re-provision for the journey ahead.

By the time evening came, my pack swollen with new supplies, I was ready to see Boston again. Since fleeing the Congo, Boston had made his home in one of Kampala's more affluent suburbs, perched on top of one of the hills west of the city. I was due to arrive at six, but by seven I was still walking in circles, lost amid the winding lanes, where gated buildings sat back from wide, tree-lined roads. I have to admit, the sensation of walking was a wonderful thing, but by the time eight o'clock came around I was beginning to grow weary. I seemed to be passing the same trees and bends in the road over and over again. We had made it all the way from the Nyungwe Forest by trusting to our instinctive skills for navigation – but now, in this sleepy city suburb, I was lost.

I must have passed Boston's house several times before I realised it was there. I hadn't expected it to be so grand. Boston's home seemed, to me, a palatial bungalow, set back from the road and surrounded by high walls and a locked gate, at which a security guard was snoozing.

It put me in mind of the kind of compounds that rich European landowners used to inhabit in the colonial days. Once the security guard had given me a cursory look, the gate drew back and I saw the bungalow itself, sitting in a vast, green garden. Boston was already waiting underneath the eaves at the front of the house.

'How did you get lost?' he demanded as I hurried to meet him. 'I thought you were supposed to be an explorer.'

'Because you gave me the wrong directions,' I grinned. 'I thought you were supposed to be a guide?'

Inside, Lily was waiting in a pair of fashionable jeans and a low-cut white blouse – every inch the beautiful wife Boston had described. I'd only seen her briefly when we rode into the city, but now that we were in her territory she appeared comfortable and hospitable, with a reserved manner. Boston's daughters had no such reservations. On seeing me, Penny marched up and held out a hand for me to shake. 'Nice to meet you again,' she announced, before disappearing to the dining table. Meanwhile, Aurore – the frizzy-haired girl who had been clinging to Lily when we arrived in Kampala – had already used my entrance as a diversion to sneak out into the garden, where she was excitedly skipping in circles – both to Boston's delight, and the security guard's evident ire.

'What about your son?' I asked.

'Jezu Adonis is in bed,' answered Lily. 'He's only one year old, so . . .'

Before his wife could finish, Boston burst in. 'I'll fetch him.'

Moments later, Boston was returning with Jezu Adonis walking tentatively at his side. The boy was obviously bewildered by the attention. He rubbed his eyes and, when he looked at me, his face creased in what I could only describe as terror. In seconds he was scrambling to get up into Boston's arms. Boston kept directing him to shake me by the hand, but Jezu didn't have the courage. He buried his face in Boston's shoulder and started to weep.

Boston could not control his mirth. 'He's not normally so shy. He just doesn't like you Muzungus. Come on, Adonis, say hello to the white man! He won't eat you!'

The reassurance, though, only magnified Jezu's doubt. Showing remarkable agility, he wriggled free from Boston's grasp and hurtled for the safety of his bedroom. With a withering look at her husband, Lily followed.

'Don't be offended, Lev. He is one year old.'

'I'm not offended, Boston.'

'I'm telling you, Lev, it is not his fault.'

'Boston, I'm really not . . .'

In the bedroom, the crying had subsided, and Lily reappeared. As she swept on into the dining room, summoning Aurore from the garden, Boston poured us two measures of whisky and handed me a glass. 'I don't like to leave them at home with the nanny,' he confided, as the smells of home-cooked food tempted me on. 'You never know if she'll sell them to a witch.'

'You must be kidding . . .'

'I'm serious, Lev. It happens all the time. Two or three kids go missing every week in Kampala. You see it in all the newspapers. Nannies desperate for cash will sell a child for a couple of hundred dollars and they'll never be seen again. Once a witch gets hold of them, it's dead.' He lowered his voice to a whisper, so his children would not hear. 'They murder them, chop off their genitalia, and turn them into lucky charms. People pay a lot of money.'

'That's disgusting, Boston.'

'Yes, but it's rife. The only way is to have your boy circumcised – that way he's a man and useless to the witch. Are you circumcised, Lev?'

I decided not to answer.

In the dining room, huge platters of Congolese food were spread out in front of me: *matoke*, a kind of starchy green banana that is cooked and pounded into a meal; baked tilapia, no doubt fresh from the shores of the lake; *ugali*, with much more flavour than any we had eaten on our travels; and more rice and steamed vegetables than I thought I would see for the next several months. Lily was an excellent cook. Boston opened beers, which he insisted we drank from the bottle, and the family all ate with their hands. As I helped myself to more tilapia, I had a sudden surge of pride; it was an immense privilege, I knew, to be let into Boston's house and to eat with his family. And, not to mention, the food was igniting taste buds I thought had died somewhere in the Tanzanian bush.

As we ate, Boston began regaling Lily with stories of our trek. Most of them I recognised, but there were moments here that I felt certain must have happened to somebody else, or else been plucked straight from Boston's imagination. Lily took it all in with a healthy scepticism and I was suddenly reminded of the stories Boston had told me of her – how Lily herself had been tortured for being at his side during the conflicts of the Congo, how she'd distributed leaflets in an effort to re-take the Congo during its wars, how she had escaped with him over the border, leaving behind everything she knew to start a new life here. Was this shy, reserved, excellent cook really the same bold mistress? Unlike Boston, Lily was not a person to speak of the things she had lived through – but I could tell, by the gleam in her eye when Boston launched into another one of his tirades, that she had an inner strength she did not often display. There was no longer any doubt in my mind: when I wasn't here, Lily wore the trousers; underneath her tiny frame and nervous smile, she was a powerful woman.

'And I hear, Levison, that you've convinced Ndoole to come with you into South Sudan?'

I shot a look at Boston, who only shrugged in a noncommittal way. 'He is a great guide,' I ventured, uncertain exactly how Boston had framed his decision.

'Do you know what's happening in the north?'

I nodded. 'We'll have to make a decision somewhere up the road.'

Our crossing into South Sudan was still some five hundred kilometres away, but it had been in the back of my mind for many weeks. We had barely set off from the Nyungwe when rumours reached us of the rumbling conflict in the world's newest country, and every time we had reached a town or village along the way the stories had intensified. Now that we were in Kampala, a modern city, I had access to the kinds of information outlets I hadn't for most of my trek, and those rumours had solidified into real knowledge: the unrest in South Sudan had grown into much more. Five hundred kilometres to the north, a country was at war.

South Sudan gained its independence from Sudan in 2011 – ending one of Africa's longest and bloodiest civil wars – but, since then, has itself been dominated by internal conflict. In December, just as my trek was beginning, the president, Salva Kiir Mayardit, declared that his former vice president, Dr Riek Machar, was behind an attempted military coup. Power politics quickly turned to real fighting when Kiir ordered the disarming of troops from all but one ethnicity inside the Presidential Guard. Like Uganda, South Sudan is a country in which people from many different ethnicities live side by side – but Kiir's act ignited the simmering disharmony between his native Dinka and Machar's native Nuer. In the days that followed, certain Dinka elements began attacking Nuer civilians in the capital city of Juba – and, though these initial outbreaks of violence were quickly curbed, it wasn't long before a conflict that had begun as political had come to be defined along ethnic lines. By the time I reached Kampala, hundreds of thousands of people were being displaced by the violence and fleeing across South Sudan's borders to refugee camps in Kenya, Sudan – and especially Uganda.

I didn't blame Lily for being sceptical and, now that I saw her children the gravity of what I was suggesting we do struck me more pointedly. Could I really ask their father to accompany me into a live warzone, to act as my guide in a country he didn't know and where he didn't speak the language? I was determined to follow the river, no matter what, but I was beginning to believe that I couldn't ask it of Boston. South Sudan, dominated by the vast marshes of the Sudd, had been one of the journey's greatest challenges from the outset; I only hoped that the current conflict didn't make it impassable.

'We'll know more when we get there,' Boston declared, draining his beer as if to put a full stop to the conversation. 'The refugees will tell us. Now, Levison, I have something you have to see . . .'

Half of me suspected a stuffed crocodile, but Boston took me through to the sitting room where photographs lined the walls and an old shoebox crammed with more had been unearthed and left on a table to pore through. It was good to see Boston so relaxed. He was the master here and I was his guest – no longer an employer or a leader – and it was a different kind of smile on his face as he showed me these old photographs. Here were pictures of him from his youth, the outrageous hair of the 1980s, his dubious fashion choices and oversized shirts; Boston and Lily standing proudly outside his first small business, a shop selling records; his old ranch in the Congo, where a young Boston – recognisable only by the smile – stood beside his mother, who looked almost identical to her son. Among them all there lay a lone photograph of Boston's father. He picked it up between forefinger and thumb and handed it to me. 'It was months before he went missing,' he said – and I noted that here, with his family around him, he said 'went missing', whereas, out in the bush, he had always intimated murder.

Later, once the children had gone to bed, it was time to make my exit. Boston, perhaps driven by one too many beers, insisted on walking me down the road. 'It's so the great explorer doesn't get lost!' he exclaimed – but, by the end of the garden, where his security guard was still fast sleep, he seemed to have forgotten.

'She's worried about the north,' I said, looking back at Lily in the door of the house. 'I am too, Boston. Look, I *have* to go, but you . . .'

Boston didn't want to hear more. This time, he wasn't smiling when he cut me off: 'There is a month between there and now. A lot can change, Lev.'

Alone, I wended my way down the twisting streets until, at the bottom of the hill, I was able to find a *boda-boda* to take me back into town. There, I sat up, long into the night, bickering with the unstable internet connection in the hotel lobby, as I tried to learn more about what was happening up north, and the challenges we would have to face.

'Listen,' said Boston, stalking across the hotel lobby for the TV buzzing in the corner. There, he fumbled to turn up the volume. We had spent the morning in the Kisenyi market, where Boston had commissioned a metalsmith to make him a catapult from smelted car parts. In the hotel, rap music began to blare out across the lobby, drawing infuriated looks.

'Talentless!' Boston fumed, insisting I watch. 'Can you believe it, Lev?'

'It's rap music, Boston.'

'But *listen*.'

I did. Only two words seemed to emerge from the mix. They were strangely familiar.

'The song is called "Levison Tembula",' Boston explained. 'Levison the Walker. You are famous, Lev, but it doesn't stop it being shit.'

We had marked today as another rest day before we followed the shore east to Jinja, where the true White Nile emerged and began its course due north, but there was to be precious little resting. Boston had promised to show me the heart of the *real* Africa and it was with his sardonic grin emblazoned in my thoughts that we hailed a *boda-boda* driver and headed for the southern bounds of the city.

After several wrong turns, we arrived at a fenced-off section of woodland, which appeared as nondescript as everywhere else outside Kampala's beating heart. Parked up inside was a brand new Land Cruiser, its windows blacked out, its wheel trims mysteriously clean, in spite of the dust that swirled around. As Boston bid goodbye to the *boda-boda* driver, one of the black windows wound down and a Ugandan man stepped out.

'Have you brought gifts?' he began.

Boston said, 'You didn't mention gifts.'

The man looked far from impressed. 'You were told to bring a white cockerel and five litres of fresh cow's milk. You should know, Levison Tembula, you cannot come without gifts.'

I looked at Boston, who didn't seem in the least perturbed. 'We'll find them, Lev. Come.'

The gifts, Boston told me as we headed into the shanties, were for Mama Fina, reputed to be Kampala's richest witch doctor. 'She prefers to be called a traditional healer,' he explained as we made for what looked a likely stall among the shanties, 'but she was in the *Red Pepper* doing things that didn't look medicinal at all.'

The *Red Pepper* had been the favourite rag among the fishermen in Kasansero, and I had already witnessed first-hand the sort of lurid headlines in which the tabloid specialised. Photographs of Mama Fina had been spread across its central section, where the paper exposed her as Kampala's most prolific nymphomaniac, who regularly used sex as part of her dark magic.

'Then why are we going to see her?'

'So you can see for yourself, what these magicians can do.'

We came to a stall where it seemed we could buy eggs, Coke and other assorted goods but our requests for fresh milk were, predictably, met with bewildered silence. In the end Boston managed to unearth five litres of UHT in battered plastic cartons and, in place of a cockerel, a small billy goat who looked at us, disgruntled, as we led him away on a length of string. Before we got back to the Land Cruiser, Boston took a detour into the shanties, managed to procure a small jerry can and, with the broadest grin, proceeded to decant the UHT. 'This witch doctor will never know the difference, Lev. It's all for show.'

On inspection of our gifts – which, though blatantly not what was demanded, appeared to be good enough – the man from the Land Cruiser led us down to the shore of the lake. Towing the goat behind us, we trailed him along the beach until, at last, we began to see people. Twenty or thirty of them – poor men, women, even a few children – were gathered along the breakers of a secluded cove, where driftwood fires littered the sand. Clusters of homemade spears were lodged in the ground beside each of the fires; as we approached, I couldn't help thinking they had the appearance of shrines.

'Are they all waiting for her?' I asked.

'You don't have to wait, Tembula,' said the man who was leading us and, together, we picked our way through the petitioners.

Ahead of us a cliff reared up, and in its shadows I saw a recess in the stone, a natural cavern in which yet more fires were burning. It was exactly as I had imagined a witch doctor's hideaway to be – peculiarly so. My imagination, stoked by Hollywood clichés, was being fed images to keep it alive. Smoke from incense sticks billowed in great reefs from the mouth of the cave, lending the cove a malign air. A group of camp followers, half-naked – and many of them disabled – gathered around one of the beach fires, stirring the contents of a cast iron cauldron. The spearheads, blades pointed upwards, suddenly took on a devilish air.

'You know what this is, Lev.' I was about to tell Boston it was downright creepy when he cut me off. 'It is *branding*. Mama Fina isn't even her real name. It's Sylvia. All of this – the smoke, the cave – she knows what she's doing. She is a clever woman, this Mama Fina.'

Boston was right. Mama Fina, he explained, had started out life as an orphan wandering the Mabira Forest east of Kampala, but, forty years on, was living the life of a fabulously wealthy business woman. This cavern we were approaching was not her home; it was her place of business, a store front for a very particular product. Mama Fina had made her cash every which way she could, first as a housemaid, a cleaner and washer girl, before taking over a textile business and beginning a chain of stores. She had even, Boston assured me, gone on to monopolise the *boda-boda* taxi service in Kampala. But it was here, in 'healing', that she had truly made her money.

'Casting spells, mixing potions, chanting and singing, praying to the gods of water and wind and fire.' Boston seemed to take great delight in recounting the list of acts she performed. 'She is an actress, Lev, but these Ugandans believe her. Did you know, she is the president's personal healer . . .'

Mama Fina was waiting for us in the mouth of the cavern. As the fog around her parted, I saw urns and pottery chalices arranged in delicate piles. Mama Fina was enormous. As she approached, she waddled like one of the ducks out on the lake. She was wearing an ill-fitting traditional dress, the bottom hem heavy with dirt, and her deep black eyes exuded what I took for a keenly focused greed. Her black hair was cropped close to her scalp and, on each of her fat fingers, huge jewels sat in rings. I was about to introduce myself when she opened her mouth and hollered four belligerent words.

'Take off your shoes!'

Boston looked to me. Half of him had the air of a naughty schoolboy, but the other half was distinctly unimpressed.

Once we had taken off our shoes, Mama Fina's hand shot out and clutched me by the wrist. 'You have kept me waiting,' she breathed and, barely concealing her anger, dragged me across the sand to one of the driftwood shrines.

'Don't worry, Lev. She is only going to bless you.'

Curiosity was driving me but I suspected I could not have backed out, even if I had wanted. We began by kneeling at a rock covered in a white sheet. This, Mama Fina explained, was a shrine to the gods of the water, and it was here that she would ask them to protect me from the evils of the river and the crocodiles who called it home. In a torrent of words I could hardly understand, she instructed me to pour water upon the ground nine times, and then to spit on the goat's head a further nine. As I dredged up what saliva I had, my eyes locked with Boston, who only nodded – whether to compel me to go on, or in amusement, I didn't quite know.

Afterwards, Mama Fina dragged me to an identical shrine. 'This,' she declared, 'is the shrine to the gods of white men.' She seemed to believe I would feel most comfortable here, but I was not sure how I felt, kneeling at this shrine. Again, I lifted a three-headed vessel, drew up water from the lake, and proceeded to pour it over the shrine.

'Now,' Mama Fina began, 'take off your clothes.'

I looked at Boston and saw, in his eyes, that he knew this had been coming.

'My clothes?'

'Do it, Lev,' said Boston. 'It is better not to argue.'

With Boston's eyes on my back and Mama Fina's implacable glare on my front, I began to disrobe. I can't say what compelled me to do it – certainly not belief in the gods of white men, nor in Mama Fina's magic. Perhaps just a morbid curiosity at what was about to happen. Once I was stripped down to my underpants, Mama Fina directed me to the water. I was, it appeared, about to have a bath.

At Mama Fina's instructions, I stepped into the lake but, before I had gone a single stride, she summoned me back.

'What?' I asked. Mama Fina was simply pointing at the poor goat. It appeared he was going to have a bath with me.

Tugging on the goat's leash, I dragged him into the water. He wasn't impressed. Only an hour ago he had been happily wandering through the shanties, chewing on whatever grasses he could find. Now, he was part of a ritual to some intangible gods. I muttered an apology under my breath and, hearing Mama Fina bark behind me, sank to my knees.

For a moment Mama Fina's enormous body loomed above. Then, she set to work. It took me a moment to realise what she was doing. Hunkered over me, she was beginning to scrub my back with tea leaves and the filthy, tepid water of the lake. The scrubbing intensified and, in the corner of my eye, I could see Boston beaming from the shore. Then, as suddenly as it began, it relented. I heard the splashing that told me Mama Fina was retreating through the lake. Turning to follow, I realised, too late, that she had only been going to the shore to pick something up.

I was about to discover what the five litres of milk she had demanded we bring were for. She was already bringing it up above my head. Seconds later, the whole five litres cascaded around me, in all its freezing glory. Gasping for air, I reeled back – and, when I could finally rub the milk from my eyes, I saw Mama Fina's face open in a wry chuckle.

'The ceremony is over,' she declared, and promptly tramped back to the shore of the lake.

On the beach I was presented with a spear and badly carved shield for my protection, charms I was entitled to as one of the blessed. Boston, I was later to learn, had given her 258,000 Ugandan shillings for her services today. That was the equivalent of around £60. Not bad work if you could get it, I thought.

'That was her magic?' I asked as we watched her waddle away across the beach, to where the black Land Cruiser was waiting. The goat tried to resist being pulled behind her, but his attempts came to nothing; he was, I guessed, about to become somebody's lunch.

'Do you feel blessed?' asked Boston.

If this had happened at home, I might have felt violated. 'Perhaps just a little . . . bewildered.'

But our display in the water hadn't even drawn the attention of the onlookers from the beach. To them, it had just been another blessing among many: an ordinary day. Uganda, I had seen, was rife with magicians like Mama Fina. At the roadsides we had passed posters and flags advertising their dubious services: remedies for malaria, for syphilis, even for AIDS; help with finding lost property and lost lovers. In the back pages of the newspapers there was more of the same: Dr Kamaagagi was everywhere, selling his services as a spiritual specialist in erectile dysfunction.

'If you want,' said Boston, 'I can take you to Owino. It is a market, in the centre of Kampala. There you can buy almost any fetish in the world. Bones, animal skins, snake poison, toads and cats. Masks and potions, herbs and trinkets, little bags of powder. You can get it all, Lev.' He stopped. 'Do you want to grow your penis by six inches?'

I stammered in reply.

'They can do anything for you, these magicians.'

KINGDOMS OF THE LAKES

Jinja and Northwards, February 2014

A week in the bustling suburbs of Kampala seemed to pass by with alarming speed, but Sunday was our final night before we walked east, along the northern shore of the lake. In the morning, on 2 February, we restored ourselves with a morning coffee at the Speke Café, and then resumed our long trek.

It was two hard days' walk from Kampala to the river town of Jinja, following the main highway through the Mabira Forest, dodging trucks laden with logs that Boston was sure had been felled illegally. Sometimes, when the road was quiet, all that could be heard was the chattering of colobus monkeys or the occasional dog-like bark of a baboon in the surrounding jungle.

Jinja appeared as a vision of such incredible relief that I was almost too exhausted to notice the view. For all the arguments about the true source of the river, Jinja presented the first stretch of river that was incontestably the Nile; it was at this point that the river took on its moniker and began its journey due north. I'm sure a lot of Ugandans would have argued that I shouldn't have wasted my time with the previous seven hundred miles, but getting to the hillside overlooking the point Speke had famously declared the 'source' was more than worth the perambulation.

Speke set foot on the grassy hill overlooking the point at which the river pours out of the lake on 28 July 1862. Clad in a tweed shooting jacket and sporting an enormous beard, he had waited for this moment all his life. Two years previously, he had looked out upon this same lake from the south, as his companion Richard Burton lay ill with fever, and declared that it was the fabled source of the Nile. It was to begin a conflict that lasted until the end of his life. Speke and Burton returned from that expedition separately, Speke going back to England whilst Burton rested in Arabia. According to Burton, the pair had made a gentleman's agreement that Speke would not make any announcements until Burton had made it home safely and they could share the glory. Speke, however, went the very next day to the Royal Geographical Society and declared that he – and he alone – had discovered the source of the Nile. Thus began a rivalry that was to continue for the next five years.

To Burton's chagrin, the eminent fellows of the RGS hailed Speke a hero and granted him more funds to return to the Nile and prove the theory by reaching the point at which the river actually exits the lake. So, in 1862, Speke – this time choosing a rather less argumentative walking partner in the form of James Augustus Grant – set off, while Burton wrote books and bitter letters from England. Burton contended that the Nile actually flowed from a number of sources and that Speke was a speculative opportunist, a bad friend – and, worse, a terrible geographer. In many ways, Burton was right. Up to that point, Speke had never actually laid eyes upon the Nile and, until he reached Jinja and saw it for himself, his theory that Lake Victoria was its headwater was pure conjecture.

Nowadays, an ugly red obelisk about fifteen feet tall, made of chipped marble and bearing a grubby plaque, marks the point at which Speke reached Jinja and uttered his famous words – relayed back to London and the eager ears of the RGS by telegraph – 'The Nile is settled.'

As I glanced out across the bay, I felt, like that rogue Speke must have done, a sense of wondrous magic – and, I must admit, a little pride.

The lake, and the emergent river, didn't give itself up until the very last moment. This was exactly how I wanted it to be revealed, like a secret being finally uncovered. The view, I knew, had changed since Speke stood here, the landscape redesigned by a great hydro-electric power station and dam, built in the early 1950s to harness the power of the river. Ripon Falls, over which he had looked, had been swallowed up by the dam, but the evidence of a wide, low cascade was still here in outcrops of drowned rocks and a small island on which a single tree flourished. Some iron girders still jutted from rock on the shore – I imagined them to be the detritus left behind by an early attempt to build a jetty. To the south, Lake Victoria opened up, a singular, glistening expanse. The southern horizon was obscured by rows of jagged islands sitting in the lake.

On this western side of the river Boston and I stood alone, but from the other side came distant voices. In the heat haze I could just make out the east bank full of vendors selling trinkets to the tourists.

The news that Speke had indeed 'confirmed' Lake Victoria as the source of the Nile infuriated Burton, who had been watching his progress with envy, so much so that he made a public declaration that, since Speke hadn't actually bothered following the river North to a point at which it had already been explored, then nothing had been proven at all. To settle matters once and for all, a debate was arranged, to be held in Bath on September 15th, 1864, where all the great names in geography and exploration would be assembled and, finally, the rivals could slog it out over maps and oratory.

On the morning of 15 September 1864, Burton and Speke sat at opposite ends of the hall, and among the crowd were some of the most famous people of the day: Roderick Murchison, president of the RGS, and the explorer David Livingstone, who was by then a household name. The crowds were all there for the stars of the show – Burton and Speke, who were to clash that afternoon – but first, as in all Victorian meetings, there were the minutes and parish notices to deal with. Speke, never one for form, excused himself and decided to kill a bit of time by doing a spot of grouse hunting at his cousin's nearby country estate. A few hours later, just after 2.30pm, a messenger burst into the hall and muttered something into the host Murchison's ear: Speke was dead. He had been killed in an accidental discharge of his shotgun as he clambered over a style. Murmurs reverberated around the room. Burton's face went white as a sheet. Some whispered that Burton had perhaps arranged the murder of his rival, others that Speke had committed suicide. Burton, aghast, had never wanted his companion dead – even the Nile wasn't that important.

After that, Burton was never the same again – he was always to blame himself for the terrible tragedy. For him, Speke had been a worthy subordinate who had let his ego get the better of him. The truth was, to Burton their rivalry was all a game – it was the journey that mattered, not the destination – and friendship counted more than winning. For Speke, it seemed, all that mattered was the Nile – and, in the end, he won. In death, his glory was secured – and Burton would forever after be seen as the quintessential eccentric traveller, whose subordinate had claimed the ultimate prize.

At the bottom of the gardens, Boston and I found a little boat that would take us onto the Nile and motored out to a little island in the centre of the river, at the exact spot where it meets the lake. Here, an entrepreneurial soul had set up a gift shop selling awful T-shirts and key-rings. It was a dilapidated shack, perched on jagged rocks, and its floor was three inches deep in Nile water – but the shopkeeper didn't care. He seemed to think of it as his own individual kingdom and welcomed us warmly, pointing out all the little souvenirs and keepsakes we could buy. Boston began to peruse the tat, but I just wanted to wade out from the outcrop and stand for a moment on this momentous spot. At the edge of the rocks a crude sign read 'This is where the river Nile starts its 4,000 mile journey to the north.' I gazed in that direction, tracking the great river as it cut a gorge through the forested valley.

Boston found me standing there, silently staring into the north.

'What is wrong, Lev?'

I couldn't put it into words. Gone was my wonder at standing in the same place as Speke and seeing the same things he had seen, more than 150 years ago. I was, I admitted, beginning to feel something very different. I wouldn't say it to Boston, but I was suddenly affected by an overwhelming sense of terror. I was going to have to walk every last one of those miles and, across history, they had defeated better men than me.

The town of Jinja began life as a fishing village but its unique place at the mouth of the river made it a melting pot too. For much of Africa's history, the Nile was a great divider, with different languages and cultures evolving along its eastern and western banks, the water itself a barrier to their intermingling. Jinja, however, was special. Jinja was one of those rare places where the river itself could be crossed, by a natural bridge of rocks at the top of the Ripon Falls – and, because of this unique geography, Jinja naturally attracted traders and migrants.

Even the name Jinja is suggestive of a place where men from different worlds could come and find one another; in the languages of the Buganda and Basoga people, who lived on different sides of the river, it means the very same thing: the place of rocks.

The fishing village became a town in 1907, when the British named it an administrative centre, and Lake Victoria first began to be exploited for travel and industry. Now, it is Uganda's second biggest town, with a population of almost 100,000. Boston and I arrived, dirty and dishevelled, and were thankful of a return to civilisation. Perhaps we had been spoiled by our week in Kampala, but from here the way north would feel increasingly rural and remote. It was time to spoil ourselves one last time.

We met my old friend Pete Meredith at the 'Nile River Explorers', a tented campsite and hangout for backpackers, ageing hippies and that most eccentric of breeds – the expatriate. Amid the lush tropical gardens, where vervets screeched incessantly from the tall branches and rock pythons slithered around the banks, long haired gap year types spoke of spiritual enlightenment and kayakers told tales of the 'Nile Special', a particularly daunting rapid just downstream. The river was beautiful and shrouded in mist. It was the weekend of the Nile River Festival, an event which saw hundreds of paddlers from around the world descend upon the white water north of Jinja.

'It's gonna be wild, bru.'

Pete Meredith's distinctive South African accent was tinged with excitement. We'd first met some years before, when I had been roaming East Africa in search of adventure. In fact, it was Pete who introduced me to Boston so, in many ways, the reunion was an integral part of my journey. It simply had to happen.

'I bet you've got some stories eh?' he smiled, but I knew better than to regale this man with any. He'd been there and done it all and there was nothing I could tell him that he didn't already know. This was a man who'd seen his best friend get eaten by a crocodile. In spite of his laid-back style, this tall vegetarian rafting guide was as hard as nails. He'd served in the South African Paratroopers and lived in the bush most of his life. Also for most of his life he'd drunk like a fish and partied hard – until recently, when he'd met Leila, a vegan yoga teacher, and together they'd travelled to India in search of enlightenment. Nowadays, they lived in a shipping container in Jinja and spent their time on the river. It was the Nile that brought Pete to Uganda; it was this river that provided the sole meaning of his existence. It isn't surprising then that, in 2004, he was the man who led the first team to travel its entire length in a raft. He'd also been the source of much help in planning my own expedition.

'Whatcha gonna do about South Sudan? It's not good there at the moment, but you'll have some fun . . .'

By fun, Pete really meant danger. I liked Pete; in spite of his new hippie leanings he was a soldier at heart.

'You're in good hands with Boston, but don't let him rip you off!'

As Pete slapped Boston on the back, Boston's face broke into an expression of disbelief. 'Mr Pete, how dare you! You know I would give my life for Lev . . .'

'Let's go have some beers,' Pete said.

In the NRE, it seemed that all the expatriates in Uganda had gathered together. Pete was unusual, having shunned life's material things to live the life of his choosing – but not as unusual as many of the expats communing here. That's the thing about ex-pats – they really are often very odd. It was fascinating to see them in their adopted habitat, carefree and wild. As Pete explained, you only had to spend a few minutes speaking to one before you discovered who coveted whose servant, who had slept with whose wife and who had bribed which local chief. In Jinja there were Americans, Dutch, French, South Africans and plenty of Brits – and, like elsewhere in Africa, they ranged from travellers to mercenaries, charity workers to missionaries. Each had their own agenda, whether it was money, oil, God – or simply the opportunity for bragging rights.

'Not me,' said Pete. 'I'm here for the river. Nothing else.'

Soon, outside the bar, the mist would burn away, and the Nile would be revealed to the hundreds of kayakers who were about to converge on it for a three-day celebration of daredevilry on the water. I had already heard Jinja spoken about as a 'black hole', a kind of vortex that sucked people in and refused to let them go – and the Nile River Festival was part of the reason. It is at the heart of Uganda's booming tourism sector and, as Pete led Boston and me to its banks, sport lovers and groupies of every nationality were getting ready. Colourful streamers and stalls lined the riverbank, and the sounds of carnival were in the air.

By the time Boston and I reached the river, the party was already in full swing. Music was blasting out of speakers, beer was being drunk, and at first it seemed that kayaking was the last thing on anybody's mind. Rather, the festival was about one thing: beer, and how it might be used to celebrate life along the water.

'Check out the Special,' said Pete, pointing to a seething explosion of foam. On the river, waves cascaded over enormous boulders to create a swirling rapid. It was the famous 'Nile Special' – unique because it performs its aquatic marvels 365 days of the year. Suddenly a red flash flipped in the air, spurting out of the rapids like an insignificant bean. It was a paddler – a professional, by the way he landed upside down in the white water but still managed to perform an Eskimo roll and get back up. The crowd cheered and he raised a fist, whooping as he passed by.

'It'll all be gone soon,' said Pete with sudden melancholy.

'Gone?'

'Because of the dam. If they build another dam here, like they plan to, none of these rapids will be left and we'll all be left without jobs. Not just us ex-pats – all the Ugandans who work in tourism too. People come from everywhere to see this water, and the government wants to fuck it up with another dam. It's a total waste of time. You know, it'll only generate 180 megawatts – but it'll destroy twenty eight kilometres of river . . .'

I'd already seen the Owen Falls Dam at the mouth of Victoria – built in 1954, that was the dam which had submerged Ripon Falls, thus destroying the famed view that Speke would have seen. But at least it created 350 megawatts of energy, and submerged only two kilometres. This new one was a false economy.

'Once it's gone, it's gone. The river will never be the same again. Fifty thousand people a year come to Uganda to get wet in these rapids. That's a lot of cash – but it goes to the locals and not the government. That's why they want to build this thing. It's just greed. Think of all the people that will lose their homes.'

It was to be a story I'd hear over and over. Dams, and the taming of the Nile, seemed to be a constant feature of local politics, not just here in Uganda but further north as well. The Nile, it seemed, was all things to all men. A source of drinking water, food, entertainment, and above all else, money. The Nile is life.

But we had dallied long enough, first in Kampala and now here, this strange riverside vortex where, it seemed, if you did not leave straight away, you were destined to stay forever – just like Pete. After one last night of relaxation, watching the kayakers out on the river, we woke with raging hangovers and set off for the north.

*

'Once upon a time, in the Congo,' said Boston as we were approaching the village of Baale, 'I met an old man near to the Ituri Forest. He lived just on the edge of the jungle and had got back from a hunting trip with his sons. He was a simple man, and he lived off wild bananas and bush meat. That day, he'd killed a porcupine and a monkey and was about to roast them over an open fire. I'd been walking for a few days and wanted to know how much further there was to go, so I asked him. "Bwana. How far to the other side of the forest?" And the old man laughed. "Son," he said, with a hand on my shoulder, "I have lived here all my life. I am an old man now and I tell you this. These trees, this forest, it goes on forever. If you walk into the woods and keep going, no-one will ever see you again. You'll be lost. There is no end."'

Three days upriver from Jinja, Boston and I stood in front of what I could only describe as a vision from hell. On one side, the river cut its course north; on the other, what had once been virgin jungle was now a fresh plantation of tree stumps, blackened by fire, the indigenous forest being forced back by flames to make way for farming ground. The Nile was growing broader the longer we walked and, at this point, was almost a mile wide. But, as it became more powerful, so too did the opportunity for harnessing its power grow – not only in the dam we had seen outside Jinja, but in the potential for irrigation and agriculture as well. The river brought farmers here, and farmers meant deforestation. The Nile, we were seeing, brings life – but it also takes it away.

'Did he really believe that, Boston? The old man?'

Boston scoffed, 'He thought the forest was endless, and in it the animals and fruit would continue to be there until the end of the world. That's the problem with Africans, Lev – they don't see a problem with chopping down the trees, especially if there's a profit to be made.

See, the Mabira Forest we passed through – it looks real, but the truth is it's like those Hollywood movie sets. It's a façade. Go into the woods fifty metres and behind the old mahogany and teak trees you'll find destruction, where the loggers have been. The government does nothing to stop it.'

It was true. In the Mabira we'd seen five-hundred-year-old trees sawn down at a rate of ten a day by teenagers who'd been paid three dollars by the landlord. This was big money for a poor villager, and with the economics of the industry working like that, what hope was there for convincing local Ugandan people to leave the forests alone? It's all well and good preaching the wonders of conservation, but not to men with families to feed and roofs to keep over their heads.

We spent the next days walking north, but the further we went the more apparent the devastation became. Instead of hacking our way through jungle, here we walked through coffee plantations, banana trees and maize fields, all planted amid the shorn trunks, the uprooting of their stumps being prohibitively expensive. Seas of white ash made it seem as if it had been snowing. In the plantations only a few living trees remained, left there deliberately to provide shelter from sun for the farmers. On the third day, instead of baobabs, vines and knotted mahogany, a flat, unrelenting sugar cane plantation stretched for as far as the eye could see. Gently waving in the wind, the twelve foot high sugar cane was eerily silent. Boston and I stopped to survey it. Of all the things we had seen, this, to me, seemed the most atrocious: a ghastly vision of man's victory against nature, and a visible statement of how consumerism, not conservation, was dictating Africa's future. Sugar – that sweet crystal craved by millions in the West – had utterly vanquished an ancient biosphere, and in it millions upon millions of creatures, from the smallest chameleon to the most intelligent of primates.

'It makes you sick,' said Boston as we took off into the cane.

But it wasn't sickness I felt. I felt trapped, just like the Africans running this plantation must have felt trapped – by economics, by industry, by the reality of putting food on the table at the end of each night. Africa has to develop, its people have to be empowered to use their natural resources – but it brought a tear to my eye, to think of the forest that had once been here, vanished forever so that we in the West can get fat and rot our teeth.

We weaved through narrow channels between the stalks, trying to keep to the river, but sometimes the pathways would go off at an angle and we'd have to blaze our own way, causing the only living creatures here – bush rats, mice and rattle snakes – to scuttle off into the cane's interior. Soon, we began to smell smoke, a tell-tale sign of further deforestation somewhere to the north. Up ahead, a thick column of black smoke was rising into the sky. I judged it to be about two miles distant and, as we wended our way closer, it became difficult to see what was on the other side.

We emerged from the cane.

Ahead of us lay mile upon mile of charred bush. This deforestation was fresh and, not far away, it was happening right now. A wall of fire, where scores of men had hacked, chopped and ploughed up the trees into a straight line of ecological debris stretching east and west, blocked the way forward. As Boston and I watched, we could see the march of the flames. They were going north, annihilating everything in their path.

Boston and I followed the fire north, walking in fresh devastation. Until now, the method by which the forests were cleared for agriculture had been abstract to me, but here it was impossible to ignore. It touched all five of my senses. When the smoke was too strong, tears budded in my eyes and I kept having to knead them so that I could see.

'It's senseless. This is what makes Africa unique, and they're killing it.'

For the first time, Boston wasn't merely playing devil's advocate when he disagreed. 'You whites cut down your forests hundreds of years ago,' he said. 'You had your industrial revolution, and when you needed wood you took it. Well, now we need ours. We need to plant crops to feed our children, and plant sugar so you can feed yours whatever shit you feed them.'

He was angry at me for getting on my high horse and, as we found a way through the fire, I couldn't blame him. We'd cut down England's forests to build a navy, to make our own charcoal so that we could power the locomotives and mills that, in their time, had made Britain great – and allowed us to take over the parts of the world through which I was now walking. Why shouldn't Africa do the same, and finally exploit its own natural resources? Yet, for all his damn logic, even Boston couldn't hide his sadness at the irreversible change going on around us. Never again would this landscape look the same. The acacias, the birds, the buffalo, the antelope and monkeys – all of that was gone. And even more difficult to swallow was the hypocrisy I felt at bemoaning it, and my inability to conceive of a single answer to what was going on all around me.

On the other side of the flames, a group of men were busy preparing the ground for the march of the fire. In order to direct it, channels of debris had to be built and others cleared, so that the march of the flames could be controlled. Half-naked, these men turned to watch us arrive. Boston approached to introduce us, but it quickly became apparent that they were half-drunk; a bottle of waragi gin was lying on the ground, by the rim of a deep charcoal pit.

'Five days,' Boston translated, as the man chattered at him in Bugandan. 'It took them five days to clear all this.'

'Imagine what they could do in fifty.'

'A man's got to eat,' said Boston and, as the other man continued to talk, his eyes were drawn to the charcoal pit. 'That's his pay,' Boston went on. 'He gets to keep some wood to turn into charcoal, which he can sell at market.'

I was about to get on my high horse again – these men charged with destroying the ancient forests weren't even *paid* to do it? – when I heard a tiny squeaking from somewhere up ahead, where the bush was still thick and green, helplessly awaiting its annihilation. Leaving Boston to talk to this man, I crossed the desolation. Before I had gone two steps inside the acacias I saw a vervet monkey, hunkered down in the undergrowth. Vervets are a small but highly intelligent monkey, with white-grey fur and tiny black faces. Studies have shown them to have almost human characteristics – vervets have been documented suffering from stress, anxiety disorders, and even engaging in social alcohol use – and I had never seen it more closely than in this little monkey. She was a little more than a foot tall and her face was creased in anxiety that looked peculiarly human. In the bush she strained to get a better view of me. I watched her, unable to descry why she was risking the fire and smoke and wasn't fleeing deeper into the forest like every other animal.

Then all became apparent. From between the trees, two boys appeared. They were no older than seven or eight and, between them, they were holding what, at first, appeared to be a small rat. Instantly, the vervet set up an alarm call. The language of vervets has been deciphered to have distinct calls for every predator of the forest, but this must have been a very specific call – because, as the boys got closer, I saw what the vervet already knew: the animal in their hands was not a rat at all. It was, in fact, a tiny monkey – a baby, not more than a couple of days old. It was clearly the offspring of the mother fretting in the undergrowth.

While I had been watching, Boston had come to my side. Apprising himself of the situation, he began to bark at the boys. 'Give it to her,' he said, indicating the vervet's panicked mother, but the boys just looked at him dumbly.

'What do they want with it?' I asked.

Behind the boys, an elderly man was appearing from the undergrowth. It seemed he had been watching our little confrontation play out, because he was grinning, with something approaching cunning in his eyes. Boston began to bark at him in Bugandan, before the man gave a sanguine shrug and chattered back.

'He says they take it to market. They can get a good price for bush meat. Then they'll use that money to buy food for their families.' Boston stopped. 'He says – does the white man want to buy it?'

I looked at the man and had the distinct impression that this was not truly an act of desperation by an impoverished family. This was a tiny movement in a much more complex economy, one that encouraged the impoverished to plunder the forest's natural resources without thought of the future. Like the drunk villagers channelling fire behind us, this man and his children were pawns put into play by much bigger corporations, whose only responsibility was to their own profit. With a little help, locals like this could be taught how to look after the land and still make a living from it – but that was too much of an effort.

'Don't buy it off him, Lev. He thinks you're a weak European. He thinks you'll pay top dollar, because you're too soft.'

'I wasn't going to *buy* it from him, Boston.' Instead, I strode towards the boys and, before they could protest, simply lifted the baby vervet from their hands.

In mine, the vervet was no less frightened. Ignoring their protestations, I strode into the bush, clambering over smouldering embers to where the mother had last been seen. Sure enough, she was still waiting – but, on my approach, she set up the same startled cry as before. To this desperate mother, I was no better than the boys I could sense stealing after me, eager to reclaim their catch.

Panic took the mother and, before I could get near, she scuttled off to the sanctuary of a bush. Creeping near, I placed the baby vervet on the ground. Behind me, Boston was barking at the boys to go back to the forest, but I remained fixed on the vervets, hoping the mother could be coaxed out of her hiding. Slowly, I beat my own retreat. Only when I was some metres away did the mother emerge from the scrub. Tentatively, she crossed to where her baby was yowling – but still she seemed unsure. After sniffing the baby from a distance, neatly evading its grappling hands, she turned tail again, and disappeared into the undergrowth. Thirty minutes later, the baby was still there, stumbling in circles, and the mother was nowhere to be seen. Who can tell what truly goes on in the minds of animals? But it seemed to me, watching the baby left alone, that the mother was afraid of its new smell, corrupted by the hands of man. She had abandoned it.

'Let's go,' muttered Boston, in sadness.

Over my shoulder, the boys were still lurking – and, even though I knew there were countless other animals being destroyed in the forest today, I did not want this one on my conscience. Ignoring Boston, I crept close and retrieved the vervet. Instantly, she set up a screech – but, moments later, still screeching, she was clinging to my neck in the way she would have done her mother. I stood and turned around. As I did, the boys scuttled off, just as quickly as the vervet's mother.

'Lev, you're not serious. She won't last an hour without . . .'

'Bring me some water, Boston.'

Boston glared.

'Boston, some water!'

After I had bathed her head and helped her drink some water from the cup of my hand, we picked our way back to the river and resumed our trek. Though she clung to me fiercely, it was obvious the stress of the situation had affected the vervet; soon, her screeching had faded to silence, and her head began to loll. Stopping to offer her more water, we picked our way north. At least the fires had not yet reached this part of the river and, for several kilometres, it was possible to believe we were back in Rwanda or Tanzania, where the bush remained wild and, in most areas, unplundered.

By nightfall we had made it to the village of Baale and, instead of our usual dilapidated shack, we were able to find a guesthouse. There were supplies in the village and, as well as soft fruit, we were able to find fresh milk. Holed up in the guesthouse, I gently roused the vervet and fed her a soft paste mixed from what we had bought. She began to perk up – until, after an hour or so, her screeching started again. Another hour later, her digestive system seemed to be back in working order – and Boston was fuming as he crouched in the corner of the room, making a simple nappy out of torn pieces of an old shirt.

'What will you do with it, Lev?' he grunted as, with the lights out, we listened to its mewling.

'We'll find *her* a home,' I said. My mother had worked with monkeys in South Africa and I knew there were sanctuaries all over the continent where a tiny thing like this could be reared and, potentially, even reintroduced to the wild.

'When?' Boston was only angry because, as he tried to sleep, the vervet was clambering all over his face.

'Soon,' I said. 'As soon as we can.'

But, right now, I had to admit I was even glad for the company of somebody – or something – who wouldn't always be launching into some new tirade at the turning of every mile.

'I think I'm going to call her Florence,' I said, 'after Samuel Baker's wife. He rescued her from captivity too.'

But Boston wasn't listening. For the time being, there were going to be three of us on this trek.

North of Baale, we followed the river for another hard day, along a dirt red track that ran parallel to the water. The road seemed endless, sparse and unpopulated, the indigenous forest razed but with so little agriculture in its place that it made what we had seen yesterday seem even more hopeless. Our goal was to reach Lake Kyoga by nightfall but, delayed by Florence's constant chewing of my earlobe, stops to catch her when she scrambled from my shoulder, and my repeated attempts to find her a safe haven, we fell 10km short and spent the night in a little village called Galiyiro. North of us, the Victoria Nile disappeared into Lake Kyoga and emerged again on the lake's most westerly point, then wending its way due west to Lake Albert. We had fallen a day behind and, with Florence, would fall even further – but that was a problem for another day. Now, hot and exhausted as we were, was a time for clean water, laundry, and clean clothes.

In the village, we shared dinner: big plates of chapatti and beans, with Florence bouncing between the two and stealing morsels from our plates. When I was finished, I looked up to see Boston stifling a smile. I thought he was laughing at the monkey, but he had a different kind of sparkle in his eye.

'What is it?'

'How did you like it, Lev?'

I had liked it well enough – but, then, I had eaten enough rotten goat and bush rat in the last weeks to make anything hot and filling feel like a banquet.

'Haricot viande!' he declared. 'Meat beans!'

'Meat beans?' I asked, noting that Florence still held one in her tiny paws.

'It's the dish of refugees,' Boston explained. 'We'll see a lot more of it the closer we get to South Sudan. You see, Lev, these beans, they're rotten. Full of maggots.'

My stomach clenched. Instinct was telling me throw up, or at least throw a punch at Boston for not warning me before.

'It's protein, Lev! You whites wouldn't understand. This is good food for starving Africans.' He leaned across the table, wearing his familiar conspiratorial smile. 'Trust me, Lev, when we cross over the border, you might be grateful to find a plate of haricot viande . . .'

At that moment, my phone rang. Boston was lucky: it was the only thing that stopped me from throwing my plate at his face. On the other end of the line was Pete Meredith. Pete had been in touch with a representative of the Ugandan Wildlife Education Centre in Entebbe, a big town sitting on one of Lake Victoria's many peninsulas, some forty kilometres away from Kampala. The endless calls I had made during the day, it seemed, had not been so fruitless after all; if I could get Florence back to Jinja, the Education Centre would pick her up and rear her in safety, before aiding her reintroduction to the wild.

When the phone call was finished, Boston was still smiling.

'You can wipe that smile off your face,' I said, refusing to admit that the memory of the beans was not so disgusting after all. Even maggots taste good when you're as famished as I was. 'We're marching again tomorrow, without this vervet to slow us down.'

In the morning, we bid goodbye to Florence. I had arranged for a taxi and local guide to take her back to Jinja and, outside the guesthouse, made certain she had a clean nappy and wished her a good journey. To me, Jinja seemed far away, but by car the journey would take only a few hours. Before Boston and I had reached Lake Kyoga, Florence would be safely with the representatives from the Wildlife Education Centre. Watching her little face peering through the glass, suddenly I understood how much I was going to miss the little monkey. My earlobe would heal, the smell of her faeces constantly dropping down my back would be gone, but for all of that I still felt torn. Perhaps it was only the heightened emotions that come with undertaking an expedition like this, but watching Florence go affected me in a way I had not anticipated. Suddenly, I was thinking of all the family and friends I'd left behind in Britain. Was this, I wondered, the first intimation of some sort of homesickness?

Boston was already half-way down the road. He turned and yelled for me to hurry up. We had taken on a local boy as a porter. Emmanuel was seventeen, of South Sudanese origin, and had a bicycle with which he could help us carry our packs. Some of the other local boys were pouring scorn on him as he trotted after us, but Emmanuel didn't seem to care. 'Perhaps if they'd gone to school, they'd be carrying the Muzungu's packs too,' he declared, though I wasn't comfortable with the idea of him being proud to be my servant.

'Are you okay, Lev?'

'That monkey's probably the closest I've ever come to having a baby,' I replied.

'You should have children, Lev. It is the best thing a man can do.'

I hung my head, half-afraid I'd prompted Boston to embark on another one of his rants. But, this time, he remained silent. 'I think I'll leave it for a while,' I said, and took my first step out of Galiyiro.

It was another ten kilometres to the shore of Lake Kyoga. Compared with Lakes Victoria and Albert, Kyoga is a shallow body of water – all of its 660 square miles are less than six metres deep, with most of the water having a depth of only three to four metres. The shallow waters are perfect for lilies and water hyacinth, and as we came to the shore we first had to pick a way through thick, glutinous swamp land. Out on the water, floating papyrus islands and acres of water lilies gave the false impression of a succession of much smaller lakes. In places it seemed as if we might even be able to walk across the surface, if we balanced delicately on the slowly bobbing green sheet.

Boston, Emmanuel and I gathered ourselves. The only clear water we could see was the expanse where the Victoria Nile fed into the lake. According to the increasingly cumbersome self-imposed rules of my expedition, we could not use the flow of the river to gain an advantage, and had to follow its length in its entirety. Right now, that meant crossing the lake and continuing our trek on its northern bank, where we would follow the shore westwards unobstructed by swamps. There, we would find the headwaters of the river where it emerged from the lake.

It took some time before we found passage over the water, paying for the services of some local fishermen and their precarious river-boats. Though we set off at midday, by the time we had crossed Kyoga the afternoon was paling, the light soft and diffuse. We had spent those hours clinging to the bow, trying not to panic at the sight of the alarmingly big holes in the basin of the boat, while Boston used a small tin dish to bail out water.

It was with some relief, then, that we came to a landing site on the northern bank. The village, the fishermen told us, was named Kiga, after the people who have lived in this region for generations untold, and we had attracted quite a welcome. Standing on the banks was a crowd of other fishermen, all staring inquisitively at the prospect of a white man intruding on their routine. A tall man stepped out of the crowd, and introduced himself as James. I was surprised to hear how clear his English was and, before I had introduced myself, he took me by the hand. 'You will come and meet the chief,' he began. 'Leave your boy and bike here.'

Boston and I looked at Emmanuel and shrugged, but if Emmanuel minded being left by the lake he didn't say a thing. Emmanuel was already further away from home than he had ever been, had already accomplished more than he could have done in his old job as a village water porter. The money we were paying him was to go towards his dream of one day owning a motorcycle, and he was happy to wait for us, thinking of the day it would come.

Up the bank, the shacks sat closely together, though there was nothing that could be easily mistaken for a road. Boston and I followed James through a dirty fishing village – every house surrounded by bones and fish guts, the huts no more than ramshackle piles – and came, at last, to a mud brick house. Inside, a middle-aged man slept sprawled on a wicker bed, his chest rising and falling with every whinnying snore.

At once, the man woke with a start and, barely pausing for breath, ordered James to provide seats. Moments later, small plastic chairs were arranged in a circle around the chief and his bed. Some other villagers were arriving, now. I took them to be villagers of note and, soon, they were introducing themselves as such. 'This is the chief, Geoffrey,' began a lanky youth in a gaudy red Arsenal football shirt, who had previously introduced himself as the head fisherman.

Geoffrey's eyes fell on us. 'Before you present yourselves, you must first sign the visitor's book.'

If I had expected a grand, leather-bound ledger I was mistaken. A tattered school notebook was produced and Boston and I scrawled our names inside. 'A relic from British times,' he whispered from the corner of his mouth.

Once the signing was complete, I prepared myself. Just as I was about to launch into a speech detailing who we were and what expedition we were on, another man interrupted. 'First, we pray!' he barked, and led us back into the light. Outside the chief's hut, it seemed the whole village had assembled. There must have been two or three hundred people here. As Boston and I faced them, I had images of how it had been for Baker, Stanley, Livingstone and Speke when they had first come across remote villages like these. Their journals are filled with stories of the contrasting hostility and welcome they received across inland Africa.

Around me, everybody lowered their head and folded their hands in their lap.

As the village pastor launched into his prayers, welcoming us to his village, Boston and I looked at each other in mute disbelief.

'Lord!' the pastor began. 'Let us pray. We pray for our guest, this Muzungu who comes across the lake from the land of England. We pray for his health, that he does not catch any bad diseases. We pray that his children are big and strong and that he has many more. We pray for his goats and his chickens, and if he is a fisherman that his lakes are full of tilapia. We pray that he will have lots of money so that he may return to Kiga and give us some of it. Lord, we pray too for this Congo man, who is clearly not of sound mind, that he survives this great journey and may return to make more children with his wives . . .'

Suddenly, there was a sharp pain in my side. I looked round, to find Boston's elbow being driven into my ribs. The faces in the crowd were all staring into me. It was time, it seemed, to add my own voice to the prayers.

'Chief,' I began, acknowledging each man with a nod. 'Pastor. James. People of Kiga!' Boston nodded in approval, but the more I went on the more foolish I felt; my skin was turning an unmistakeable shade of crimson. 'My name is Levison Wood. *Tembula Muzungu* from over the water. And this is my companion, Ndoole Boston of the Congo. We have come from Kampala and beyond – from the mighty Lake Victoria . . .' In spite of myself, I realised I was actually enjoying this. Beside me, Kiga's collected dignitaries were nodding away, while the faces in the crowd were rapt. A flash of inspiration struck me, and I remembered the copy of the *New Vision* magazine in my rucksack, in which the journalist Matthias had written about our trek. As I produced it and Geoffrey handed it round, I continued my tall tale. I spoke of the greatness of the Ugandan people, the kindnesses we had come across in our journey, the beauty of the land and generosity of the tribes. As I concluded my spiel, rapidly running out of superlatives with which to describe the people of the north, the pastor translated the article and, at last, the chief's face seemed to brighten up. Once we were done, he stood and surveyed the crowd.

Now it was time for a speech of his own. With his white string vest, fat belly and ragged trousers, I did not expect the voice that came out of his throat to be so bold. Yet, in seconds he had the village transfixed. James whispered in my ear, translating as he went.

'The chief welcomes you to Kiga. We are blessed by your arrival, and may God bring you safety on your great journey. For the moment, Kiga is yours and you must feel at home. The chief has told the people of the village that they must not disturb you, harass you, or ask you for money. Nor,' he added, 'must they threaten to kill you.' I made eyes at Boston, who was only beaming. 'He has told them you are not only a white man – you are a Britisher, and must be afforded our respect. We hope that you will go away from here and tell people that Kiga is a good place. We expect that you will tell your queen and your president, and your minister for development, that Kiga needs the help of the white man to develop, and that we need the government here to give us more money so that we can buy better fishing nets. Also, Levison, we need another toilet. The one we have is almost full.'

As James continued to translate, each sentence one behind the chief, the crowd burst into laughter, loud enough to drown out what he was saying. Only when the laughter had died down, could James carry on.

'He tells the people they must not be afraid. Even though you are English, you have not come to turn him into a homosexual. No matter how hard you try, he will not marry you.'

I cast a look at Boston, expecting him to be as outraged as I was, but his laughter was as loud as any of the villagers, and seemed to cut through the general throng.

Moments later, I found the copy of *New Vision* being pressed back into my hands. 'Fetch your boy,' said James. 'You may spend the night in our police station. Not as a prisoner, Tembula. You are our honoured guest.'

As James led me there, I was not sure how honoured I actually felt.

It was too late to continue our journey, and the fish that the villagers supplied was enough to convince me to spend a restful night here, rejuvenating ourselves for the day to come. Inside the lock-up, Emmanuel was asleep almost as soon as dinner was done, so it was only Boston and I who sat up, watching the sun setting over the lake. Around us, posters clung to the walls. In England they might have been declaring "Don't Do Drugs!" or "Report Suspicious Behaviour!", but this one was different. "SAY NO TO CHILD SACRIFICE" were the words that glared out at us from the wall. I made a silent gesture to Boston. 'Just like your nanny,' I whispered – but Mama Fina was in my thoughts as well.

'Only human sacrifice is guaranteed to bring wealth to the man who consults a witch doctor,' Boston snorted. 'It used to happen in Congo until we banned it. Not so in Uganda. Here, everyone believes this shit. It's like I told you – these people need education, Lev.'

I glared at him, compelling him to be silent in case any of the villagers heard, but sometimes Boston could not be stopped. He was standing in the door of the station, drinking bitter coffee from a chipped glass. 'The problem with Africa,' he went on, as a dying sun reddened the endless stretch of papyrus, 'is that people are short-sighted. They follow any mafia hard man or jumped-up village bully if he offers them cheaper gin or free firewood.'

The sound of crickets was almost drowning out the waves lapping against the lake's rocky banks, but they could not drown out Boston when he decided to get on his soapbox. 'The chief doesn't seem like so much of a bully here in Kiga.'

'Don't you believe it, Lev. Give him half a chance, and he'd be . . .'

'He's hardly Idi Amin.'

'Well, why not? Amin is a classic case of a jumped-up village bully. But take the Congo, for example . . .'

I hung my head. I had already heard Boston's war stories ten times over.

'In the Congo,' he continued, 'we have eighty million people. Eighty million! That is more than you English. And do you know how many of them were educated when the Belgians left?' The Belgians, Boston had repeatedly told me, had left the Congo in 1960, part of the first great wave of African independence. 'Not a single one!' he exclaimed. 'The Belgians had banned it. At least you British educated your natives. Not so the Belgians – they were total bastards. How can a country be expected to start from scratch when even the leaders haven't been to school? That's how it happens, Lev. Without education, it's the thugs who rise to power – they're the only ones who can take control and rule. It's the law of the fist.' He paused, seeming to contemplate his own words. 'People without education don't think about the future, so these villains take over, and because the villains are short-sighted too, they're corrupt. They steal and pillage their own country. You get generals who are only in command because they're related to the president – just like here in Uganda. And those same generals have three or four big mansions each, just like those Sudanese! And the politicians, they're all murderers these days. You can't be a politician in the Congo without having been a fighter. And do you know what that means, Lev? It means you've probably raped women and killed children. That's what qualifies you for government.'

'Boston,' I ventured, '*you* were a fighter.'

'Not like that. I didn't rape. I didn't murder. And *that's* why I'm here, tramping along this river with you, instead of in government. It's a disgrace.' He hesitated. 'Do you know what I'd do if I was an MP, Lev?'

Whether I wanted to know or not, I was about to find out.

'I'd start again. I'd wipe out corruption and ban the tribes. I'd kill anyone that dissented and force peace on people.'

'Do you know, Boston, you're beginning to sound like Idi Amin yourself. Kill anyone who doesn't agree with you because you know you're right. You'd be a dictator.'

'I'd be a great leader of a great nation. How do you say in English? You cannot make scrambled without breaking eggs.'

'Omelettes,' I interjected.

'What?'

'You can't make omelettes without breaking eggs.'

'Precisely,' Boston barked. 'I think I'd probably need to kill at least half the population though. Maybe as much as two thirds. By then, we'd be left with decent people.'

There was a glimmer in Boston's eye that told me he was aware of how outlandish he sounded, but the way he could nonchalantly profess all this after what we had seen in Rwanda, not to mention Uganda's own recent past, struck me as bitterly ironic.

'So you're advocating mass genocide?'

'Somebody's got to clear up this mess,' he replied, and after that Boston would brook no more conversation. It was time, he declared, for some well-earned rest; before dawn, we would be heading west.

INTO THE WILD

The Victoria and Albert Nile, February – March 2014

At the westernmost point of Lake Kyoga the river rose again, depositing itself into Lake Albert two days further north-west. By fall of next night we had reached the outskirts of Masindi, a favourite haunt of, among others, Winston Churchill and Ernest Hemingway, the kind of place that drew adventurers and explorers from times past. The chief town of the Masindi region, it has a population that far exceeds the towns and villages we had tramped through since Jinja, with almost 50,000 Ugandans calling this home. An urban sprawl of red dirt roads and shanty shacks gathered around a square where modern banks and a public hospital suggested a tiny corner of modernity, it was the last significant town we would come to before we reached the vast Murchison Falls national park.

Masindi was an important milestone for another reason: it was here that the British explorer Samuel Baker had based himself from April 1872 until June 1873. Baker, beaten by John Hanning Speke to the source of the White Nile at Jinja, had turned to his other overriding passion in life – the abolition of the slave trade. And it was from

Masindi that Baker locked horns with the local Bunyoro king, Kabalega, to kill the trade at its source.

Samuel Baker was born in June 1821, the eldest son of a London merchant family, whose considerable wealth had been built on the thriving trade in sugar. Marrying young, Baker, his wife and extensive brood left England to oversee the family's plantation in Mauritius and, later, Ceylon – but, after his wife was stricken with typhoid fever, Baker found himself a widower at the youthful age of 34. Leaving his children in the care of an unmarried sister, Baker embarked on a new career, constructing railways and bridges in central Europe.

Baker's life was to take a startling, almost fairy tale turn when, in 1859, circumstances brought him to Vidin, then part of the Ottoman Empire. Visiting the slave market in the city, Baker became enraptured with one of the girls about to be sold. A white slave, she seemed destined for the harem of the Pasha – or honorary Lord – of Vidin; but Baker had other ideas. Though he bid to buy the girl himself, the Pasha's resources far outweighed Baker's own – so, if he wanted to acquire her, some nefarious tactics had to be employed. Baker decided that he would have to bribe the girl's guards and, though she had legitimately been bought by another, he and the slave girl escaped in a carriage. Baker soon discovered that the girl was the orphaned daughter of an aristocratic Hungarian family, whose parents and brothers had been massacred during the uprisings of 1848. She was later to tell him that her nurse had helped her to a refugee camp, from which she had been abducted and sold to an Armenian slave merchant. It was this merchant who had brought her to market in Vidin, having groomed her to join the Pasha's harem.

The girl, whose name was Florence, would go on to become Baker's lover, wife, and companion in his African adventures. Together they set out to explore central Africa in 1861. By this time

Speke and Grant had already discovered Lake Victoria, but – following clues left by them – Baker and his wife would go on to discover Lake Albert to the north-west. Although Baker wanted to claim this as one of the Nile's various sources, he was never taken quite as seriously as the other African explorers. Even though the river rising from Lake Albert did feed into the Nile further north, providing as much as fifteen per cent of the river's northerly waters, Baker's standing amongst Nile explorers never rose to the heights achieved by Speke or Grant. In part this was because he was always shunned by Queen Victoria, who refused to meet him because she was certain he had been intimate with his partner Florence long before they were formally wed. A civilian scandal involving his brother, a decorated colonial officer later convicted of sexually assaulting a lady on a train, also damaged Baker's reputation – but it didn't damage his zeal for Africa. By 1869 he was back, commissioned by the Khedive – or viceroy – of Egypt and Sudan to lead a military expedition into central Africa and quash the slave trade there, opening up great swathes of the interior for commerce and the advancement of civilisation. It was this quest that brought him to Masindi, and into direct conflict with the local kings.

Boston and I stood at the river port on the outskirts of the town, beneath a baking sun. Here, the river turns north, before banking west to flow through Murchison Falls National Park and finally enter Lake Albert. This is the ancestral land of the Bunyoro tribe. Traditionally they were colonial resisters, and fought bitterly against Baker, seeing his expedition as another way Europeans were bringing British influence to bear. But, after a year of establishing his presence here, it was Baker who won out, with the king of the Bunyoro captured and exiled, and the whole tribe severely weakened as a result.

'Lazy bastards,' said Boston, after yet another local porter had deserted us. 'Even worse than the Bugandans. We'd have been better off with a woman. This Bunyoro couldn't carry a bag for more than five minutes without complaining. What we need is a Sudanese or a Nilot. Maybe a Kakwa. They were Idi Amin's old tribe. They're warriors. They don't usually carry things, but at least they're strong. If you pay them enough, Lev, they'll do it.'

Walking through the kingdom of the Bunyoro had been much more challenging than our earlier trek through the southern parts of Uganda. Perhaps memories of Baker lingered, but it seemed outsiders were not looked upon kindly here. The local Bunyoro people had given us little by way of help, and for the most part had been suspicious to the point of being hostile.

'It's because of the LRA,' said Boston as, circumventing Masindi, we sat at the side of a red dirt track with our rucksacks piled up. We had one spare rucksack that neither of us could carry and in that was our food, water, tents and electrical gear – all the spare batteries, cameras and solar panels we needed to charge them up. Emmanuel had left us on the road to Masindi, returning proudly to his village with enough money to fulfil his dream of owning a motorbike, only to be stopped and searched by police who, after giving the matter some careful consideration, decided to liberate him of all his hard-earned wages. Since then, we'd managed to find lads with bicycles who'd been willing to come along for cash and a bit of adventure, but one after another they absconded. We waited in the midday sun, with only a banana tree for shade, and hoped that someone would come along and offer help.

'The LRA ravaged this area,' Boston went on. 'They stole kids and raped women. That's why these people are scared of foreigners. Did you see the way the children run away and hide in the bush whenever we get near?'

I had, and I'd wondered why. It wasn't like in Rwanda, where they'd done it smiling, for fun. Here they were genuinely scared.

'And all that was only a few years ago. The LRA were in these parts until about 2007, before they ran further north.'

The LRA were the Lord's Resistance Army, a militant movement – and, in many ways, a religious cult – with their heartland in northern Uganda and South Sudan, and bases of operation as far afield as Boston's beloved Congo. Formed from the remnants of a civilian organisation called the Holy Spirit Mobile Force, which fought against the acts of terror perpetrated by the government against the northern tribes in the mid-1980s, the Lord's Resistance Army claims to be founding a theocratic state out of northern Uganda and southern South Sudan, a nation based on a strict understanding of the Ten Commandments, as well as on local traditions. This unique blend of African mysticism and Christian fundamentalism has manifested itself in frequent bouts of violence and human rights' abuses all across the region. Boston was talking about rape and child abduction in Masindi, and stories like this are not uncommon. The LRA has been accused of engaging in child-sex-trafficking, female genital mutilation, as well as forcibly enlisting abducted children to their armies and ritually preparing those enlistees as rapists of the future. The International Criminal Court has had warrants out for the arrest of its leader, Joseph Kony – who proclaims himself God's spokesman on earth – for war crimes and human rights abuses since 2005, but he has somehow evaded capture. As Boston and I sat by the bank of the river, I gazed north and had the unshakeable feeling that the country we were walking into was hiding him.

'Some of these kids are barely old enough to remember all that,' I said.

'It's the memories that live on, Lev. Their parents tell them about what happened. They're terrified of northerners, of Nilots and

Sudanese, the Kakwa and the like. And it's not just them – they're scared of all foreigners here. They're so superstitious. They probably think you're here looking to steal children for witchcraft or something. You know . . .' And here Boston winked at me in delight. '. . . you Muzungus eat babies! That's why my son was so scared of you when you came to my house.'

'Yes,' I said, 'you might have disabused him of that notion. Do you want him to grow up scared of white people? Isn't that irresponsible?'

'It's only tall tales, and a bit of fun.'

I wondered what my reaction would have been if, back home, a friend told me they were raising their children to be afraid of black Africans. 'But these villagers,' I went on, 'they actually believe it.'

There came the sound of an engine. When Boston and I peered down the road, we could see a cloud of red dust slowly moving towards us. Moments later, a shape started to form in the dust: a motorcyclist was coming towards us. I motioned to Boston to grab our packs and we scrambled to our feet, ready to flag him down.

'It's because that stuff happens,' Boston went on. 'Not the whites – but people do go missing here all the time. Only last week they found a woman just outside Masindi – murdered, with her breasts cut off. That's witchcraft. I'm telling you.'

The motorcycle rider slowed down as he approached, and we launched into our familiar haggle. This time we were lucky. For a fee, he agreed to tag along behind us, with our spare rucksack strapped to his saddle. Wearily, we took off. There were still some hours of daylight left and Boston wanted us to reach the village of Bweyale before nightfall.

And so, we followed the river north. Although vast areas of the bush here have been burnt down to make pastures for cattle, it still felt bleak and wild, so much so that Boston and I had to find some local herdsmen to guide us through the maze of scrub until we could rejoin the river. A day further on, the Nile makes a sharp turn west and enters the ancient land of Murchison Falls National Park. Murchison Falls is the largest wilderness area left in Uganda, and is steeped in history. It was traversed by Samuel Baker and his wife Florence in 1864, and it was Baker himself who named the spectacular waterfalls at the heart of the park, in testament to the president of the Royal Geographical Society, Sir Roderick Murchison. Baker entered this area of wilderness from its western extremity, sailing upriver in the opposite direction to the one Boston and I were walking. What he discovered was beauty untouched. As he described it in his journal, 'the fall of water was snow-white, which contrasted with the dark cliffs that walled the river, while the graceful palms of the tropics and the wild plantains perfected the view.'

Baker's journey had been fraught with difficulty. Already frustrated at his relative failures when compared with his contemporary explorers, he had faced hostile tribes and a civil war that had blocked his path and caused many months' delay. The area he would name Murchison Falls was the fault line between the Nilotic Lwo and Acholi tribes, as well as other Sudanese groups and the Bantu-speaking Bunyoro, all of whom were engaged in battles for land and cultural primacy. This land of disparate people was almost impossible to navigate safely.

In the early 20th century, when Uganda had become a British protectorate, Murchison Falls became something of a magnet for travellers consumed by the idea of seeing Africa in its rawest state. Winston Churchill came hunting here, searching for big game, and was as impressed by the falls as Baker had been a generation before. Word must have spread, because soon other world leaders and luminaries were making this a regular haunt. Roosevelt found wilderness here to surpass the American West, Ernest Hemingway crashed two planes in the park in less than a week, and the film stars of the early Hollywood era were drawn to this unspoiled landscape. Humphrey Bogart and Katherine Hepburn filmed *The African Queen* here in 1951 – though, by all accounts, it was not an experience Hepburn was keen to repeat.

The park was gazetted as a game reserve under the British in 1926, becoming famous for its wildlife. Host to twenty thousand elephants, as well as thousands of rhino, lion, buffalo, and all the varied forms of African antelope, it became the glint in the 'pearl of Africa', so much so that, in the 1950s, the Queen Mother had a bungalow built here especially for her safaris. This golden age, however, was not to last. During the Ugandan Civil War, Idi Amin plagued the region with his militias, and finally renamed the park Kabalega, after the famous king who had battled with Baker here. War drove away the tourists and, when Amin ascended to the leadership of Uganda, he closed the gates to foreigners. After this, the park was ravaged. What had been a place of bounty quickly became decimated, as conservation activities in the park ceased, making its wildlife easy prey for poachers. By the end of Amin's rule, in 1979, elephant numbers had been reduced to just over a thousand. During the turbulent 1980s, when the country lurched from one leader to another, the slaughter continued unabated; a succession of military factions occupied the park, and started to eat their way through the wildlife. By 1990, fewer than two hundred and fifty elephants and a thousand buffalo survived, the hartebeest and kob herds had plummeted to around three and six thousand respectively, rhinos and African hunting dogs had been hunted to local extinction, and giraffe and lion were on the brink of going the same way. Since then, fortunately, the tourists have gradually started to return, conservation activity has begun again, and populations are slowly starting to grow.

Boston and I had already been given permission by the Uganda Wildlife Authority to walk along the river. We had been summoned to see its chief, Colonel Andrew Seguya, in Kampala; Andrew had heard we'd been broadcasting our opinion that the true source of the Nile belonged in Rwanda – and only by our conceding that the source of the *White* Nile was in Uganda did the bespectacled colonel agree to help us. Two days out from Masindi, we came to the small town of Karuma, where another power station straddled the river and the falls, gentle compared with what we would find further west, still looked dramatic. Boston had told me that the Ugandan government had plans to transform Karuma into a new, modern city – not organically, by attracting investors and settlers, but by imposing growth from above and the building of yet another dam. Right now, there was no evidence of this. Ahead, the national park was a verdant line of green, and I was glad to be walking into it, leaving the deforested devastation behind.

At a UWA ranger station on the outskirts of Karuma, we met the guides and porters who would take us into the park. A motley collection of crumbling buildings, the station didn't look much like the headquarters of an operation tending to more than three-and-a-half-thousand square kilometres of wilderness, but inside we were introduced to Simon, the lead ranger, Francis, his right hand man, and Maureen, a gun-toting lady of such considerable girth that I had to quickly stop Boston from asking her how she intended to walk with us *all* the way to the Falls. Accompanying us there would also be two porters, George and Julius, who knew the park intimately as locals and had aspirations of becoming rangers themselves.

As we were checking packs and Simon was showing us a map of the park, another ranger appeared in the station, dragging a handcuffed local after him. I watched as they crossed the station floor to disappear into its recesses, where Boston assured me the cells were waiting.

'Poaching?' I asked.

Simon nodded, wearily. 'Illegal fishing, this one.' As he said it, I noticed Julius, one of the porters, looking particularly shifty. 'He'll be prosecuted and fined, but it doesn't stop them.' The fine, he explained, was ordinarily around 300,000 Ugandan shillings, roughly approximate to £70, a fortune for an impoverished fisherman, but nothing when stacked against the need for food for a man and his family. Simon and his rangers enforced the law as it was, but something was fundamentally broken that even subsistence fishing had to be policed like this. 'It's not him we have to worry about,' Simon conceded as, finally resupplied, we left the ranger station to head for the park. 'It's when it becomes commercial. There's meant to be no fishing, without a licence, inside the whole of the park, but boats come onto Lake Albert and up the river. That's not subsistence. That's industry.'

Outside, Karuma Falls Bridge – originally built so that military could move swiftly over this part of the river – took us to the north bank and, from there, we entered the park. As we crossed the boundary line, Boston dug his elbow into my side and gestured for me to look up – but he needn't have bothered: I had already seen the grotesque, decapitated head sitting proudly on the edge of the trail. Once, it had belonged to a buffalo. Flies swarmed the sockets where its eyes used to be.

'It can be dangerous in there,' Francis said as we passed. 'Just yesterday that buffalo charged a ranger and injured one of the villagers inside the park. And only a week ago, a lone elephant killed four villagers. They can do that, when they're not part of a herd. It turns them bad.'

With that, Francis began the march again, leaving Boston and me to stare at the decapitated head. 'I wonder what happened to the body,' I muttered.

'You should have learnt by now,' Boston said, shaking his head. 'These Bunyoro have eaten it.' He paused. 'Don't look so surprised, Lev. There's good meat in a buffalo. Idi Amin treated this place like his moving larder. That's what the locals do too.'

Then it was off, into the wild.

The contrast with the Uganda we had been trekking through could not have been plainer. The bush was thick and green, and before we had walked a few steps we were treading in elephant dung, and there was an overpowering smell of ammonia, a sure sign that wildlife was close to hand, marking its territory everywhere we trod. Almost immediately we were greeted by the sight of bush buck flitting away, and before we had stopped for a first break we had seen warthog cross our path, and the majestic necks of giraffes bending to graze from the uppermost branches. Down by the river, with the sounds of Karuma Falls now having faded completely away, we heard the unmistakeable grunt of hippopotami. Venturing down the bank to fill our water bottles, I saw the grey hummocks of several lurking in the shallows only ten metres away. As I marvelled at them, Maureen idly filled her mug from the river and crouched as she drank. It was only then that I properly heard what the rangers were saying: hippo meat, they all agreed, was very tasty indeed.

Boston gave me a knowing look, and then we took off again.

This was the restorative I needed after the bleak walk north from Jinja. For ten kilometres we hacked our way through steaming, sweaty forest, until we broke for the first time on the beach near a river eddy. Julius took delight in telling us that this was the exact place he came to fish, and, though he was keen to stress that he had a licence to catch fish inside the park, Boston was under no such illusions. 'His licence will let him catch a fish a day,' he said, 'but he'll be taking more. Trust me, Lev. All these Bunyoro are on the take.'

It took three more days to push north to the falls. Along the way, we camped wild by the banks of the river, or in poachers' camps deep in the bush. With no food except that we could carry on our backs, and no water except the Nile's frothy offerings, it was the most visceral experience I had had on the expedition. We spent the days in agonising bliss, the forest jagged and dense, the air thick with tsetse flies that made a mockery of our exposed flesh. Hacking across scrub, or through impossibly tall elephant grass, we dodged crocodiles disturbed from their slumber, and steered clear of the hippos who snorted in the shallows. This was African wilderness untouched since Samuel Baker walked here all those years ago; here the river was no longer paralysed by dams, no longer being bent to the needs of man, straddled by bridges or plundered by fishermen. The country it fed was not being razed to make way for plantation land, and the forests were not being destroyed at the altars of industry. It was my African idyll and, for a few days at least, I was able to forget thoughts of South Sudan and whatever else lay head.

We would have made the falls much sooner, but after a day it became clear that the rangers themselves were holding us back. Francis had become a ranger simply because he liked guns, while Maureen – constantly lagging behind – had signed up so that she could spend her time among animals; but neither had fully appreciated the stamina it would take to complete a trek like this. Julius had begun the journey eager to test his mettle in the hope of one day becoming a full-blown ranger himself but, by the end of the second day, he was recanting his former ambitions; Murchison Falls, he declared, was just too much hard work. Nor was our other porter, George, in better spirits. On the third day, when we came across the remains of an elephant trap lying in the bush, he announced that he, too, had changed his mind: now he wanted to become a soldier and fight the rebels in South Sudan, not a ranger whose only battle was against the 'honest' poachers working in the park.

By the end of the third day we were close to Murchison Falls itself. Across the scrub we could see a herd of over twenty giraffe, marching north to better grazing, while antelope flitted in their shadows. At the head of the procession, Boston cast disparaging glances at the rangers lagging behind.

'We should push on until the falls.'

I knew how aggravated he was. Only an hour earlier I had heard him barking at Maureen to hurry up, telling her that she ought to be ashamed at wearing the Ugandan flag on her uniform, but the truth was the heat was getting to me as well. It was near forty seven degrees, the tsetse flies were unbearable, and the thought of coaxing another twelve kilometres out of the rangers today was just too much. Ignoring Boston's lament, I led the rangers back to the riverside and, amidst yet more swarms of tsetse, we made camp.

In the morning, we made the decision to leave Maureen and Julius behind to make their own way back to the ranger station, and pushed on through the heat. The bush seemed to get thicker and thicker and the going was hard. Sometimes it was so steep we'd have to shimmy up or down vines, doing awkward impressions of Tarzan, the lord of the jungle himself. Danger lurked at every step – one false move could result in a slip to the bottom of a chasm filled with rattlesnakes.

'Stop!' said Boston in a whisper. He raised his hand towards me but his eyes didn't move from a spot ten metres away. Grinding to a halt,

I opened my mouth to listen for movement around me. 'Hippo!' he said, in evident alarm.

We froze.

There, right behind a tree, was a large, boulder-like lump. Until now, it had lain motionless, wallowing in the shallow mud of a half-dry creek. But now, disturbed from its slumber, the enormous beast was slowly emerging from the hole.

Hippos are the biggest killers of humans of all the large animals of Africa. They kill more people than lion, buffalo, crocodiles and elephants combined. Incredibly territorial and defensive of their young, they don't like people – and nowhere are they more dangerous than on land. 'The most dangerous place in Africa,' Boston had repeated several times along our journey, 'is between a hippo and the water . . .'

I looked at Boston, who was usually so unflappable, treading slowly backwards. Behind me, Francis and the porters were doing the same. I followed suit. As it stood, the hippo began to sniff at the air. Suddenly, it caught our scent and inclined its massive head towards us.

'Run!' I cried.

In an instant, we darted for a cliff face, intent on scrambling to safety. Behind us, the monster began to charge, its cavernous mouth open to reveal skewer-like teeth. Every animal has different instincts and any human foolish enough to invade their habitat must know what they are thinking. For instance, you should never run from a lion – its cat instinct will always compel it to chase you down. Rhinos have terrible eyesight so, if you can hide behind a tree, you'll quite possibly lose it. With elephants, you need to give them plenty of warning – spook them and they'll run away before getting aggressive. But, if you come across a hippo on land, there's nothing to do but climb. There's no way you can outrun a hippo on the flat as, despite their clunky appearance, they are fast, able to charge at thirty kilometres an hour. Believe it or not, hippos are actually cousins of the horse.

As the beast gained ground, we grappled with thorns and vines, without regard for pain, until we had hauled ourselves to the safety of a ridge overhead. Beneath us, the hippo gave a dismissive snort and then slumped away into the undergrowth. As one, we all breathed a sigh of relief. For the longest time, we basked in silence. Fresh from our close call our hearts were pounding, our bodies full of adrenaline. Short of patrolling through a minefield in Afghanistan, I don't think I'd ever felt quite so vulnerable, or so exhilarated.

'Are you ready, Lev?'

'Ready for what?' I asked, as I doused my face in water.

'Ready to do it all again. Well, we need to get to the river, don't we?'

We picked ourselves up and hacked on through the spiny acacia, the river's presence felt rather than seen. Eventually, blue shimmers could be made out – and then a beautiful glistening beach onto which our bedraggled party emerged. It was a relief to be able to replenish our water and, moreover, be out in the open where we could at least see where danger lay. There were dozens of hippos in the water, noisily grunting – but as long as they remained in the river, we were relatively safe.

We walked along the soft sand westward but, as we progressed, the beach narrowed to the point where it became less than a metre wide. Occasionally, fallen trees blocked the path so that we had to scramble over them or risk the water and wade into the river.

Then, as if we had escaped the frying pan and fallen into the fire, the unimaginable happened.

On the far side of a log, a massive, eight feet long crocodile was blocking our path. I froze. Francis raised his rifle in its direction but

Boston, this time emboldened by his successful escape from the hippo, picked up a stick and moved closer to the reptile. Only when he was almost at the point of touching its tail, did the prehistoric lizard snap out. With the speed of lightning, it launched itself at my guide and snapped its jaws shut. I stalled, convinced Boston's hand had been lost to the beast – but the monstrous teeth had clamped shut just an inch away from where his fingers still hung.

In that instant, the crocodile ran, disappearing into the placid water of the Nile. Moments later, it reappeared only metres away, this time just its eyes and the end of its nose poking out of the black depths. I looked back along the beach, from the direction we had come. More crocodiles, five or six huge beasts, had emerged out of the forest, awoken no doubt by the commotion on the beach. There was no way back, no way to retreat. Our only option was moving forward along a twenty metre stretch of narrow sand that probably contained more of the lurking beasts.

Perversely, Boston seemed to be enjoying the experience. 'Like the one in the museum, Lev!' he was shouting, a demented grin on his face. Beside me, Francis was gripping his AK-47 tightly and the porters simply looked terrified.

As one, we began to run, raving like mad men as we dashed along the beach. As expected, the forest alongside us came alive as gigantic crocodiles darted out of the undergrowth to take shelter in the safety of the water. At one point, as I ran, I had to jump over the tail of one crocodile as it slithered past me into the depths. Finally, and with all our limbs intact, we made it to the security of a rocky headland. We were safe, for now.

The fierce heat made the rest of the day intolerable but, by dusk, we had reached our first destination. It was the noise that came first – a clash of water that marked the top of Murchison Falls. As we approached the top, from the opposite direction to Baker – who had come from Lake Albert, still some miles further west – the roar of the rapids grew louder and louder. At last, we crested a hill – and there, in all their glory, lay the magnificent Murchison Falls. Below us, all the pure white water of the Nile was forced through a chasm of hard rock only a few feet across, the entire power of the river converging into one almighty chasm. Even from the top of the falls, the force seemed tremendous. More than the rapids outside Jinja, more than the dams we had seen harnessing the power of the river, this was a sight to prove how mighty the Nile truly was. From where we stood, the bottom was totally obscured, only a dense mist of spray from the falls to say there was a river there at all.

THE GATHERING DARK

Murchison Falls to South Sudan, March 2014

Two days later, as refreshed as it was able to be in the blistering forty-seven-degree heat, Boston and I were preparing for the final leg of our trip through the park. We had spent the days exploring the vicinity of Murchison Falls. Patrick, a contact from the Uganda Conservation Foundation, had taken us out on a marine patrol. Lake Albert loomed in the west, beyond a vast estuary of papyrus marshes, and it was here that the patrols picked up illegal fishermen and poachers. According to Ugandan law, fishing is illegal within two hundred metres of the borders of the National Park, but this didn't stop enterprising fishermen crossing the imaginary line in the lake and casting their nets.

Illegal fishing, though, was the least of the threats Patrick exposed on our patrol. Far worse were the floatation markers we saw along the river and cast across the lake. These were the early signs of seismic testing – the first stage in oil companies looking to take advantage of the park. According to Patrick, the deals had already been struck at the highest levels of government; there was a predicted $55 billion worth of oil waiting to be tapped inside Murchison alone – and, whenever riches like that await, conservation is quickly forgotten. Drilling was already happening on the outermost stretches of Lake Albert. Soon, it would creep inside the park itself – changing this wonderful, wild part of Africa forever.

On the morning we resumed our trek, turning north where the river met Lake Albert, we heard news from further north: in South Sudan, the fighting was spreading in intense bursts across the north of the country. Boston and I listened to the news soberly before hefting our packs onto our backs and making for the estuary.

The river meets Lake Albert near its northernmost point, but the few kilometres walking along its shore before seeing the river re-emerge seemed to take forever, the heat and entangled bush hindering us with every step. At last, we made the northern tip of the lake and saw the Albert Nile rise. At the tumbledown town of Pakwach we crossed the river again, this time by an old military bridge constructed during Idi Amin's rule, and arrived at the Heritage Lodge before dark. The owner, William, seemed a shadowy sort, with a smile vaguely reminiscent of the hundreds of crocodiles we had seen lounging along the banks of the river – and, though he had arranged for our arrival to be greeted by a troop of Acholi dancers, taking part in their elaborate ritual was the last thing on my mind. Exhausted, at last I could retreat to my bed. Tomorrow, Boston and I would meet up with Matt Power and Jason Florio, two journalists who had been keen to accompany us on part of the journey. But, before then, we needed the comforting blackness of sleep.

It was evening before Matt and Jason arrived, to be greeted by Tamarind juice – just like Samuel Baker, all those years ago. While Boston had spent the day scrambling for a phone signal to contact his family, I had wandered from shadow to shadow, seeking some respite wherever the sun was not casting its most destructive rays. For long hours I lost myself in Hemingway's *Green Hills of Africa*, but his ruminations on Tanzania were difficult to concentrate on, with one eye always on the sun hanging in the sky.

I was holed up in the newly built bomas of the Heritage Lodge – a camp built in the traditions of the Nilotic tribes, with thatch huts covered with colourful decorations on the adobe walls – when Matt and Jason finally arrived. The rooms looked out over the river which seemed to melt into the vast forest around, and the town of Pakwach was nothing more than a grey smudge in an otherwise verdant landscape. When Boston introduced them, the day was paling to dusk, and with it the edge came off the heat. I was glad of it and we gulped down the Tamarind juice with relish. For the moment, Matt and Jason were just glad for the chance to drink something; I could tell they'd had a long journey to get here, and probably weren't acclimatised yet. Debilitating as it was for me and Boston, at least we had been introduced to it, one degree at a time.

'Captain Wood, I presume?' said the man before me with a grin. He was all teeth and smiles, with a pair of dark sunglasses and an air of cheery mischief.

I suspected I was going to like him straight away. Matt Power was an American travel and adventure journalist, who had been commissioned by his new editors at the US magazine *Men's Journal* to accompany me for a week and write about the expedition.

'Hi, mate,' said Jason. I broke into a smile at the familiar sound of an English accent. Jason was perhaps forty, with an enormous beard and long, straggly hair. There was something about him that had the air of a guerrilla fighter, a kind of English Fidel Castro with a camera. It didn't surprise me, therefore, to find he'd travelled all over

Afghanistan with the Mujahideen and happened to be in New York for 9/11. For all his tame demeanour, this man was the real deal, and I was intrigued to find out more of his adventures. Matt and Jason had been friends for a few years and had long planned on working together on an assignment, but, while Matt had plunged straight into this fierce Ugandan heat from the tail end of a bitter New York winter, Jason had come from the Gambia in West Africa, where he lived and worked as a photographer. Jason had made Africa his speciality and was well-versed in the conditions we would be facing.

'Come and settle in,' I said, motioning them to take a seat in the shade of the thatched hut.

'God, it's hot out there,' said Matt. He was still sweating, but he had a smile on his face that belied an excitement at being here, about to embark on a great adventure. Even though he'd done this a million times before, he seemed to be feeling the shivers down the spine that always precede the start of a journey. I felt the same way.

As they relaxed by an electric fan, I took the opportunity to look them over. We'd had some email contact but, since I'd been out in the bush, I hadn't been able to find out all that much about the two men who would be joining the expedition. Matt was originally from Vermont in the USA and had carved out a career in adventure and travel journalism in an era when the industry was in tailspin, writing for *National Geographic* and countless other publications. He'd walked in places of the world of which I could only dream, trekking along the Great Wall of China, through India's Sikkim State, and had even spent time with Ed Stafford, an adventurer whose journey, to some extent, mirrored my own: three years before my own trek began, Ed had completed walking the length of the Amazon river, an expedition that had taken almost three years of his life. Softly spoken, Matt's voice had an almost nasal quality – but, as the night wore on and barriers broke down between us, I saw he was exactly the same as me: energised, not by the idea of a world-first-record, but by the opportunity to be out here, walking, just because the world was there and we didn't want to miss a single thing. I liked his style of documentation.

'Lev,' he said calmly, 'I'm here on a job. A very exciting job. I'm gonna tell the world your story. Do you mind if I just keep my Dictaphone handy and record stuff you say?'

'Sure,' I replied.

'It seems to me that we could learn a lot from Africa. On the way here, I saw a kid with a bike made entirely from wood. From *wood*.' He said it with such passion that everyone in the room turned. 'And kids in America whine that they don't have the latest PlayStation . . .'

I'd seen so many wooden bicycles in Uganda that they'd lost their novelty, but Matt brought me down to earth and I realised that what he said was completely true.

Soon after we met, Boston departed; there was, he told me, a man living in Pakwach who owed him money. This was a tale I had heard in several towns and villages along the way, but with Boston gone, Matt, Jason and I got down to the business of planning and preparation.

'We're here for six days,' said Matt, who looked rather out of place with his little glasses and notepad. 'Don't worry – we'll be out of your hair before you reach the border. God, you're on one hell of an adventure. I wish I could stay longer. How far will that take us?'

I looked at a map, glaring out of my computer screen. I'd only got paper maps for the most remote areas in South Sudan. Here, like the first sections of the journey, I figured I'd be able to get power from villages and be able to charge my laptop and navigate off that. It had worked well so far.

'One hundred and fifty miles,' I said, estimating the distance between Pakwach and the town of Adjumani, where they'd be able to catch a ride back to the capital. Looking at their rucksacks, I also knew that they had way too much gear, much of it unnecessary. 'I know you've done this before, but I hope you'll agree to a porter to carry these loads . . .' I said, trying to be as diplomatic as possible before the seasoned adventurers.

Luckily, I wasn't in the company of fools. 'Of course,' said Jason. In spite of his experience, he was more than happy to take advice.

The night was wearing on, and it had already been a long day for Jason and Matt. As well as their flights, they had driven for seven hours through the fiercest Ugandan heat to reach us – so, before the darkness was absolute, William showed them to their rooms.

'Are we set?' he asked.

'They've got far too much kit,' I said, 'but we can sort it in the morning, send half of it on to the end. What about you? All sorted?'

Boston gave a mysterious mutter and ordered himself a drink. 'If there's one thing you should learn in Africa,' he said, 'it's don't lend money.' He paused. 'Lev,' he went on, 'could you buy me a drink?'

In the morning, we spread Matt and Jason's kit around and began weeding out the bits of apparatus we wouldn't need: snack bars and super noodles, spare trainers and more. Some of it we would send on to Adjumani, and the rest we would assign to a local porter to carry. One of the lodge staff, a youngster called Innocent, was happy to earn some extra cash by accompanying us north, and for a few Ugandan shillings we were able to buy an old bicycle to use as a two-wheeled packhorse. By the time we had sorted ourselves, it was already 9.30am and the day was rapidly growing hotter. We had lost the good hours, around dawn, when the heat is more bearable – but, with the sun searing overhead, we returned to the heart of Pakwach town and set off.

The road we followed was around a kilometre west of the river itself. This, Boston explained, was Alur country, though its peoples could still speak many of the Acholi languages that had been the norm around Murchison. The Alur people dominate the border between north-western Uganda and the north-eastern Democratic Republic of Congo – and, of all the kingdoms inside Uganda, only theirs had been unaffected by the ban on traditional monarchies that was enacted in 1966. The first villages we came to were constructed entirely of square adobe huts. In every doorway and pool of shade, the villagers were drinking homemade palm wine with abandon. They called out as we passed, clearly uncertain if what they were seeing was real, or some apparition brought on by their inebriation.

'Why is everybody so . . . drunk?' ventured Matt, incredulously.

Boston gave a simple shrug. 'It is Saturday,' he declared.

By midday we had covered ten kilometres, but the effects of the heat were plain to see. Jason, who had been based in the Gambia for some time, was still unaccustomed to heats Boston and I could just about tolerate, and lagged some way behind. Matt followed at even more of a remove, and every time we came to a village or likely resting spot, where the track was dominated by bush and we could take advantage of the shade, we stopped to regroup and rehydrate. According to Boston's watch, by midday the temperature had reached an intolerable forty nine degrees and, after that, we lurched on in fits and starts. It began to feel as if we were constantly running a relay, beginning together before fragmenting along the paths, and by the late afternoon I knew we couldn't complete the miles we had planned. We came to a village where the chief permitted us the use of a schoolroom as a camp for the night, and there we squatted under the rotting desks amid piles of notepads and stacks of chairs. Boston set out to replenish our supplies of water, while Matt, Jason and I built a fire in the yard. The kindling we collected was so dry it took no effort to cultivate flames and, soon, we had one of the village chickens butchered and roasting on spits. As children gathered outside the schoolhouse, Boston returned with water and – like tiny cylinders of heaven – cans of Coke with which we could top up our electrolytes. For a moment, it felt like we were in Rwanda again, constantly keeping the children at bay, listening to them dare each other to get our attention.

In the morning, we made sure we were up well before dawn and, having fuelled ourselves with coffee brewed on a device Matt had brought along – a tiny stove powered by twigs, leaves and whatever other detritus we could find – we were on our way. At first the going was easier than the day before but, when the first rays of sun broke in the east, setting the waters of the river aflame, I knew we were in for another scorching day. Within an hour the temperature had reached its zenith of the day before, and from then on it only climbed. In silence, each contending with it in our own way, we trudged on – and soon we began to space out again, first Jason lagging behind, and then Matt even further behind. After a little way they both committed all of their packs to Innocent's bicycle, but lightening the load didn't diminish the heat. After we had completed eleven kilometres, we stopped to rest in the village of Nyakumba to fill up on water. As we stood in the shade of one of the tall adobe huts, the unmistakeable roar of engines could be heard on the other side of the village: motorbikes, scrambling up and down between the houses.

It was Jason who said it. Matt was off, handing out some of the rice we'd brought along to the village children, and a horde of them were scrambling eagerly for his attention. He seemed to be loving it. 'We're going to take one of the bikes,' he said.

As I looked at them, I nodded. 'It makes sense. There's no reason you have to walk the whole way.'

Jason nodded. This wasn't a decision he'd come to on the spur of the moment, but rather one he and Matt had debated that morning as the realities of the walk set in. 'We'll take the bikes north to Pawar.' He paused. 'We'll rest up and see you there.'

What Jason was proposing did make sense and, if I am honest, there was a small part of me relieved – without Matt and Jason, Boston and I would cover the remaining seven kilometres we had planned for the day much sooner. After our water supplies were replenished, we watched Matt and Jason disappear up the road into clouds of dust, riding pillion with the locals they had persuaded to taxi them to our camp.

Though the road took us up and down a succession of arid hills, Boston and I were able to complete the final stretch of the day in only an hour and a half, and found Matt and Jason making themselves at home in Pawar, where Matt was in deep conversation with the village headman and Jason was taking photographs of the scrub that overlooked the village. Both seemed revived by their restful afternoon, and Matt had already negotiated a campsite with the villagers. As a group, we followed a small game track down to the bank of the river where, thankful for the cool breeze coming in off the water, we pitched tents and opened our ration packs for the night. Soon, the headman – a drunkard with a longbow over his shoulder and a string of children hurrying behind – brought us firewood and three jerry cans filled with purified water. We sated ourselves greedily, and Matt was already standing over our fire, warming through the dehydrated ration packs of chilli he had brought with him. After weeks of rice and fish, and whatever other inedible foodstuffs the bush had thrown up, it was a feast beyond my imagining.

Later, as more and more children flocked out of the village to watch from the edge of our camp, Jason and Matt took photographs of the crowds. Boston and I lay by the banks of the river. The night was curiously silent, the river barely seeming to move. There were no crocodiles or lowing hippo to remind us where we were.

Before dawn, Matt was awake and brewing porridge on his little twig-burning stove. Jason was refilling the jerry cans while Boston was already in Pawar, locating the headman and the local ranger station. Today we would enter the Ajai Wildlife Reserve, a small conservation area surrounded by seasonally flooded swampland and forested savannah. Ajai had been the traditional home of the endangered white rhino in Uganda for decades, with the species hunted to near-extinction in the 1960s and the survivors all relocated to protect them from poachers. Entering Ajai would mean we would not pass any villages, and water would be more difficult to find. Even with the rangers Boston was procuring to take us into the park, the amount we could carry would be limited. Even more than the days we had just completed, this was going to be tough.

Matt's thoughts had evidently been headed in the same direction. As we lined our stomachs with porridge, leaving generous leftovers for the children inching down to camp, he said, 'I think we'll only go half way. We'll treat it the same as yesterday – come into the reserve, then hitch a ride to the next camp.'

I nodded. 'How are you feeling?'

Matt only shrugged. 'I knew we'd be tired, but I've done these treks before. You have to pace yourself. Being tired is to be expected. It's half the challenge – plus I've got a few blisters, which is slowing me down . . .'

We had planned to walk twelve miles that day, but we would no longer be following a well-beaten track, instead hacking our way through the scrub as we'd done on the way to Murchison Falls. With the going so tough, we spent the early morning looking for porters from Pawar, but the local men seemed too hungover from their night's excesses – and, in the end, the two rangers Boston had acquired agreed to be our pack animals as well. Moses and Charles were experienced guides and knew the area well, even if they did turn a blind eye to the occasional villager stealing firewood from the park. Moses spoke good English and evidently loved his job. Charles was big and strong – but, sneakily, only picked up the smaller of the bags.

The first miles of Ajai were dominated by tall, elephant grass savannah, with only a few trees growing up, like islands in a sea of green. All we could see of the Nile was the green papyrus swamp sitting on the eastern horizon. The grass was dense and tall, and we had to hack a way through – but it was not so tall that it could shield us from the worst of the sun. This was going to be another punishing day and every mile was going to be earned in sweat and toil.

By the time we emerged from the grass to make our way across the remnants of a dried swamp, we had seen so little wildlife that the reserve seemed eerie, sun-baked and dead. In fact, the only game we had seen at all were a few kob, a small sub-Saharan antelope, spooked at our approach. 'Has it been hunted out?' I asked the rangers, but Moses and Charles only looked up and pointed to the sun. The animals of Ajai, I understood, were more canny than we were being – they didn't tolerate this kind of sun when they didn't have to.

Though we stopped in every pool of shade we could find, by eleven o'clock the islands of shadow were dwindling rapidly – and soon, with the sun directly overhead, there would be nothing at all. I looked at Boston and saw that his gaze, too, was directed at a line of forest some distance to the west. When he turned to me, a simple nod was all it took for me to be sure of my decision. I turned to Matt and Jason; today, because we had been moving at such a sluggish pace, they had not lagged behind – but their exhaustion was palpable, mirrored in each other's face. 'We're going to head for the shade under those trees.'

If I had expected them to whoop or cheer, I was mistaken. 'How are you feeling?' I asked, as I saw Matt sip from the tube of his camelbak water bladder.

'I'm fine,' he said, sweat pouring from his forehead. 'Just a bit warm today.'

'It's fucking hot . . . The hottest day we've had. Are you sure you're okay?'

'Yeah.' Matt nodded. 'I'm fine.'

'Well, let me know if you're struggling,' I said. 'We'll take it easy.' I looked at Jason. He, too, was struggling with the heat – and, even though neither of them was carrying a bag, I knew they couldn't bear more than about two kilometres per hour. As we set off, I resolved to take it steadily and keep an eye on them. Boston, who looked the most sprightly of the group, began trampling down the long grass to make life easier for the rest of us.

Between us and the tree line, there was about a mile of sun-stricken land. In single file, we set out: Moses at the front, then Boston and me, with Matt and Jason bringing up the rear with Charles. Not for the first time, with all of us cringing from the overhead sun, our trek had the air of a military patrol as we all kept a watchful eye on one another. The Ajai park was wavering in the intense heat.

Moments later, I heard a call from behind me. I turned, to see Jason.

'Matt feels faint,' he said. 'Can we break, for just a few minutes?'

I nodded. The tree-line was only a hundred and fifty metres away, but those hundred and fifty metres felt like miles.

I found Matt hunkered down in the elephant grass. He was sipping from the water pack attached to his rucksack, through a thin tube. There was something almost ghostly about his face: pale white and flushed red in equal measure. 'Are you okay, Matt?'

He nodded. 'I'll be fine. I just need a moment.'

Boston was at my side. For a time he stared at Matt. Only then did he pull me aside. 'We shouldn't linger here, Lev. Not with . . .' He rolled his eyes to the sun hanging directly overhead. 'Better rest when we get to the trees. The longer we spend out here . . .'

Boston didn't need to finish the sentence, and nor did I need to convince Matt. He was already using Jason to get back to his feet. 'Are you sure?' I asked. 'Have you got enough water?'

Matt nodded. 'Plenty,' he said. 'The trees aren't far. Come on, let's go . . .'

'Well, keep drinking. We can rest just there . . .'

Together we lurched across the plain, finally entering the relative cool beneath the branches. But we had barely shed the sun when I heard Jason's cry, turned, and saw Matt face down in the dirt. By the time I reached him, he was trying to pick himself up, only to crumble again. He looked at me, his eyes open wide, with something approaching bewilderment on his face. Then, as we gathered round, stripping him of his trousers, his shirt, fanning him endlessly, anything that might cool him down, his expression changed again: he had come to some moment of epiphany, a simple, chilling realisation. 'Oh my God,' he uttered, and I wish I could say it was in disbelief, 'I'm going to die.'

Jason knelt at his side. 'You're not,' he said. 'You'll be fine,' he insisted.

I had seen this before, when I was in Afghanistan. This was heat exhaustion: hyperthermia, the overheating of the body, is just as deadly as hypothermia, but – beyond summer sun-stroke – is barely ever talked about. I had never had a man die on an expedition, not even in my tour of Afghanistan, and this could not be the first. I scrabbled in my pack for my satellite phone and, as Jason arranged Matt's body into the recovery position, I made my first emergency call.

In the forest behind me, Jason was feeding Matt water, but there were no longer any words coming from his lips. Now he only made odd, whimpering noises – noises that will remain with me through all of my years. On the phone, I reached our insurance company – but, this deep in the wilderness, their options were limited. I called home, to ask a contact to arrange a medevac helicopter. I called my old friend, the army doctor Will Charlton, for medical advice. In desperation, I called the Ugandan Civil Aviation Authority – but they didn't feel able to send a helicopter, not in this great heat, and not with nowhere for it to land.

'We need to cool him, *fast*,' I told Jason.

The river was too far away to submerge him, so we emptied all our canteens into a bowl and used it to cool his head and body. 'Find a village,' I told Boston. 'Go and bring help . . . and more water!'

Boston needed no other impetus. Taking Charles with him, he hurried back into the sun to follow one of the game trails to the edge of the river. Meanwhile, I turned to Moses. 'If they send a helicopter, it'll need somewhere to land,' I said. 'Burn a landing zone . . .'

Moses took off, while Jason and I remained at Matt's side, sponging him with what little water we had left, fanning him in a vain attempt to cool him down.

By the time Boston returned with water, half an hour later, Matt's breathing was ragged and faint. He had not opened his eyes and, though he had tried to make words, they came out as stunted groans.

I smelt fire and hoped the smoke would attract attention – but, with mounting horror, I realised the smoke wasn't coming from the elephant grass on the plain. For some reason, Moses had lit the fire on the hill above us – in completely the wrong place. The flames were raging – and, what was worse, the wind was driving it in our direction. Every time I ventured to the treeline, they had intensified.

We bathed Matt. We sponged water onto his lips. When we thought he was lucid enough to understand, we told him that he was going to be okay, that he would soon be back in New York where the African heat could not touch him, where his wife Jessica and family were waiting. When we could, we helped him tip his head back and drink some of the water – but, by two o'clock, he seemed to have lost the ability to swallow. On the edge of the woodland, I searched the skies for signs of a medevac helicopter and made repeated calls to the aviation authorities and insurance providers – but there was only endless blue above.

Back beneath the trees, I said, 'We've got to get him out of here.'

'The helicopter . . .'

'We can't wait for any helicopter,' I snapped. 'It's the fire.'

For more than two hours now, the fire had been coming our way. Coaxed by the wind, and fuelled by wood so dry it was perfect tinder, the flames were growing frighteningly close. Already the smell of smoke was strong, tendrils of grey wafting through the branches. 'Matt can't stay here,' said Jason.

By two thirty, the fire was less than fifty metres away. Bent low over Matt's chest, Jason confirmed what we had been fearing: his breathing was fading fast, now barely perceptible as a rise and fall of his chest.

'We need to move!'

Boston and Jason helped me lift Matt, but he was too heavy for one man alone. Urgently, listening to the crackle of the nearby flames, Jason rolled out a tarp from his pack. We laid Matt gently on top and, taking a corner each, bore him off. Moses and Charles, meanwhile, rushed back towards the fire, hoping to cut around its edges and find the nearest ranger station – and the help we desperately needed. As they went, they loosed rifle shots into the air – anything that could draw attention.

Two hundred metres on, the weight was too much. We stopped, momentarily clear of the grasping smoke, and laid Matt down to trickle the water Boston had brought from the river into his lips. Only, this time, when Jason bent over him, there was no breath coming from his throat.

I dropped at his side. I tipped his chin back and put my lips to his. Instinct had taken over: I breathed out, into his lungs, and began to make compressions on his chest. I continued: two short breaths and thirty sharp chest compressions; two short breaths, thirty compressions, over and again. I was lost in the attempt to keep him alive, convincing myself that all he needed was a few more minutes, anything until a helicopter or some rangers arrived, when I heard Jason shout out on the edges of my vision. It took me a moment to understand. When I looked over my shoulder, Jason was holding Matt's wrist and looking as hopeless as I have ever seen a man. 'He's dead,' he said. There was no pulse.

Some time later – I still cannot tell how long – we bore Matt to the very top of the forested hill, two hundred metres of steep, agonising climb. There we waited, at the top of the world. Matt's empty eyes gazed up at us, his skin finally cold. As Jason threw himself to the earth in exhaustion, and even Boston looked faint from our charge up the hillside, I wrapped Matt in a tarp and whispered a prayer. Three nights ago, I was drinking a toast of Tamarind juice to the explorers of the Nile with this man. Now, because of my expedition, he would never see home again.

It was five o'clock by the time the rangers returned, bringing with them ten more rangers from one of the reserve's stations, several miles away. By then the fire was dying of its own volition and, up on top of the hill, the first intimations of dusk were drawing in. It was cooler, now – and, staring at the bundle that was all that was left of Matt Power, that seemed the cruellest irony of all.

As we sat in disbelief, the rangers cut a makeshift stretcher from the branches of an acacia and, in a sombre procession, we bore Matt's body back across the plain. After some hours we emerged from the bush and took shelter at one of the rangers' outposts, where local police were waiting to take our statements. Numb, we recounted the events of the day at a strange remove. There was already a feeling that they had happened in a different age, in a different time.

Once the statements were taken, it was already night, and a pick-up truck was waiting to take us away from the reserve. Alongside Matt's body, we made the lonely drive west, forty five kilometres to the town of Arua, which sits on the western border with the Congo. Ordinarily, Boston would have begun some tirade about his years in the DRC, while simultaneously declaring the country's superiority above all others, but as we approached he was silent. The only sound was of Jason, starting up his mobile phone and – now we had a signal – dialling a New York number.

'Who are you calling?' I asked.

'Matt's wife,' he answered. 'Jess.'

In an Arua hotel, we sat together in the bar, staring into our beers. Every time I opened my mouth to speak, words failed to come. But I knew what I wanted to say: 'Screw the Nile. To hell with the Nile.' I wanted the cold comfort of English skies again. I wanted the familiar surrounds of London, or the plain, safe drudgery of the Staffordshire village where I had grown up. I wanted to be anywhere but here, thinking of the man who had died so that he could write about me on my indulgent, pointless, selfish trek.

It was Jason who broke the silence. 'Thank you,' he said, lifting his glass.

I looked at him numbly, and lifted mine to join his. I could scarcely believe what he was saying.

'We did all we could,' he said.

'It was simply his time,' said Boston sadly, as he drained his glass.

But, all through the long night, I wasn't so sure. I would never forget the gesture Jason had made, but whether I could ever exonerate myself of blame is a question for which I'm not sure I'll ever find an answer.

In the morning, after making yet more statements at a police station which seemed ripped straight out of the pages of some farce, we made arrangements for Matt's body to be returned to Kampala – and, thereafter, to be handed over to the US Embassy. I couldn't bear to think about the shockwaves his death was sending around the world to his friends and family, so instead lost myself in the practicalities of his trip. There would be no helicopter to take Matt back to Kampala, but – after much haranguing – we sourced a coffin and persuaded the police to take him there themselves. Jason was to join the convoy. Before he left, he shook my hand, and made us a gift of the last of the ration packs he and Matt had packed for the trip. As they left, I got to thinking how well Jason was handling it; to me, Matt was a stranger, but to Jason a close friend. I was glad it was Jason who would see him back home.

We spent the day in long silences. Boston walked, for hours, alone. At the hotel, I toyed with my phone. Half of me itched to pick it up, tell everyone I was coming back to England, that the expedition was over – but half of me wanted nothing more than to get back on the road, anything to put miles between me and the memory of Matt's eyes rolling back in his head. Today, night approached so much more swiftly than it had the day before. That was what the days were now: an endless succession of hours, each blurring indistinctly into the last. I tried to write in my journal, but I did not have the words to capture how this felt.

On 13 March, three days after Matt Power died, I emerged from a dream. As I woke, the memory of being beneath those trees as the fire advanced and we tried to beat life back into Matt's chest receded, and I staggered down to meet the day. Dawn was breaking in the west, and in the corner of the hotel lobby a grainy television set broadcast news of the intensifying fighting in South Sudan. In the shade outside, Boston was already waiting. It was the hundredth day of our expedition and, in that moment, every one of them felt like a sentence.

'How are you feeling, Lev?' Boston asked, without emotion.

I didn't know how to reply to that. I was feeling as cold as Boston sounded. But everything about Arua was bearing down on me this morning: the hotel walls, the empty, endless sky. There was only one thing I could think of that would break this spell, but it seemed sacrilegious to suggest it. I still did not know whether I wanted to complete the expedition, whether I wanted to go even as far as South Sudan, whether there was anything I could have done differently for Matt Power. The only thing I knew with any certainty was there was only one thing in the world that could bring me out of myself for the moment: the simple, blunt, monotony of putting one foot in front of another, empty and unthinking, for hours on end.

'I think we need to walk.'

Boston and I found transportation back to the river, close to the point at which Matt Power had died. In silence, we tramped north. In the distance, lush green hills began to flank the eastern bank of the Nile. By midday, storm clouds were brewing in the distance, and the first droplets of rain began to fall. Not one of us remarked on the irony; if Matt Power had joined us scant days later, his life might not have ended here, so far away from home.

By fall of night we had entered into Madi country. The Madi people, claiming to have come from Nigeria, moved into new homelands in Uganda, via the Sudan, in the mid-1800s – and seeing them in their villages, their skins so much darker than the Ugandans of the south, their homes bedecked in bright orange and black paint depicting simple pyramids, made me think how far we had come. We took refuge in a village where the chief granted us permission to sleep in the empty store room of the district shop, and listened to the bustle in the village square. This, the chief had told us, was the night market: a place to which the Madi people came from near and far to buy and sell fish and other commodities in the pitch black.

Soon after the market began, the heavens opened. The storm clouds we had seen during the day had followed us down river, and now the rain came down in violent torrents. Torrents that might have saved Matt Power's life.

Boston and I barely slept that night, but it was not just from listening to the rain hammer down on the rooftop. I was lost in thoughts of home, and of a home to which Matt Power would never return.

In the morning, we did the only thing we could to keep the terrible feeling of sadness at bay: we continued north, soon to meet the border.

THE FOG OF WAR

South Sudan, April 2014

At Adjumani, the last town of any real note before we came to the border, the signs of the conflict in the north were already plain to see. More than once we had seen stragglers coming down the roads, and in the villages along the river talk was of the sprawling refugee camps springing up along the border. The further north we came, the more evidence we saw of foreign NGOs and charitable organisations flocking to the camps. As chaos brewed ahead, it seemed Boston and I were fighting against a current – not of the river, but of people hurrying south.

In the days following Matt Power's death, Boston and I had walked in silence. On the east of the river, mountains of boulders emerged from the savannah. Perhaps it was only the memory of Matt's death playing tricks on my mind, but I began to feel as if we were somehow walking back in time, into a prehistoric past. The villages we encountered were small and rough, with ramshackle huts open to the elements and no stores to buy food. On the night before we reached Adjumani we camped on the outskirts of a village where the locals watched us as if we were bandits, and only begrudgingly let us buy the only food they had available: bush rat stewed in a pungent peanut sauce. It had black, rubbery skin and, though Boston devoured it with relish, I could barely stomach the taste. In the end, as I watched the leftover skull in my plate being picked clean of flesh by some of the local children, I resolved that it was because of what had happened in the Ajai Reserve. I had lost my appetite since then. I was beginning to wonder if I had lost my appetite for the trek.

On the 103rd day of our journey, we picked our way through thirty four kilometres of Acholi tribal land, finally crossing back to the east bank where the air was somehow cooler and black clouds spoke of the rains to come. I was eager for them; the heat was as fierce as it has been on the day Matt Power died, and I would rather have tramped endless days in the downpour than risk that again. By mid-afternoon, we followed the sweep of the river – and there, up against its banks, was the town of Adjumani.

Adjumani was smaller than Masindi, but it was clear that the local population – nineteen thousand at the last official census – had been swollen dramatically by the influx from over the border. It had the feel of a frontier town, its main strip flanked by crumbling colonial buildings and a small roundabout where a policeman waved through traffic and goats. It was in the swarmed roads that we saw evidence of the fleeing South Sudanese. New Land Cruisers with RSS plates and tall, smartly dressed men with facial scars had set up camp here; these were refugees with money – and lots of it.

'Some of them have fled as far as Kampala,' said Boston as we picked our way into the centre of town. 'The house prices have rocketed because of these Sudanese. They're buying all the biggest houses in the city.'

'Where do they get their money from?'

Boston only laughed. 'They steal it, Lev. Even you can see that! South Sudan is one of the most corrupt places in the world. All that aid money and charity donations going in – where do you think it goes? Not on aid . . .'

Now that Boston said it, I remembered reading about how the president of South Sudan, the cowboy-hat-wearing Salva Kiir Mayardit, had admitted that over four billion dollars of public money had 'gone missing' – the implication was that it had been stolen by members of his own government.

'This is why African aid will never work,' Boston muttered, and we stopped for the goats to pass.

Adjumani was welcoming the rich South Sudanese fleeing the violence on the other side of the border, but it was the next day that we discovered what was becoming of the less well-off. After a night in the relative civilisation of the town, where good hard cash could still buy a decent bed for the night, we followed a winding path north, keeping our eyes firmly locked on the mountains that marked the border of the world's newest country. From our vantage point, on a rocky plateau overlooking the Nile, we could see small villages on the plain below. It all looked so wild and untamed, and as the mountains grew bigger so did their air of menace. Beyond them, only thirty miles to the north, lay a warzone.

Nestled in the mountains' black foothills I could just make out the telecommunications masts of the border post of Nimule, and the columns of faint smoke rising from a village fire somewhere between us and the hills. As we progressed across the plain, through elephant grass twelve feet high, and waded waist deep across a tributary from the river, the smoke grew thicker, and at last we emerged to find what I knew instantly was a refugee camp on the cusp of great crisis.

Nyamanzi had once been a tiny village, like any of the other ramshackle ones we had stopped at on our way north. Now, it was a refugee camp threatening to outsize Adjumani itself. The line of UN-issued shacks, made from plastic sheeting over simple wooden frames, was only the beginning – Nyamanzi was vast, and only growing bigger. Boston and I stopped to take it all in. From the shadows beneath the plastic sheeting, countless South Sudanese eyes watched us. Boston was shaking his head, half in sadness and half in barely controlled rage. 'It happens every time,' he uttered, and I could feel his frustration: he had lived through innumerable moments like this, Africa forever fighting against itself.

The fighting on the other side of the border was now four months old, and many of the refugees had been here since the beginning. There were now almost twenty thousand refugees from across the border, mostly ethnic Dinkas from South Sudan's Jonglei state – and they were still coming. Between the clusters of shacks, Boston and I saw buses and trucks rolling through the red dirt, hundreds of other refugees disembarking with plastic chairs, mattresses, cooking pots and cases containing their most precious possessions – anything they had been able to save. As we wandered, we found no structure to the site. This was a city that had come into being overnight, without planning or order. There were no fences, no roads, just arbitrary groupings of families, friends, and work colleagues, each demarking their little piece of land with sticks or lines etched in the dirt.

At last, after picking our way through the tents for an hour, we came to the centre of the encampment. Here, bordered by yet more tents, a clear patch of land had become a designated market. The stalls that lined the square were not run by refugees, but by entrepreneurial Ugandans – the kind who had seen, in the sudden influx of desperate South Sudanese, less a humanitarian catastrophe and more an opportunity for commerce. Still, they were providing a service vital to the camp. The stalls here sold firewood, nails, soap, bags of rice – as well as hazardous-looking home-made phone chargers, powered by motorcycle batteries.

We were about to disappear back into the sea of tents when I saw a sign outside one tent offering the services of a barber, another where people sat at white plastic tables drinking tea, and another where pretty little girls could get beads and hair clips. Boston and I lingered, watching one girl having her hair put in braids.

'Life goes on, Levison,' Boston announced, and then it was time to go.

Ever since Kampala, I had been catching up on the official news whenever I could. What had begun as political posturing and backbiting had rapidly spiralled into ethnic violence, with the Nuer 'rebels' regrouping in the north and attacking key towns along what reporters were calling 'ethnic fault lines'. Towns such as Bor, Bentiu and Malakal had ended up becoming front lines and had changed hands several times over the winter. The rebellion had, if anything, only grown stronger since then, as the government forces pushed the so-called rebels out into the bush. Army defections became rife, with entire battalions moving over to rebel command – and others simply going rogue to become independent militias. The Jonglei, Unity, and Upper Nile states had been the worst affected – and these were the ones that straddled that nemesis of all Nile explorers, the vast Sudd swamp. The Sudd had been my greatest worry on undertaking this expedition; I had always known that, if I reached it too late, I risked the rainy season making it impassable. But now there was another variable to add to the mix: the very impassability of the Sudd made it a perfect base for rebel militias. When not attacking towns, they were said to disappear and melt into the emptiness of the Sudd where they could hide amongst the papyrus for weeks on end, waiting for new supplies of ammunition and armaments to be smuggled across the nation's fluid borders in the north and east. There was so much information and misinformation flying around that to see a full picture was impossible, but it seemed that northern Sudan – led by Omar al-Bashir, who had himself come to power in a military coup twenty-five years before – was covertly supporting the rebels, whilst publicly giving shows of solidarity with Kiir's government. In the east, meanwhile, the Ethiopians had adopted a neutral, mediatory stance, offering to hold peace talks – while Uganda, and even the USA, were sending in troops in support of the government. Hundreds of Ugandan soldiers had already lost their lives patrolling the roads and towns along the border they shared, and the USA had seen several of its own killed in the fighting when they attempted to extricate American citizens trapped inside the constantly shifting zone. More than a million people had already fled their homes, either seeking sanctuary across the border or settling in Internally Displaced Persons' camps. With the country's infrastructure rapidly collapsing, and the economy barely functioning, famine was being spoken about by the NGOs on the border. And, though the UN were involved in trying to broker a ceasefire, this was proving more problematic than it ought to have – the head of its mission, Hilde Johnson, had been accused of siding with the Nuer rebels instead of taking the UN's mediatory stance when it transpired she had once been the lover of the rebel 'leader', Riek Machar himself.

'Are you sure you want to do this, Lev?'

I turned to Boston. We were standing on the edge of Adjumani, facing the border – though there was no road to speak of, only untamed bush. 'I was going to ask you the same question. You don't have to come with me. It wasn't part of our agreement. You could go back to Kampala, to Lily and the girls. To Jezu Adonis.'

But Boston only said, 'I would not leave you to it alone!' At first I thought he was being brotherly and felt almost touched. Then his face broke into one of his wildest grins. 'Without a guide, Levison, you would not even make it to the border.'

We began to walk.

There is no road to Nimule that runs parallel to the Nile so instead we hacked our way through the bush, following the curve of the river. The Nile widened here, running east for some miles before tracking north again, and on its banks elephants still roamed. Ordinarily the herds lived in the Nimule National Park on the South Sudanese side of the border, but sometimes they would swim across the river in search of better grazing and trample Ugandan crops, uproot Ugandan trees, and generally leave destruction in their wake.

The first sign of Nimule, as with many other African villages, was the phone masts reaching into the sky. The tower rose out of the scrub but, before long, I could hear the rumble of trucks coming from the south, the buzzing of motorbikes and the barking of feral dogs. 'Must be a main road near here,' said Boston, and before we knew it we had stumbled onto the track. Soon, we were standing among the shanties. Nimule was as busy as Adjumani before it; the refugees who hadn't yet made it to the camps were lingering here and some, it seemed, had even made the frontier their home. Juice sellers lined the road and radios blasted out the latest news from the frontline. Somali truck drivers sat around chewing *khat* and Sudanese Arabs in white *jellabas* smoked *shishas*. People of all nationalities crowded the street, dodging lorries full of Ugandan supplies bound for the empty stores of Juba, the capital of South Sudan.

'It's the Wild West,' I said as Boston and I made our way to the checkpoint. My nerves were already intensifying, because neither of us had the appropriate visa to get into the country. I hadn't been able to get one before leaving home because of the outbreak of war, and Boston had decided too late that he was accompanying me this far. Not having a visa isn't always an issue in a continent where a fistful of dollars still goes a long way, but I was feeling increasingly on edge.

'It's enterprise,' said Boston. 'Opportunity. An African knows where to make a fast buck. There are people who specialise in it. The second they hear of war, off they go.'

It wasn't just Africans, I reflected, as we joined a queue at the checkpoint. Businessmen from all over the world were here to make a quick buck. So were the NGO workers – it was a mistake to believe some of them weren't here for the money as well. As the traders, merchants and soldiers headed north, the refugees – some in rags, some in shiny new suits – headed south. Nimule was a place in constant flux. Slowly, we made our way down the line.

It took a long time to reach the front of the queue at the checkpoint but, when we handed over our passports, our entry to South Sudan went without a hitch; the border guard didn't even look at our visas before stamping the pair of us out and barking for the next in line. There was no turning back now. Without looking back, we walked across a stretch of barren no-man's-land where Ugandan soldiers mingled with their South Sudanese counterparts. On the South Sudan side, the immigration building was virtually empty – there could not have been too many tourists looking for visas, and, within five minutes, we had been granted a two-month entry stamp and were being welcomed by a beaming equatorial official. 'Welcome to South Sudan,' he said, with a smile that spoke of a thousand things.

In the scorching light of the South Sudanese morning, a figure was waiting. Outside the immigration office, he watched us through dark glasses, reflecting the sun. Wearing boot-cut jeans and short-cropped hair, his barrel chest and biceps threatened to tear open his shirt. As if to complement the look of a human monolith, his neck and shoulders bulged.

A shovel-like hand extended and grabbed mine in such a crushing hold that I couldn't have torn away, even if I had wanted. 'Alright mate!' he said, with a perfect English accent. 'How's it going? Welcome to the republic of South Sudan! *Tamam?*'

'Tamam?'

'It means cool, good, awesome . . . Well, something like that. It's Arabic.'

Ignoring Boston's suspicious looks, I said, 'Well, in that case, Tamam to you too.'

'It's me,' he said, lifting his glasses for an instant. 'Andrew Ray Allam.'

Now this smiling behemoth made sense. I'd been expecting to meet up with a man named Ray Allam somewhere this side of the border, but hadn't anticipated his being at the checkpoint. All I knew of the man was what I'd heard from a friend back home, who'd helped arrange the logistics while I'd been dealing with Matt's death. Allam was a military man, somebody who could advise me as we tried to make a way north. He was newly promoted as a colonel in the SPLA, on a part-time basis – a sort of Sudanese reservist, whose day job was to arrange logistics for television crews and journalists. The SPLA was the Sudan People's Liberation Army, South Sudan's newly official military force, which had begun as a guerrilla organisation in 1983 and finally won the country's independence in 2011. It was now engaged in suppressing the 'rebels' of the current crisis. If anybody could help me continue the expedition by navigating between the shifting sides of the conflict, it would be Allam. Or so I hoped.

We agreed that he would meet us at several junctures on the journey north – first, here, at Nimule, and later on the outskirts of Juba, the capital city, which was now held safely by government forces. Further north, things became more problematic, with several key towns along the Nile being fiercely contested, but that was a bridge to be crossed another day. For the moment, Allam led us around Nimule as we resupplied our food and provisions. The town was incongruously calm – the only signs of conflict were the refugees passing south, back into Uganda. Breeze-block mansions and restaurants lined the main Juba road, and among them, Allam had found us a compound-style hotel. In the morning, he told us, he would introduce us to the rangers who would escort us north, through the Nimule National Park – but, for the moment, it was time to hear his story.

'I was twenty-one when I arrived in England,' he told me, in the hotel bar. 'Before that, I'd escaped the civil war by heading to the north – to the side of the enemy. I'd been told that was the place to receive a good education, but when I got there I met an Englishman who arranged for me to get refugee status in the UK. When I arrived, I couldn't speak a word of English – but they sent me to college in Winchester and I studied hard. I ended up with a diploma in media studies and was on track to get a good job in England . . . but I couldn't stop thinking about my homeland, about Africa. In the end, I came back. I wanted to serve the SPLA, so I volunteered as a soldier. But they said to me – Andrew, the pen is mightier than the sword. And the camera is even mightier than that! So use your new education, and be our voice. Well, that's exactly what I did. I reported for the government, and worked in media, telling good news stories – victories and so on . . .'

'Propaganda?' Boston said, in his usual brusque style.

For the first time, Allam's teeth flashed menacingly – and I thought I caught a glimpse of the true man, beneath his jovial exterior. 'Yes, my Congolese friend. Propaganda! The stories we told were an important way of winning the civil war, and South Sudan finally getting its independence . . .'

'And then?' I asked, wanting to steer Boston away from quizzing him further.

'That was twenty years ago. I've been in and out of South Sudan and England ever since. I have a family in England – in Dorset, where my beautiful wife lives – but I make my money here. Who'd have thought it? I make money here in Africa and send it back to my family in England! This is a topsy-turvy world, my friends . . .'

After Allam had left, promising to send our arrangements for the start of our trek tomorrow, Boston muttered, 'He is not the man for us, Lev.'

'What are you talking about, Boston? He's already sorted the rangers for us to . . .'

'He's a government agent.'

I was used to this by now – Boston seeing spooks everywhere he turned – but, this time, his assertion didn't seem nearly so wild.

'I promise it, Lev. A part-time colonel with the SPLA, helping media and foreign guests? He's a spy, Lev. He isn't here to help us. He's here to keep an eye on us, to make sure we're who we say we are.'

'Well,' I began, 'we *are* who we say we are. If Allam can help us cross this country . . .'

Boston laughed – as much at me as at the situation. 'He won't help like you think he will. He's a government man. Do you really think they'd want us walking in areas they don't hold, where they can't control the people we talk to, the things we see . . .?'

I had to concede: Boston had a point. I lay awake for a long time that night, thinking of the strange pact we had made with this strange spy catcher.

There are almost three hundred kilometres of river between Nimule and Juba, and in the morning we set out, guided to the edge of town by Allam himself. Before we embarked properly, there was a surprise awaiting us. Outside Nimule, where the Nile does a sharp northerly turn when it hits the hard rock of the Nimule plateau, a tamarind tree was growing from an outcrop of smooth boulders. Beneath that tree's gnarled branches, a collection of village elders awaited our arrival. Allam was grinning as we approached, and one by one he introduced me to the chiefs of the area, and of the Madi people.

The Madi have made this part of South Sudan their homeland for many generations – and, though nobody really knows from where they came, Madi folktales suggest they may have emigrated from Nigeria to find a new home here, along the banks of the Nile. Certainly, the Madi had already been living here for aeons when Samuel Baker first explored this part of the world, following the Nile upriver from his base at Gondokoro, a trading station that sat on the river near present-day Juba. It was here, at Nimule, that Baker first set eyes on the plains of northern Uganda, and succeeded in travelling further south along the river than any other white man. To his great relief, he was greeted with open arms by the local Madi chiefs, who quenched his thirst with a cup of their famous tamarind juice. And, to my surprise, today, they were going to treat me exactly the same.

Three old men and their wives presented me with my own

tamarind juice. Soon after, a troop of village ladies in traditional clothes appeared from beyond a hillock, formed a circle around me and started to dance, with the leader of the group banging on an ox-hide drum. The rest of the women held papyrus wands and shuffled in unison.

As we watched, Andrew Allam winked at me. 'I thought you might appreciate a "Baker's Welcome". They adore him here. He's like a god.'

After the dancing, the chief performed a simple ceremony – first spitting, and then sprinkling Nile water, over my hands. 'You are now considered as Madi,' he announced. Out of the corner of my eye, I saw Boston surreptitiously wiping his own hands. 'You are following in the footsteps of the great Sir Samuel. With the Nile as your guide, and God as your witness, go in peace and safety.'

It was the most foolish thing, but as we set out, that simple blessing gave me succour and, for a little while, I could almost forget the terrible events that had happened in Uganda.

Allam had instructed us that we would need at least three rangers to guard us as we went north: Nimule National Park was a tiny conservation area with a herd of elephant and occasional hippo, and sometimes the elephants turned rogue and could act aggressively towards visitors. On the morning we set out, though, only one ranger was ready: Severino, a grisly looking warrant officer who barely said a word. The shortfall, Allam explained, couldn't be helped – given the country's current crisis, the government was in the process of 'security screening'. In effect, they were interrogating all of their own soldiers, police officers and rangers to test their loyalties – all a result of recent mass defections. The other two rangers we had been allotted had either disappeared into the system, or not been through their interrogations in time. Severino, it seemed, would have to do.

North of Nimule, we entered the park. Most visitors to the park, occasional aid workers and the more adventurous UN staff, come to see the Fola Falls, a small set of cascades in the Nile that mark the last real obstacle for boats before the cataracts of the Sahara desert, still a thousand miles further north. By the afternoon, we had passed by the falls, and come upon a crumbling set of brick and timber buildings. For the first time, Severino muttered words: this place, he told us, was called 'Commando'. It was a place with which he was very familiar – the park's rangers used it as an outpost. But then, he lifted his hand and pointed to one crumbling shack, in the heart of the others. 'That's the place,' he said. 'That was Garang's hideaway.'

Slowly, we approached. Now, it was only a collection of shattered bricks, gradually being reclaimed by the wild. But Severino was lifting the lid on the story of South Sudan's origin, and one of the longest civil wars that Africa – and, indeed, the world – has ever known.

Dr John Garang de Mabior was a Sudanese politician and leader of the rebels who initiated the Second Sudanese Civil War in 1983. A member of Sudan's native Dinka tribe, Garang had been born in 1945 in the upper Nile region of Sudan. Orphaned at the age of ten, he tried to join the army when the first civil war erupted in Sudan in 1955, but, because of his age, the army sent him abroad to continue his education – first in Tanzania and later in the United States. Garang was a bookish young man and quickly excelled at his studies, but, though he was offered a scholarship to pursue graduate studies at the University of California, he made the decision to return to his Sudanese home. It was a decision that would ultimately change the face of Central Africa for ever.

Civil war still raged in his home country and Garang was soon numbered among the rebel soldiers of Southern Sudan, fighting the government in the north for greater representation and regional autonomy. In 1970, the rebel army sent him to Israel for military training, and, although the first civil war ended in 1972, Garang had already taken his first steps towards becoming a career soldier. Subsumed into the Sudanese standing army, for eleven years he rose through the ranks, becoming first a captain and later a colonel. Then, in 1983, his sympathies still with the rebels of the South, Garang masterminded a defection of a battalion stationed in the southern city of Bor. It was the opening gambit in what would become the Second Sudanese Civil War. By the winter of that year, Garang had brought various rebel commands into his control, effectively founding the Sudan People's Liberation Army, a professional rebel outfit that would resist at all costs the north's military rule and brutal imposition of Islamic law.

The Second Sudanese Civil War was to last twenty-two years and cost one-and-a-half million lives, drawing in the armies of Uganda, Libya and Ethiopia along the way. In 2005, after two years of peace talks, a resolution was finally reached – with the southern regions of Sudan being given the status of an autonomous region for six years, before a referendum would decide their ultimate fate.

What we were looking at here, Severino explained, was the final hideout Garang had used during the most desperate phase of the Second Civil War. In 1993, things were at their lowest ebb for Garang and his SPLA. The Arab army, in support of the Sudanese government, had recaptured the city of Juba and reached the Ashua River, just twenty kilometres to the north of where we now stood. 'They were broken,' said Severino, 'forced into hideouts in the bush and the hills. Lots fled into Uganda. But, somehow, Garang brought them all back together, all those ragtag soldiers from the SPLA.' It must have been a desperate situation. Allam had told me how his men had been so desperate and low on ammunition that they had thrown fishing hooks into the river to slow down the advance of the Arabs. That was back in 1993, at the height of the Second Sudanese Civil War, but somehow, against all the odds, they pushed them back.'

Looking at it now, it was hard to believe that these tumbledown buildings had been the epicentre of one of the civil war's most famous last stands. The hut was overgrown by thorns, its windows smashed, reeking of the excrement of wild cats and baboons – but, inside, the legacy of war remained. As I ventured in, I saw bullet casings littering the floor. On the walls, faint etchings in chalk showed the names of commanders, diagrams of tactical formations, lists depicting orders of battle. As I traced my fingers along the brick, trying to imagine what it had been like, Severino grunted and simply waited outside. He was, I was beginning to understand, an old SPLA soldier himself, and had no desire to remember the past.

'It must have been hell,' I said, but Boston wasn't listening. I found him lingering behind a smashed brick wall, where he was considering taking a piss into John Garang's old toilet. It was only that image that brought me back to reality. It was time to continue our walk.

Severino left us on the seventh day. We had come through the national park, the path like a tunnel beneath thick baobab trees with branches tangled in vines. After a time, we were able to walk directly along the banks of the river, and I was glad of it. Severino had told us that the area was still pockmarked with landmines, but on the riverside we would be safe. Huge boulders dotted the banks, Nile monitors skittering away at the sound of our footfalls, and solitary huts made from dried grass and wattle looked like constructions from some bygone age.

Severino had had enough, and I was not sad to see him go. There was something resigned about him that made me think he was dangerous – here was a man who truly did not care – and, as we watched him hitch a lift back towards Nimule, I felt a weight lifted off my shoulders. There were still a hundred miles between us and Juba, and though Boston quickly found a replacement as porter – Martin, a village pastor, agreed to help shoulder our packs further north – the sense that I was truly alone on this trek had never been keener. I found myself walking, for long miles, ahead of Boston and Martin. Occasionally, I'd hear them having a heated theological debate, always laughing, always smiling – but I was in no mood for conversation. Only a few weeks ago, I would have loved to listen to Boston, the fervent anti-religionist, and Martin, a devout Creationist, battle over whether Adam and Eve were black or white – but now I shrank from their arguments. They seemed so frivolous. I couldn't stop my mind from flitting back to that Ugandan hillside where Matt had died, nor flitting forward to what we were walking into. At every village we passed, the news from the north intensified. As the road progressed, we saw more people fleeing. Toyota minivans seemed to be the exodus vehicle of choice, piled up with mattresses, chairs, tables, cooking pots, goats and entire families. The mangled wrecks of pick-ups, buses and lorries littered the roadsides, and beyond, in the bush the entire landscape was filled with landmines. More families than I cared to think about had lost their lives in traffic accidents, all in an attempt to flee the mounting hostilities. It was those hostilities towards which I was willingly walking – and, for the first time in my journey, I began to question the sanity of what I was doing. Matt Power had already lost his life, all because of my indulgent quest to be the first man to walk the Nile. Was I really so selfish as to ask Boston to risk his life as well, or risk the lives of any of the other companions we would meet along the way? I began to think about home more and more often: of the family and friends whose lives I was missing out on; of the loved ones who must have forgotten about me while I was here, walking – just walking. I wanted to be in a world in which I didn't stand out. I craved the anonymity of London's streets, where police didn't stop you for your papers, and you didn't have to fear that the ground beneath your feet was littered with explosives.

At the edge of the road, where I had stopped to take in the view, Boston and Martin caught up with me. They'd been aggressively arguing over the age of the Earth.

'What is it, Lev?'

I didn't want to tell him the truth – that, for the first time, I was tempted by the thought of giving up – so instead, I pointed to the north. Over the horizon, the black storm clouds were gathering, heralding the rainy season to come. We were close to the borders of the vast swamplands of the Sudd now, and when those rains began to fall, the country would become impassable.

'Then we'd best be walking!' declared Boston and, for the first time, marched ahead of me down the road.

On the 122nd day of the journey, Boston and I – having said goodbye to Martin on the road – pushed our way into the outskirts of Juba. If Kampala is a teenager of a capital city, then Juba is a petulant infant. Founded in 1922 by a group of Greek traders who came to supply the British Army camped along the Nile, it was one of the most fiercely contested battlegrounds in the Sudanese Civil Wars, and became the official capital of South Sudan after the peace agreement of 2005.

Dusk was hardening into night as Boston and I entered, and everywhere we saw the detritus and filth left behind by the fleeing population. The first casualty of war, it seemed, was not the truth – it was hygiene. Piles of plastic bottles were strewn among the shanties, Marabou storks looking like pterodactyls plucked from some forgotten world as they picked through the waste looking for anything edible.

At my side, Boston said nothing. Perhaps his silence was the most fearsome thing of all. The walk really had begun to feel like a march into the bowels of hell. We had reached the frontier, the very edge of safety. Juba had been a battlefield only four months before, with thousands killed in the streets. No sooner had we crossed through the first shanties, to see the great conical mound of Rajaf Hill marking the southern boundary of town, and Jebel – a craggy ridge to the west – domineering the skyline, we began to see the soldiers. The streets were filled with SPLA. Machine-gun posts and sangars – temporary fortifications constructed from sandbags and stones – sat on every corner. Every hundred metres, figures lurched out of the shadows to demand our papers and send us on our way with a warning: the nightly curfew, designed to keep combatants from moving under the cover of darkness, was about to come into effect. Whole areas of the city were off-limits to civilians, and anyone caught taking photographs would be immediately arrested, perhaps even shot.

By 7 pm, we had entered the old town and reached Juba's bridge over the Nile – and there, to my relief, Andrew Allam was waiting for us, just as had been promised. I was grateful to see him. Allam might have been a government agent, but the government was in control of Juba and the further we walked into the city the tighter the security became. Enthusiastically, Allam shook my hand and guided us towards the iron bridge. One of the oldest landmarks in Juba, it had been built by the British long before the civil wars tore the country apart, and, Allam insisted, was testament to the good work the British had done for the region. This bridge was the only crossing to span the Nile in two thousand miles and was part of the reason Juba had grown from trading post to capital city in only eighty years.

'You've had no problems?'

'Some,' I said, 'but nothing we couldn't handle.' The lower-ranking soldiers who had stopped us were the most problematic: they seemed to think they had to shout first, ask questions later – and, if you showed any fear, they were quick to exploit it. Along the way, I had learned that the only way to deal with them was to demand name and rank, do my best impression of an indignant commander; tell the bastard to stand up straight, smarten his collar, and trust that they fell in line. Officers, I had found, were much easier to deal with: all they wanted was a nauseating show of servility and they usually let us go.

'Well,' said Allam, 'you have nothing to fear for now! Everything's in order. You'll find Juba a calm enough place, once you—'

We hadn't even set foot on the bridge when Allam's voice faltered and, out of the gathering darkness, appeared two unmarked Land Cruisers, gleaming in black. With a screech of tyres, they drew alongside us, the first banking slightly as if to bar the way ahead.

Allam's voice returned. 'Stand still,' he whispered – and, for the first time, I heard real nerves behind his words.

The doors of the first car opened, and a shady-looking man stepped out. At first, I didn't know why I found this man any more unnerving than the soldiers who had so regularly been stopping us. Perhaps it was because he wasn't wearing any uniform. As he studied us, the doors of the second car opened and two other figures emerged, the first a particularly vicious-looking Dinka – with scars across his forehead. In dark sunglasses and a scuffed leather jacket, he didn't look the sort of privileged officer who ought to have been stepping out of a gleaming new Land Cruiser, but it took me a moment to properly understand: these men were not soldiers at all; they were members of some other, shadowy security force. South Sudan's secret police.

The man in the leather jacket strode towards Allam, who held up his hands. In seconds, they were barking at each other in a language neither Boston nor I understood. I was beginning to curse myself for bringing Boston here – not only for putting him in danger, but for fooling myself that I could do this without a committed, local guide. As Allam and the man engaged in heated debate, I flashed a look around. Apart from us, the bridge was silent. Beneath us, the waters of the Nile rushed by. There was nowhere else to turn.

In an instant, the security agent rounded on me. For the first time, he spoke in English – broken and slow. 'How long you have in South Sudan?'

I fumbled for my passport and the visa stamp within. 'Two or three months,' I began, handing it over.

'It says here you entered on 26 March.'

'That's right.'

He snapped my passport shut in a flourish that seemed to betray some hint of triumph. 'That wasn't three months ago. That was only two weeks.'

I could see Allam's face turning to stone, but I persisted: 'I meant I *will* spend two or three months here . . .'

'Your story doesn't calculate. You told me you had been here two or three months.'

'No, I said—'

He cut me off with a victorious snarl. 'You're lying. I can see this. Your story does not calculate.'

Allam responded to him in the Juba Arabic. By the tone of his voice, I knew that he was flustered – and, all the while, the agent's eyes remained on me.

'Are you saying my English is bad?'

'I am a colonel in the SPLA, comrade,' Allam interjected. 'We are brothers in arms! I have been serving this country for twenty-five years. The *khawaja* is just a little simple . . .'

But this final plea for my stupidity didn't pacify the agent. 'Get in the car,' he said, indicating Boston too. 'In silence. You are all under arrest.'

For a moment, I only hung there in disbelief. Then, Allam mouthed two words: 'Do it.' To see Allam suddenly so servile left me with no misapprehensions. Boston and I got into the car. In the back, as the agents bickered among themselves, Allam kept his head down and whispered from the side of his mouth: 'These people are stupid, Lev. They don't know anything except paranoia. Just stick to the story.'

'What story?' I snapped. 'I told them the truth.'

'Just keep it simple. They'll kill you if they think you're taking the piss out of them.'

And as the Dinka climbed into the driver's seat, one of the other spies forcing his way into the back, I heard Boston mutter under his breath: 'These Dinka, Lev. They have no education.'

It wasn't until the Land Cruiser was pulling away that I saw both men in the car with us were wearing pistols at their sides. Outside, the darkness had solidified, and the hulking towers of new-town Juba were subsumed in the night. The 4×4 swung around, returning the way it had come. We were, I understood, bound for the centre of town. The light from street fires, where locals were burning rubbish, plastered itself across the glass. More than once, I saw dark figures at the edges of the road. Lone electric lights flickered in open doorways, while cows and goats grazed between the buildings, picking through piles of human excrement.

Even before the war, this had been a frontier town, the government desperately trying to drag it into the 21st century. Many of the shanties had been bulldozed to make way for development: NGO compounds, banks, shops and more vulgar government ministries. Half-built high-rises sat uncomfortably between the more traditional South Sudanese dwellings, unfinished since the boom years that had followed independence. There was a tragic air about this landscape: Juba, only a year before was a boom town – a frontier settlement full of Africans of every nation trying to make a buck. Ugandans ran the taxis and motorcycles, and the fruit markets. Somalis ran the logistics and foreign exchange, Indians ran the garages and shops, Chinese built the road and factories and Eritreans ran the hotels. Juba, which should have been South Sudan's shining beacon to the world, was being reclaimed by the wild.

I whispered to Allam out of the side of my mouth: 'Where are we going?'

'The Blue House, Lev. Security HQ.'

A kernel of fear hardened in my stomach. I knew of the Blue House only from hearsay. Its colloquial name didn't sound terrible, but even so it inspired dread in the minds of the South Sudanese. It was an infamous construct, known to expats as the 'Ministry of Torture', and sat in the centre of town, its innards hidden from view by reflective glass windows and shiny blue walls.

'What for?' I asked – but my only reply was a glare from the Dinka guard at my side, and a deliberate flashing of his pistol.

At around 9 pm, the Land Cruiser entered a stretch of highway cloaked in absolute darkness. On either side, the buildings had been blacked out. What few streetlights remained had been turned off, and even the cars that we passed moved with their headlights turned off. Five hundred yards on, the Land Cruiser slowed to a halt and, as the Dinka driver emerged to get us out of the back, I saw the fortress of the Blue House itself. Its gates were surrounded by soldiers in a dizzying array of uniforms; some I took for SPLA, but others I didn't recognise, and still more were in plain clothes, hanging around in packs along the edge of the road.

Behind me, Boston stumbled up onto the road. Allam was protesting to the agents again, but his arguments fell on deaf ears; with few words, they directed us towards iron gates, where yet more soldiers manned a gunnery point. Moments later, the gates were open and we were through, shepherded into a black courtyard bordered by tall, concrete walls.

'Sit down,' one of the soldiers barked. In silence, we took seats on a cold, metal bench, watching as the other two agents disappeared into the building. At my side, Allam drew a cigarette from his pocket and fumbled to light it – but, in a flash, the Dinka guard ripped it from his lips and ground it beneath his heel, cursing in Arabic. I could only assume it was to do with the blackout engulfing these streets.

The minutes stretched on, each one seemingly longer than the last. Boston, preternaturally quiet, had his gaze fixed on the floor and, every time I tried to get his attention, he seemed to inch further away. It was only now that my feelings of guilt truly solidified. I found myself thinking of Lily and his children in flashes: here was Jezu Adonis, wearily climbing out of bed; here, his daughter Aurore welcoming me to their house. I had been foolish in coming to South Sudan myself, but even more foolish in bringing Boston.

Movement erupted in the corner of my eye. The barriers were opening again, and through them marched six or seven men, with their hands tied behind their backs. I took them to be Nuer, captives from the opposing side of the conflict, and watched as more armed guards followed after. Only twenty metres from where we stood, one of the soldiers barked and the Nuer were forced to their knees, heads bowed against the compound wall. Now, they were lost to the shadows on the fringes of the courtyard. I could no longer see them; all I could see were the soldiers bringing batons back to rain down blows. For a short time the air was alive with screams of pain, and for a long time after all I could hear were muffled groans.

Allam could not meet my eyes, almost as if he was embarrassed. 'You don't fuck around here,' he muttered, darkly. 'If they torture us, Lev, don't say a thing.'

For the first time, Boston lifted his head, his eyes flared. This, I remembered, would not have been the first time he was tortured.

Moments later, the doors opened and our government captors returned. This time, they were not alone. Accompanying them came a corpulent officer, dressed in army fatigues. As he approached, the soldier ordered us to stand. Warily, we obeyed. The fat chief had come bearing a torch, and one after another he focused it on our eyes.

'Why were you at the bridge?' he demanded.

'We were crossing it . . .'

'You were filming,' he declared.

Behind him, one of the Dinka lifted my backpack and spilled its contents onto the ground. There, among all our camping gear and ration packs, rolled the camera, small laptop and recording equipment I was using to chronicle the expedition. The agents, I saw, were already holding my journals in their hands.

'You were recording the bridge. The artillery pieces. Why?'

I opened my mouth to respond, only to be cut off again.

'What if we were to come to England and take pictures of bridges there? What would your government think? Why are you here, disrespecting the sovereignty of South Sudan?'

I wanted to shout out, to tell him he could take all the pictures of English bridges he wanted, that we were only passing through – but the absurdity of the notion stalled me. What kind of a fool would be simply 'passing through' Juba at a time like this? I floundered for the words and, before I could find them, another officer had emerged from the doors behind.

In the edges of the courtyard, the groaning of the captive Nuers went on.

The officer who approached was evidently superior to the ones whose faces I could not see for the torchlight dazzling my eyes. He was dressed in smart plain clothes and shiny black shoes, the mark of the African spymaster, and, as he approached, the agents who had apprehended us stepped aside.

At the new colonel's gesture, the agents collected my camera, laptop and Dictaphones together, scrabbling through the packs to make certain there was nothing they had missed. From a pocket, one of them retrieved another digital memory card, the one that held all my photographs of Lake Victoria and the journey north: photographs of Kampala, of Kyoga, of Murchison Falls and Matt Power.

'You are free to go . . .' he told us.

It took me a moment to understand. By then, the soldier had thrown our packs at our feet and were half-way across the compound, carrying all our electrical equipment.

'. . . pending an investigation,' the colonel concluded. Turning, he summoned one of the soldiers who had been attacking the Nuer up against the compound wall. 'Take them to Bedouin Lodge,' he began. 'The investigation will be complete by morning. You are to return to us then.'

I began to protest, but a single look from Andrew Allam stopped me. He was already tramping across the courtyard, back to the gate. Not even Allam, it seemed, could wait one more second to be rid of this place. Heaving my ransacked pack over my shoulder, I hurried to follow.

THE IMPENETRABLE SWAMP

Juba to Bor, South Sudan, April 2014

'Missionaries, mercenaries and misfits,' said the man behind the hotel bar. 'Everyone here's a lunatic with nowhere better to be, but if you find the right one, they might be able to help you get north.'

Two days after we had been dragged to the Blue House, I was prowling the hallways of Bedouin Lodge – a popular hotel crammed between an abattoir and a graveyard where dogs regularly dug up human remains – intent on finding a way to further our expedition. The morning after our arrest, our equipment had been returned and the spies' specious charges all dropped – half of me understood that, when the soldiers had found nothing suspicious, they had decided to let us go; but I also suspected they had been looking for money, some kind of bribe. Whatever it was, I didn't want to stay in Juba long. The problem was how to go further. Allam had prepared papers that would allow us – mindless government agents aside – to get to the city of Bor, a further 120 miles downriver. But, after that, there were still five hundred miles before the border with Sudan.

The man in the hotel bar was Andy Belcher, a white Kenyan pilot who had turned hotelier and refused to leave Bedouin Lodge even when Juba erupted into ethnic violence. Belcher was a gregarious man with a sardonic sense of humour; you had to have a certain kind of mania to live and work in a warzone.

'I can . . .' Belcher began, '. . . make some introductions.'

'Introductions?'

He gave me a knowing smile. 'Leave it with me, Lev.'

Boston crossed the bar and went into the hotel lobby. Once or twice he tried to venture outside, only to reappear moments later, seemingly unwilling to wander too far. In the past days, I'd been watching him closely: he was peculiarly skittish, refusing to engage me when I'd tried to broach the subject of his family and what they would make of me dragging him further north. 'You are not dragging me, Lev,' he kept saying. 'I want to see the river's end.' My dream, it seemed, had become Boston's too, but every time I considered taking him further I remembered Matt Power and felt my stomach tighten.

Belcher spent the next days introducing me to a roster of every defiant ex-pat he could find, while I sourced out every remaining aid worker and NGO in Juba, only to hear the same: to travel north was to invite disaster; if one side didn't kill me, the other certainly would. Alone among them, only one of Belcher's contacts thought differently. Three nights later, I walked into the bar at the Bedouin Lodge and, in a fog of cigarette smoke, Belcher introduced me to Ken Miller.

Miller was not the first suspicious associate that I had met thanks to Belcher. There had been a man known to all as Commander Dan, a sixty-year-old former Catholic Irish priest who'd had to leave the church for marrying a Dinka woman and running guns for the rebels under the pretence of aid work. But Miller seemed different. Dressed in a Hawaiian shirt and dark glasses, he seemed to have modelled himself on a rogue CIA agent from a Bond film. Belcher had described him using only three words: 'Mad as fuck.'

'Everything's possible,' he said in a thick Scottish accent, as I took my seat. 'What's the plan?'

There was no plan. At this point, I was running out of ideas. 'I've got papers that can take me to Bor, but after that . . . I've tried every NGO, every aid worker. The UN are running a barge down the Nile to Malakal, but nobody there's returning my calls.'

Miller nodded. There was a funk about him that told me he was stoned, seeing me through a miasma of smoke. 'It's all about the cash. Cash can get you anything you want. How much have you got?'

'Not all that much . . .'

'See,' drawled Miller, 'you could walk to Bor. That should be okay. But, go on the west bank, through Lakes State. Then you have two choices. Stay west and go up to Wau or Yei – stay away from Bentiu, mind you; those Nuer are planning an attack any day now – then cross in Abyei and Sudan. But you'll need to avoid the Nile . . .'

'It's the Nile I'm walking.'

'Aye, but the rebels are regrouping and they've just got a resupply from Ethiopia. They will attack before the rains come. That means you've got less than a month.'

I caught Belcher watching from the bar and was reminded of what he'd said: Miller knew what was going on with the rebels because he'd travelled every inch of the country, smuggling guns, supplies and vehicles to every militia out there.

'Otherwise, from Bor, you could try and make contact with the rebels and get into Ayod, then get a rebel escort up to Malakal, and then hand back over to the government. It's the front lines you'll have to worry about. Normally, I'd say go up the Jonglei Canal – but, if you try that shit now, you'll get fuckin' shot, me laddie.'

Miller was speaking with such nonchalance that, for a moment, his vision sounded possible. He slumped back in his chair, taking a long drag of his cigarette. 'I'll come with yer!' he said, raising an eyebrow. 'It'll only cost yer seventy-five grand. US dollars, cash. New bills, of course.' He must have seen the way I was staring at him, trying to suppress my astonishment, because then he said, 'That would be all in. No expenses required.'

Slowly, I stood and backed away, stepping out of the cloud of sweet smoke that surrounded us. 'Let me think about it,' I said.

The last thing I heard as I walked out of the bar was Miller mutter, 'Aye, you do that, laddie . . .'

That night, I found Boston kicking his heels nervously outside the hotel. Across the rooftops of Juba, the sky seemed steelier each day – a sure sign that the rainy season was descending from the north.

'Boston,' I said, 'we need to talk.'

Boston tramped along the hotel wall, where the brickwork had been opened up by the spray of automatic rifles. He had been like this for days, pacing up and down like a captured tiger, eager to get back on the road – to be anywhere but here.

'What did Miller say?'

'Miller's after money. It's hand him everything and risk failure, or get to Bor without him and risk failure. It's a no-win situation. The only hope is getting to Bor on Allam's papers and making a decision there. This expedition's thrown enough at us already that . . .' I paused. 'Miller says to take the west bank, through Lakes State and into Unity. Once you get past Terekeka and Minkaman, you reach the edge of the Sudd. Seems that's the way to get to Bor.'

In an instant, all the nerves evaporated from Boston: 'When do we leave?'

I steadied myself. There was something I needed to say, a thought that had been blossoming in the back of my mind ever since we had crossed the border into South Sudan. 'Boston, we've been travelling together for four and a half months. Day in, day out, we've never been further than a few metres apart. I don't think I can say that about another human being in my life. So . . .' I hesitated. 'This isn't an easy thing to say, so I'm just going to say it: Boston, you're not coming with me to Bor, for a start your visa is about to run out, and it's just too dangerous. Come to Terekeka by all means, but after that I just don't know.'

At first Boston didn't speak. Perhaps he had known, all along, that sooner or later, I would have to tell him this. But it seemed he was only gathering his thoughts: 'You can't do this, Lev. This is my expedition too. Above everything else, I want to see the pyramids. I want to see the sea.'

'I should never have brought you into South Sudan. You know as well as I do what's waiting up there. It's walking into a warzone. Miller says the rebels are planning another counter-attack. It's fight and fight back all the way to Sudan. Look, it's one thing taking risks for myself, but it's another doing it for somebody else. And . . . think of Matt Power. You have a family, Boston. You should go back to Kampala, be with them.'

'I have been in warzones before, Lev.'

He said it with steeliness, and I could see the desperation in his eyes: he wanted to see this journey through. I didn't want to tell him the other thoughts that had been circling my mind – that, even now, Boston had stopped being a guide, that, once we reached Sudan, he wouldn't even know any of the native languages. The truth was, he had stopped being a true guide some months ago; first and foremost, he had become a friend. He'd looked after me when times were tough and, on more than one occasion, forced me to my feet when walking was the last thing I wanted to do. But, now that he was a friend, the thought of risking his life outweighed everything else.

'Come to see the Sudd but after that, unless your papers come through and the security improves, you're going home, Boston,' I said – and, after that, we said nothing, just tramped back into the bar, where Belcher was waiting with two cold beers.

If I had had my way, I would have headed north without any minders – but the ever-watchful Allam insisted that I take two local gunmen as protection. After some delay, and protracted negotiations with a local security officer about how far they would come and how much of a 'tip' I'd give them – despite their being SPLA officers with government salaries – I awaited my new companions with a heavy heart. 'This is Africa,' I had to keep reminding myself, refuelling on yet another plate of over-smoked tilapia. 'Nothing comes for free.'

The two men who walked into Bedouin Lodge were both Dinka, NCOs in the SPLA. Shorter than I'd imagined, they marched up, wearing mixed uniforms and flip-flops on their feet. Each carried an AK-47, but there was something open and friendly about their faces that immediately endeared them to me. Nevertheless, if these were to be my companions on a perilous trek north, I wanted to get off to an appropriate start. The guards Allam had supplied for us on the road to Juba had all let us down.

'Okay, you two,' I said, thoroughly fed up with mutinous soldiers. 'We are walking to Bor. Not driving, not hitch-hiking. *Walking*. Understand? By foot.' I pointed at my feet, but the pair only looked at me, expressionless. 'We will sleep wherever we can, and eat whatever we can,' I continued. 'I am told you two can be trusted, that you're strong men.' For the first time, they nodded enthusiastically. 'I am told you will not complain, that Dinka are the very best soldiers, and that you will not run away or give up.' Solemnly, they shook their heads. 'Good. I will pay you well, but you will not get a penny until we arrive. Do you understand?'

The elder of the two, who introduced himself as Ariike, began to rummage in the child's schoolbag over his shoulder and produced a dog-eared notebook. 'Sir,' he said with an unusual smile, 'let me write this down.'

He produced a pencil.

'*Warking de Nayl,*' he wrote at the top of the page, stopping once to look at me. '*An exhibition to wark thru Youganda, Ruanda, Tazmania, Kenya and Ethyopia.*'

'That isn't quite what . . .'

He looked at me with an earnest frown. 'I was a teacher of English and speak it perfectly. See?' Proudly, he pointed at the gibberish.

'Excellent!' I said. 'Then there can be no mistakes.'

'You will sign?'

I took the stubby pencil from him and scrawled my name at the bottom of the page. An agreement had been reached, a contract signed. I had two new guardians on the way north, and it was time to see how far we could get.

Heading north out of Juba, the river soon became a vast entanglement of channels banked in vast swamps and flat, lush flood plains. All around, the grass was kept short by the thousands of cattle that roamed the river looking for new pastures, all under the watchful eyes of their herdsmen, members of the Mundari tribe. Back in

December this area had been torn apart by rebel fighters, who had swarmed through the villages massacring all the foreigners and soldiers they could find – but now the district was safe, thanks almost entirely to the efforts of the Mundari themselves. The Mundari are traditionally cattle herders and agriculturalists, but their reputation as a peace-loving people is matched only by their capacity for violence in times of need. That, a local woman told us, was the reason even a white man could walk this stretch of the river unmolested: where the Mundari held sway, the rebels were too frightened to come. I could tell why. The Mundari live on a diet of milk and fish, but look as if they supplement it with steroids. They are as imposing and statuesque a people as any in Africa.

The Mundari are also a very stoic people. One day, I was passing the fishing village of Terekeka which lies on the west bank of the Nile as it begins to widen and become the Sudd. I'd been looking for a place to sleep, when one of the soldiers suggested we take a boat across to one of the islands and make camp amongst the Mundari herdsmen. Thinking it was better than the usual corner of a filthy police station, I heartily agreed and we took passage on a tiny rowing boat. Twenty minutes later, having navigated the floating islands of matted rushes, we spotted what we were looking for.

'There they are!' shouted Ariike with glee.

In the distance, on a bare grassy bank, stood what I hoped would be welcoming hosts. Ten men, utterly naked except for loose pieces of cotton covering only the bare essentials, stood guard to a corral in which several hundred head of long-horned cattle lowed. Smoke poured out of campfires where cow dung was burnt as way of protection against mosquitoes, both for the cows and people. As I jumped off the boat, an enormous hand appeared out of the crowd to help me up.

It was the biggest hand I've ever seen, and unsurprisingly attached to a behemoth of a human being. His name was Sirillo, and he pulled me onto the island like he was lifting a rag doll. Seven feet tall, in his spare hand he carried a spear that seemed like a toothpick compared to his massive muscular frame. Slung across his naked back was an AK-47 with a feather poking out of the barrel for effect. 'Welcome!' he said with an honest smile.

At twenty-two, Sirillo was the head of the clan youth, and, leaving the elders to relax, was in charge of keeping the cattle safe and settling matters of the community. I looked around. Naked children, covered in ash, were busy rubbing more into the hides of the cows. Some of the young men were wrestling each other whilst women, bare-breasted, looked on to decide who would be their husband. Boston and I gleefully joined in the proceedings, covering ourselves in ash and trying to keep our dignity whilst being thrown to the deck by teenage boys twice our size. It was a moment of beautiful serenity, an island of peace in a land ravaged by war. There were hundreds and hundreds of cows, just returned from grazing and now pegged out with bells around their necks. Walking through them was a perilous business, as horns, some of them five feet long, were shaken in disgust at our intrusion. Some of the women were milking the cows, and would often drink straight from the udders.

As Sirillo was showing us to a bare piece of grass on which we could pitch tents, a cow began to piss nearby. Suddenly, there was a commotion and three grown men ran towards the cow as fast as they could. But it was Sirillo that won the day. Pushing the other men aside, he put his head straight under the cow and took what can only be described as a golden shower. As I stood watching in utter disbelief, Ariike grinned wildly. Sirillo stood back up and rubbed the urine from his eyes.

I was speechless.

'It's good for your hair,' said the giant.

'Makes it go red, and then the ladies like it.'

Still speechless.

'And, anyway, we don't like to wash in the river.'

'Why ever not?' I finally uttered.

'Too dangerous,' said Sirillo, looking solemn as he peered over his shoulder to the mighty Nile. 'Too many crocodiles, they always eat people.'

Of course, I knew of the danger of crocodiles – but in most places where humans live, the crocs stay away. The chances of getting eaten are usually pretty slim.

'Not here,' he said. 'They are monsters. My brother was eaten by a crocodile.'

'I'm so sorry.' I said, again on the verge of speechlessness. 'When was that?'

Sirillo, covered in piss and glistening in the sunset, looked at me benevolently.

'At eleven o'clock this morning.'

He shrugged his shoulders, picked up his spear and weaved his way through the cow horns and smoke back to his home, a teepee of dried grass. In the golden light of dusk, it looked like nothing so much as a bird's nest.

The time had come to say goodbye to Boston. For some reason there had been a mistake at the border office and he'd only got a month instead of two, and what's more, the fighting was intensifying and I wasn't prepared to put him in danger. We'd spent a solemn week north of Juba, but since our conversation things had been difficult in the knowledge that he was going home. We'd hardly spoken, and when we did it was just the mundane, daily practicalities of the walk. We'd reached the edge of the Sudd, and for Boston, the end of his journey. Standing on the banks of the Nile, we kept the goodbye short and I made Boston the promise that one day we'd meet again, and with that he got into a minibus which had been idling, waiting for fleeing Dinka from across the swamp. Without so much as a rearward glance, the car disappeared down the dusty road. In a moment it was gone, lost in the bush – and so was Boston.

It wasn't until some hours later, as I was poring over a map of Lakes State and trying to synthesise all the information Miller had given me that the prospect of heading into the wilderness without Boston began to feel real. Boston had been my ally and protector for so long that being at the mercy of strangers was going to feel strange. I tried to shake off the feeling. I was going to miss his tales of Congolese misadventure, his wildly inaccurate conspiracy theories – not to mention his pigeon hunting – but I had started this expedition alone and that was how it would have to continue.

Outside Juba, we'd enlisted the services of a young Ugandan man named Siraje, to help ferry our packs further north. For a week, we walked north through the Central Equatorial State, through tiny villages where food was scarce and where the locals, desperate since December, stared at us warily. Harbouring a foreigner, here, had seen more than one person murdered when the rebels last swarmed through, and every few kilometres the road was blocked by police barricades and army checkpoints. Very quickly, I was glad for the two Dinka accompanying me north: at every village, they somehow charmed the local chiefs into allowing us the use of an empty schoolroom or police station for a camp; at every roadblock, they regaled the security officials with tales of my derring-do – explaining to the commanders how I'd been walking for five years through a hundred different countries. My voyage was growing in the telling – and, by the time we had crossed into Lakes State, it turned out I had walked through Liberia, Senegal and Ghana, spending a million dollars along the way. With Ariike and his comrade John at my side, I didn't have my paperwork checked once.

The further north we pushed, the more visible the signs of war. Some nights, we heard short volleys of gunfire, somewhere in the indeterminate distance. Once, a blistering quake seemed to tear open the sky, only for silence to quickly resume. But clearer yet were the convoys that ploughed the same roads. On the main roads, the Red Cross were in action, ferrying supplies further north; sometimes they moved alone, and other times alongside UN trucks, peacekeepers bound for the centre of the conflict. There was a UN compound in Bor that was still staffed; perhaps that was where these soldiers were heading. Along the way, we scavenged whatever news we could. The rebels, we were told, had just attacked an oil refinery in Unity State, directly north of Lakes State itself, and still held the key town of Ayod, on the Nile's east bank. The main road between Bor and Malakal was still closed – and, more than anything else, this gave me pause for thought. I had meant Malakal to be a key staging post on my journey to the Sudanese border; I was going to have to rethink those plans.

The town of Minkaman sits on the border between Lakes State and Jonglei State, with only twenty miles of entangled papyrus swamp separating it from Bor. Here, the Nile forms the border between the states, plunging into the brown vastness of the Sudd. From a distance, it was clear that Minkaman had been transformed. The Red Cross trucks we had seen ploughing the Juba–Bor highway had been bound for here, because Minkaman was no longer the small fishing settlement it had once been; now it was a sprawling expanse of white-plastic sheeting, tents, homes built around cars, and open-air campsites. What had once been a small fishing village had become home to more than 80,000 displaced people. Some of them had come from Bor itself, but the vast majority had come from the further reaches of Jonglei State. Fleeing the rebels – who still controlled great swathes of the state – the refugees had found, in Minkaman, a place to survive.

The camp was dominated by a succession of walled, barbed-wire enclosures, the base of operations for each of the NGOs who had come here. Flags were flying, declaring not nationalities but charitable organisations. Every tree along the riverbank had become the home to a family. Children still scampered in the shade beneath those trees, while the branches suspended pans, cooking utensils, mosquito nets and all the other household possessions with which the refugees had escaped. Drums were beating, sounding out the gathering of new committees or makeshift churches, the kind of institutions a camp like this needs to keep itself from sliding into anarchy. In many ways, Minkaman was a miracle, a city sprung up from nothing, in a matter of months.

Down at the port, I chartered a motor boat that would take me out onto the swamp. It was the only way I could make the crossing to Bor and find out if there truly was a way forward. At the small dockside, I bid my SPLA stalwarts goodbye, and climbed into the boat. Siraje, too afraid to return to Juba alone, clambered in afterwards, helping to haul aboard the packs. Soon we were assailed by refugees hoping for a free ride – some citizens of Bor eager to get back and rescue more of their possessions, some traders working the water between here and the city, others soldiers returning to base in town. We took as many as we could, only driving them away when the boat could take no more.

As we began the slow navigation through the papyrus channels, a single droplet of rain landed on my head.

I looked back at the white-plastic sheets suspended from trees, at the tents and open-air campsites where people were living. 'What will happen to all the refugees when the rains really come?' I asked.

The man at the tiller only shook his head; he did not want to imagine the answer.

Some hours later, Bor loomed above our little vessel. The journey had been spectacular. Cutting through the wind, we had soared across miles of Sudd, through tangled fields of papyrus and reed. Sometimes the channels were only two metres wide; this was a landscape only a true local could properly understand. Under the boatman's direction, we weaved north and east, driving legions of storks before us. Sometimes we rounded tiny islands where more refugees camped – internationally displaced persons (IDPs) who hadn't made it to the greater camp at Minkaman but still preferred the solitude and relative sanctuary of the swamp. At least here, there were plentiful fish to catch, and the threat of sudden violence was kept at bay by the miles of entangled papyrus. This, I thought, was as good a place as any to wait out a war.

At my side, a young Dinka soldier clung to the edge of the boat. Garang was twenty-seven years old, returning from Minkaman to join his unit in the city. Already a soldier for thirteen years, he had joined the SPLA as a child to fight against the Arabs, and had since risen through the ranks to become a sergeant major. Now, he told me, he was only a part-time fighter, taking up his gun only when it was needed. 'I fought with the Dinka Youth when the Nuer rebels came to take Bor,' he said. 'The city's changed hands four times now, but it's back under government control at last.'

'Bor belongs to the Dinka then?'

'It's more complicated than that. Some of the rebels want to think of it as just government Dinkas fighting Nuer rebels, but . . . I don't hate the Nuer. In fact, my girlfriend's one. But I do believe in government, and I do believe in unity. The rebels need to understand that we're all one nation. And the only way to make them understand is to defeat them here.'

The port in Bor was ramshackle, but somehow it buzzed with activity, stevedores and fishermen pursuing their daily business as if this was not the epicentre of a war. Among them, a rabble of different soldiers moved back and forth. Siraje and I had not left the docks behind by the time we knew we had crossed the front-line.

Soldiers, policemen and hundreds of armed civilians flooded the muddy streets. We walked on, barely speaking a word. My only idea was that, once here, I could find some soldiers to accompany me northwards, convince them to hand me over to the rebels, and then pay them to shepherd me through the rebel-controlled territories until, eventually, I reached Sudan. There would be no shortage of soldiers to ask, but suddenly I doubted whether any would agree.

The streets leading into the heart of the city had been razed. Blown-up tanks rusted at the sides of the roads. Death was everywhere. Mass graves had been the only way to bury those who were killed, and before we had reached the city proper, I could see the freshly churned earth where victims had been buried.

We hadn't reached the town centre when a voice hailed us from a roadblock and, seconds later, SPLA soldiers flocked to our sides. In my urgency to retrieve the papers Allam had given me, permitting me to travel as far as Bor, I explained about the expedition. The soldiers scrutinised the papers carefully. When they instructed me to follow, I knew there was no other choice.

The soldiers led us deeper into Bor's old town. On the banks of the Nile, a cathedral had been raked by gunfire, portions of its stone wall charred black by fire, and a grave dug for the seventeen clergymen and nuns who'd been murdered here a few weeks before. The market place was empty, burnt to the ground three months ago, and ATMs hung from walls like eyeballs from their sockets. Everywhere, the walls were daubed in crude graffiti: FUCK YOU NUER! declared one pillar. DINKAS DEFEATED! exclaimed another.

After navigating several patrols and checkpoints, the soldiers deposited us at the state compound in the middle of town. It was here that the state governor's representatives gathered, co-ordinating the defence of not just the city but the whole of Jonglei State. The local SPLA commander was sitting under a tamarind tree as we approached, surrounded by men in camouflage uniform. Many of the militia were sporting sunglasses and flip-flops, and all crowned their heads with a simple black or maroon beret. The madness of the moment put me in mind of some terrible '80s action movie – only this was real.

'Let us start at the beginning. I have seen your papers, but I would hear it from your own mouth. Who are you?'

'My name,' I began, 'is Levison Wood. I'm . . .' It felt churlish, all of a sudden, to say 'explorer', so instead I told him I was a geographer, leading an expedition to walk the length of the Nile. I showed him the press cuttings I had saved from Uganda, my papers from Andrew Allam, spoke about how two SPLA soldiers had valiantly guided me from Juba to Minkaman. 'I'm here to pass through,' I finally explained. 'To follow the west bank north.'

The local commander paused a moment, as if to scrutinise me further. Then he gave an emphatic shake of the head.

'Now is not a good time to be in Bor, not for an Englishman, not even for South Sudanese. Do you know what is happening here, Levison Wood?'

I told him I did.

'If you truly did, you would not be here, asking for soldiers to take you north. The UN base in town has just been attacked. We cannot tell what happens next. My advice to you is to leave Bor and not think of this expedition again. This is a war.'

The local commander afforded us four soldiers to escort us across town, to the ruins of the South Sudan Hotel. What we found was a compound in ruins. The South Sudan Hotel had once been one of the most progressive places in the newly formed nation, a place for international leaders and businessmen looking to invest in the new country to stay. Now, it was an empty shell. Hunching close to the river, its walls were strafed with bullet holes and, in the road outside, a minibus had been destroyed by more gunfire. Across the hotel courtyard, the doors had been kicked in or torn from their hinges. Windows were shattered, and I could see the black marks where fire had licked up the walls.

The manager had little to say – only as he showed us to rooms along the veranda did he reiterate what the local commander had said: this was no place for a foreigner to be, and certainly not a white man. Dinka soldiers, he said, had stormed the UN compound in town to attack the Nuer who had barricaded themselves there. In the fallout of the attack, the UN peacekeepers had opened fire – forty-eight Nuer now lay dead, along with seven Dinka, and a group of Indian peacekeepers. As he left, I found I was grateful for the protection the local SPLA commander had given us – but the thought grew in me: what use were four men against a city spiralling out of control?

For a few hours, the South Sudan Hotel was our refuge. Only when hunger started to gnaw at my guts did I return to the veranda, to find Siraje in his room next door. It was time, I told him, to venture back into town – if only to find something to eat.

Under the watchful eyes of our SPLA guard, we left the compound and ventured back into Bor. The heart of the old town was awash with armed civilians. Everywhere, eyes turned to follow us; groups of Dinka gunmen loitered on the intersections, dissuaded from approaching only because of the armed guard. This was no time to explore what Bor had to offer, and the guards led us to an Ethiopian restaurant, where we hurriedly ordered food. Even here, the diners were armed to the teeth: AK-47s hung across shoulders or rested in laps. Eyes considered us from every corner. By the time the food had arrived, I could tell Siraje had lost his appetite; the terror, visible on his face, was hardening in his gut.

'They think we're UN,' he whispered.

'It's okay,' I told him. 'We'll be back at the hotel soon – but you have to eat . . .'

Our bellies filled, we left the restaurant in haste. Dusk was already settling – or perhaps it was only the storm clouds thickening overhead – but we had not yet reached the compound when a man lurched out of the shadows between two buildings and staggered into the street to confront us. In a second, he had cocked his rifle, raising it up to point directly at me.

He was screaming in a language I didn't understand, but the hatred in his eyes eclipsed all words. His eyes rolled madly. In an instant, Siraje threw his hands into the air; in another, the SPLA guards had their weapons raised, striding in front of me to drive the man back. There was a terrible moment in which nothing happened and everything was possible; then the man lowered his weapon, hawked up phlegm to spit at the ground, and slunk off through the door of a nearby house.

'What did he say?' I asked.

One of the soldiers answered: 'He said . . . he will kill you, because you are here with the UN.'

For a moment, I remained silent. There would have been no use protesting I was here for my own expedition, that I was not part of the UN in any way. Reason and logic didn't count for anything in situations like this. Emotions were running too high in Bor; anti-Western sentiment leached out of every pair of eyes. I looked at Siraje: 'Are you okay?'

He nodded, no longer shaking so visibly. 'I put myself in the hands of God,' he answered.

'Let's get out of here,' I said – and, without another word, we raced for the hotel.

No sooner had I settled into my room than the darkness smothered the hotel. Lying in the comforting blackness, I tried not to think of what tomorrow had in store. My plan was to go back to the local commander and talk again about leaving Bor for the north – but, the more I thought about it, the less real it felt. Bor was only the front line of the ongoing war; whatever the north had in store, it would be much, much worse.

It was only moments after I closed my eyes that the first gunfire sounded. Immediately, I sat up, listening to the fighting erupt. Somewhere, close to the hotel, a running gun battle had broken out. Perhaps the Dinka were storming the UN compound again, or perhaps rebels were making a play for Bor. All of a sudden, the room was illuminated in a wash of bright red. I got to my feet and crept to the window.

When I drew the broken blinds back, I could see tracers lighting up the night sky, illuminating the rooftops of Bor in snatches of brilliant colour. With every passing second, the gunfire seemed to grow closer. I heard the familiar crack of 7.62-calibre AK-47 rounds as they pounded the compound next door. The dull thud of DSHK rounds reverberated through the ground. The question was: who was firing? Was it a rebel incursion? My heart began to pound, keeping syncopated time with the gunfire. Shit, I thought. Were the rebels bent on recapturing Bor? Surely, we would have got wind of this?

I told myself to calm down – it was more likely to do with the attack on the UN base. The battle might have been moving to the streets, flocking this way. I waited for a lull in the gunfire and made a decision: if I was going to survive this night, I had to know what was going on.

Racing out onto the veranda, I found Siraje already emerging from the room beside mine. The way he looked at me, he was desperate for direction. 'Where to?' he asked.

Across the courtyard, soldiers and armed civilians were already gathering in the shadows. Who were they? A sudden burst of gunfire sundered the silence and Siraje threw himself back behind the door, trying his best to look calm.

'Maybe we should go over the fence, get to the Nile,' he said. 'We can hide in the reeds until morning . . .'

I hurried to the wall and peered into the west, over the black murkiness of the river. The smells of the Sudd swamp were rich and earthy. Slowly, I backed away. 'I'd rather risk a stray bullet than get chomped by a croc in that bloody river,' I said. There was only one other way to go. 'Up,' I said, and started to run.

Across the courtyard, close to the river's edge, a half-finished five-storey building stood as a reminder of better times. We burst through the shattered door and swept away the hanging wires that blocked the stairwell. Running up the concrete stairs, we didn't stop until reaching the open rooftop, which glistened with spent brass bullet cartridges and shards of glass.

From here, we could see the street fight being played out in snatches of light, machine-gun fire in the thoroughfares, fires erupting in buildings a few streets away. The night was warm, and the sounds and smells put me in mind of my tour in Afghanistan, which seemed such a long time ago.

On the rooftop, Siraje and I settled down. The minutes seemed endless. For three quarters of an hour, the fighting was intense. Flurries of gunfire fought flurries of gunfire, the sounds ebbing and flowing along the streets. More than once, I peered over the edge to see dark shapes charging past the hotel compound. I reached for the cell phone in my pocket, but the signal kept flashing in and out. Below, the gunfire intensified for one enraged minute, and then . . . only the silence.

By midnight the fighting had almost abated. Apart from the occasional shot, whoever it was had had their fun for the evening. Coaxing Siraje out of his hiding, we tramped gingerly back down the concrete stairs, past the trashed rooms, and to our terrace. SPLA soldiers had, by now, filled the open spaces, gathering in the relative safety of the hotel car park. To my relief, they ignored us completely as we made for the veranda.

'Get some sleep, Siraje.' He only stared at me, as if nervous to go back to his own room. 'Don't worry, Siraje. If you hear another attack, if you hear anything, just come and knock on my door.'

He made as if to leave, hesitating only once. 'Are we . . . staying?' he asked.

I could not answer. I told him it would be alright and retreated to the gutted shell that was my own room.

In the darkness, I reached for my phone again. As the reception flickered in and out, I saw that I had several missed calls. I was scrolling through them when the phone began to vibrate again. The name ANDY BELCHER was illuminated on the screen.

'Belcher,' I said, picking up the phone.

'Lev?' buzzed a voice in my ear.

'It's me.'

'I'm glad to hear it,' came the sardonic reply. 'Are you okay up there?'

'What's happening here, Belcher? Are the rebels storming Bor?'

Belcher had been keeping close tabs on the progress of events from the relative safety of Bedouin Lodge back in Juba. 'It's not rebels, Lev. It's Dinka Youth – armed civilians. They're so pissed off with the UN, they're ready to attack anyone associated with the organisation.' He paused. 'Do you hear me, Lev?'

'I hear you,' I said, wearily.

'Get out of there,' said Belcher. 'Look, there's a Cessna. I can have it with you in three hours. Don't take any risks.'

I had opened my mouth to reply when fists hammered at the door. Siraje, I thought, come to get me. 'Belcher,' I said, 'I've got to go . . .'

When the door was drawn back, it was not Siraje staring at me from the veranda, but the manager of the hotel instead. 'There you are,' he breathed. 'I thought, for a second . . .'

'We went to the roof,' I said. 'Just in case.'

'They'll kill you if they find you in here. These Dinka Youth, they'll think you're UN and then . . . you have to go.'

'Go? Now?'

'First thing in the morning, as soon as you can. However you can. Do you hear me?'

There was not only desperation in this man's eyes; he was begging me for my sake, not for his. 'Thank you,' I said, and watched him hurry back along the veranda.

Sleep wouldn't come to me that night. For long hours, I prowled up and down the circumference of the tiny room, listening out for voices, half waiting for another knock at the door. When it did not come, I tried to close my eyes. I wanted to think about the north, about the four hundred miles of wilderness I had been hoping to traverse – but all I saw, in vivid splashes across the backs of my eyelids, were memories of the day in Bor: the burial mounds listing in the earth beside the river; the black blood stains where the clergy had been massacred inside the cathedral; the burnt-out tanks and the smell of death.

Before dawn, I returned to the veranda, to watch the soldiers still gathered in the car park. I still couldn't shake those images from my mind. Compared to what was happening in South Sudan, my own expedition was as insignificant as a single raindrop in the storms that were soon to come. Even if there was a way to go downriver, I knew, now, that it wasn't worth it. How could I justify putting other people in danger by walking through a warzone where people – real people – were starving and being killed every day? I wasn't one of the Nile's first explorers, and this wasn't the 19th century, when it was acceptable to pay for your own militia and battle your way through spear-wielding tribes and impress your superiority upon them with a Gatling gun. I'd set out on a mission to discover more about the River Nile and its people, not simply to prove a point.

For the first time, I understood: I had no place being here. I thought back to the other conflict areas I'd been in: Afghanistan, Iraq, Kurdistan, Burma, the Caucasus and others. Of them all, this was undoubtedly the worst. Bor was a place without hope – so devastated, so lost and so violent that it sent a shiver of horror down my spine. I thought back to Baker, who had been thwarted by tribal wars in Uganda and took revenge by shooting dozens of 'natives' as he cruised upriver on his barge; I thought of the Romans, who had been driven back by the impenetrable Sudd; I thought of how Stanley had sacrificed two hundred men following the flow of the River Congo. In the final moment, I thought of Matt Power, dead on a Ugandan hill-side, never to go back home. Africa seems to take lives without regard and with impunity. Somewhere in Bor, it was happening even now. I'd seen enough death in my time to understand that there is just too much to live for, and if there was one place I didn't want to see my own end, it was South Sudan. The Nile, as far as I was concerned, could wait. She wasn't going anywhere, and maybe one day I would come back and complete this journey in more peaceful times.

Without fully realising it at first, I had made my decision. A world record simply wasn't worth getting shot in the back of the head for. In the morning, we would beat the road back south, following the edge of the Sudd, through the empty carcasses of villages decimated by war to the relative safety of Juba. No world record, no expedition, was worth the risk of walking blindly onward.

I lay back in bed, staring at the ceiling, and waited for the dawn's first light.

A NEW BEGINNING

Sudan, May 2014

The plane banked out of the clear blue skies above Khartoum, coming to a smooth landing on the runway below. Outside, the city rippled in the haze of a fifty-degree heat. I stepped, squinting, onto the asphalt of the runway and sighed. The expedition was now broken – but somehow it had to go on.

On fleeing Bor, we had returned to Juba, where Siraje and I parted ways. Boston, by then, was already back in Kampala, his own expedition cut short – and, for the first time, I understood how he was feeling. The honour of becoming the first man to walk the full length of the Nile had been denied me, and it hurt. The Sudd had beaten me, like it had tormented so many other travellers along the Nile, and the disappointment was difficult to put into words.

Escorted by SPLA security, we had holed up in the airport at Juba until a plane was ready to take us out of South Sudan. The plan, hastily rearranged, was to reach Khartoum, the capital of Sudan, and back-track to as close to the border with South Sudan as we could get.

There, the expedition would begin again, north to Khartoum and the Sahara Desert beyond.

The man waiting in the airport, holding up a sign that read simply 'LEVISON' was to be my guide from the southern border to the crossing into Egypt, a journey of over a thousand miles. He was also a complete stranger. Tentatively, I shook his hand.

I had been to Sudan once before, four years previously, when I'd volunteered to lead an expedition driving two ambulances from England to a hospital in Malawi. It had been an eventful trip, not least because we were arrested in Egypt and detained for ten days by the secret police, a stop that had left us scrabbling to make up time by driving across the Sahara Desert in less than thirty-six hours. To say that I don't remember much would be an understatement – those hours passed in such a sleepless blur that I can barely recall crashing through a police roadblock on the outskirts of the Sudanese town of Dongola, and almost being cast from the side of a cliff in the ensuing carnage. But one thing that did come out of that journey was my chance meeting with Mazar Mahir, a tour guide of Ancient Nubian descent whose family business controlled the tourist trade in Wadi Halfa, the town on the Nile that marks the border between Sudan and Egypt. Mazar was known throughout the world as the go-to man for Sudan, and over the past years, we'd stayed in intermittent contact. At first, I'd hoped Mazar himself would accompany me for the Sudanese leg of this expedition, but – perhaps wisely – he had declared himself too busy. I didn't blame him – his life was consumed with hosting tourists and helping them get out of trouble with the Egyptian authorities. But it is not for nothing that the Sudanese are hailed, the world over, as the most hospitable of hosts. 'I have a suggestion,' Mazar had said to me, 'and his name is Moez. He is my little brother. He'll meet you at the airport. See if you like him, Lev. He says he can walk.'

And that was all I knew about the man waiting for me in the airport: not that he was a good guy, nor that he was very experienced, only that he could walk.

It was, I decided as he silently led me to his car, an inauspicious start.

After a night at the Acropole Hotel, I wended my way to meet Moez at his office in downtown Khartoum. Less than a week had passed since that fateful night in Bor, but already it felt like a lifetime ago.

With the morning light filtering through the shutters of his tiny first-floor room, nestled between a spluttering air-conditioning unit and a lethal-looking fuse box, I was able to consider Moez more thoughtfully.

'*Salaam Alaikum*,' he said, respectfully.

'*Inta Kwies? Tamam?*' I smiled back. 'Sorry,' I added. 'I've forgotten most of my Arabic.'

'*Mafi Mushkila*. No problem. I will teach you. *Tamam?*'

'*Tamam*,' I said.

'*Chai?*'

Well, that one was easy. I gratefully accepted his offer of tea and followed him to the corner of his claustrophobic little office. Here, the walls were covered in photographs of Moez with tourists, scientists and archaeologists. In between hung traditional paintings: African masks, posters of the famous Pyramids of Meroe, shelves of Bedouin knives, fossils, pieces of broken pottery and even some bones. 'It's all original,' Moez said with a smile. 'Sudan is full of these things. I like rocks, particularly: granite, quartz, gold. Anywhere you go, you can just pick it up.'

'Gold?'

'Oh, it's everywhere. It's where the word *Nubia* comes from.'

'What is?'

'Gold. Nub means Gold. Like my guiding company – Nub Kush. And the Nuba mountains – the Golden Mountains. This is where the Ancient Egyptians came to find gold, and then the Phoenicians, and then the Arabs, and then the English. And now . . . the Chinese. Sudan is a golden country.'

I looked at Moez as he poured the sugary black tea into two small, chipped glasses on a silver Chinese tray. He looked to be in his late thirties, with curly black hair. His face, finely featured, with big almond eyes, looked almost feminine and complemented his high cheekbones and rather large ears. He didn't look Arabic, but nor did he look black. He was pure Nubian, an ancient Semitic people who have been the fathers of Sudan since ancient times, and whose homelands are in northern Sudan and southern Egypt. In the half-light of the room, I wondered how this man might fare as my guide. I didn't have the luxury of time to decide. The plan was to be at the southern border tomorrow, back with the river. It had been too long.

I asked him outright: 'Can you walk?'

'Yes.' He smiled. 'But where are we walking?'

I had presumed Mazar had told him. It seemed inconceivable that he hadn't – and I began to wonder if this was all a practical joke between the brothers.

'I'm walking the Nile. I have been ever since Rwanda. Only . . . the fighting in the South drove me out. I'm here to start again. Tomorrow, I'm going south to the border and, from there, I'm following the river – all the way into Egypt.'

With a studious air, Moez wandered across the room and consulted his diary. 'How long will this take?'

'Two months,' I said, 'more or less.'

He contemplated it further, lost in the diary. 'I'm free,' he said with bewildering nonchalance, 'but I'll need to pack a bag first.'

The deal was done, whether I liked it or not. I had a new guide – one, I suspected, who would be as different from Ndoole Boston as water from sand.

The mountain at Al Jabalain loomed like a giant black hand over the arid savannah. Stepping out of the car, palming payment to Salaah, the fat Nubian driver who had driven us the two hundred miles from Khartoum, I stared into the south. Only two hundred kilometres further south lay the northernmost edge of the great Sudd. I must have been staring at it too long, because as soon as Moez had lifted the cheap bicycles we had bought from the back of the van, he came to my side.

'At least you're still alive.' He smiled. 'If you'd gone into that place, you'd be dead by now – and I'd still be looking for work. Do you know how few travellers come to Sudan in the summer?'

We had come as close to the border as local security agents would allow, into a land of arid plain and desert scrub. As Salaah disappeared into the north, it seemed unbelievable that this landscape could border the mightiest swampland on Earth. The only things to break the endless flatness were outcrops of evil, thorn-ridden acacia bushes – and, of course, the river itself. Here, the Nile surged due north, for a short time forming the border with South Sudan itself, before piercing the heart of Sudan. Along its length ran a bullet-straight tarmac road, gleaming black against the parched wilderness.

All of a sudden, the vastness of the journey ahead seemed impossible. Even the two hundred miles back to Khartoum felt inconceivable. Whether it was the defeat in South Sudan, or just the simplicity, the starkness of staring out at hundreds of miles of open scrubland, I wasn't sure – but a strange sense of doubt was starting to bubble up within me.

'You should ride,' I said, as Moez balanced his packs on one of the bicycles.

'Ride?' he said, aghast. 'Why should I ride? If you're walking, then I'm walking. This is *walking* the Nile, not riding the Nile.' He finished wrapping the straps around his bag and, without another word, began to push up the road. I looked at him, in his black jeans, polo T-shirt and baseball cap, discreetly covering a balding head. On his feet was a pair of fake-leather shoes, with one sole already hanging off. Moez might have claimed to have escorted archaeologists and scientists around the vast emptiness of the Sahara – but I suspected it was probably from the comfort of a Toyota Land Cruiser. Under my breath, I muttered to myself, 'He won't last the week.'

The truth was: I didn't know if I would either.

The next days seemed to last for ever. Sudan was a new beginning, but for the first time, the walking seemed a pointless exercise. I found no comfort in putting one foot in front of the other. Flanked on one side by huge electricity pylons and featureless scrub, every day was the same. The road was so straight it began to feel interminable.

We reached the town of Kosti on the second day, crossing to the river's eastern bank to continue the endless trek north. Behind me, Moez struggled on without words. It was difficult to push the bike, especially along the riverbank where the sand was deep, but I kept my head down, ignored his travails, and barrelled on. Soon, Moez and I were walking some distance apart, saying nothing to each other for long hours. He was struggling in stoic silence, but I had no words of encouragement for him, and he in turn had nothing to say to me. I began to hanker for Boston's wild conspiracy theories, his diatribes against the state of Africa, anything that might have distracted me from this vicious silence. Sights, sounds and smells – all of these were extravagant luxuries now, devils that slowed me down: all I wanted was this inane trek to be over. Even the river seemed a phantom. Pain had become irrelevant. The blisters, sores and cramps no longer mattered. Every day, I got up, walked another marathon – and either the pain would go away, or it wouldn't. Whatever the case, the next morning, I got up and did it all again.

I would have walked through the night to reach Khartoum, anything to be rid of this endless expanse, but memories of Matt Power slowed me down. Pushing Moez too hard might have been fatal – but, by halving my pace, I doubled my frustration. Every slow day was a half-day, and a half-day wasted; half a day that I could have been closer to the finish, closer to home. I woke every morning, feeling sick to the stomach at the thought of the long months of nothingness, of endless dunes and unchanging horizon. The comforting greenery of the jungle was far behind – the variation, the hills, the wildlife that had kept madness at bay. With so much to see, it had been easy to be distracted, but here in the wasteland of Sudan, it seemed all I had to look forward to was an endlessness of searing heat and sleeping in roadside shacks amid piles of rubbish. The desert wasn't supposed to be like this. I'd had romantic notions of sleeping under the stars against a backdrop of ancient ruins – but all of that lay somewhere to the north, in a very different desert. I had to get there first.

Conversation, when it came at all, was a laboured thing. 'How long have you been working with tourists, Moez?' I asked, and had to force myself to listen to the answer.

'Since 2001,' he said. 'I like the tourists here.' He winked at me, with the look of a devil. 'Especially the Japanese ones . . .'

'Oh, yes?'

'They have skin like the waters of the Nile, so smooth and soft,' he said dreamily.

Moez might have been a teetotaller, who bookended his days with prayer, but it seemed he had an eye for different things as well. He had trained as an artist, studying at the University of Sudan in Khartoum, and the paintings I had seen hanging in his office were, in fact, his own creations. He had also travelled widely. Somehow, he'd convinced several former – female – clients to show him around their home cities in Europe. 'I even went to China once,' he began, 'and to Libya. We went over the border illegally, looking for gold. And prehistoric rock art. It's amazing, the things you can find.'

'Do you know,' I said, 'you might be even more opportunistic than Boston.'

'Who?'

I pushed on up the road. 'He was an almighty blackguard,' I chuckled, and Moez just smiled.

There were imperceptible changes in the landscape. The villages we passed were no longer the thatched round houses of the south, but all adobe mud with high compounds. The men of these villages all wore white *jellabiyas* and the women – what few could be seen – wore the *hijab*, or the *niqab*. It was my first real reminder that Sudan is an Islamic nation. Indeed, this was the reason South Sudan had fought so long and hard to secede – to gain self-determination for the Christian and Animist peoples of the South.

I woke, that morning, as I did every morning: on a string bed, at the side of the road, listening to the morning traffic – Nuer refugees fleeing the South for the inner-city ghettos of Khartoum – hurtling past. From the houses that lined the road, men emerged to piss in the street and hawk up great globules of phlegm into the sand. As I did every morning – if only to remind myself that the days were continuing to trickle by – I checked the date of my diary: it was 5 May.

'What is it, Lev?'

Moez was already up, refastening our packs to the bicycles.

'Do you know what today is, Moez?'

'Another fine day in the Republic of the Sudan?'

'No,' I said, tramping to the bicycles. 'Today is the first fifth of May in my adult life that I won't be able to get hold of a cold beer.'

Moez just looked at me, dumbly.

'Today is my birthday,' I said woefully, wiping the sand out of my matted hair and grimy beard. With shock, I realised it was now well over an inch long.

Moez reached out and pumped my hand vigorously. 'Happy New Year!' he declared. 'Today is a great day! You will not forget this birthday. Here you are, in the middle of Sudan, surrounded by beautiful desert and friendly people . . .' He grinned wildly. 'How old are you?'

'Thirty-two,' I conceded.

Moez let go of my hand, shaking his head in disbelief. 'I thought you would be thirty-seven, thirty-eight. More like my age?'

I took a deep breath, squinting into the morning sun. Thirty-two, and had it not been for the diary in my pack, I would have forgotten. There had to be something better than this. Unknown months of walking still lay between me and the river delta. I couldn't spend every day of them in abject misery and self-pity. I drew myself up, fixed my eyes on the road ahead, and spoke out loud: 'Lev, you are walking the Nile. You have set out to do it. You *will* do it. It will be shit at times, but you will reach the end. Nothing you can do will make it any easier, or any quicker. Just accept it.'

Moez drew his bicycle alongside mine. 'Lev, what are you doing?'

'I am giving myself a birthday present, Moez.'

He looked at me, perplexed. 'What present?'

'I am becoming a fatalist. Fatalism is my present to myself.'

As Moez walked off, up the road, he looked back down. 'You could get yourself a new pair of boots, too,' he said, grinning, and the day's walk began.

By the time we reached Khartoum, another week had passed. Moez's body seemed to be in a better state, and so too did my mind. Somehow, reaching that epiphany on my birthday had transformed me. Whatever black clouds had been smothering me since the failure to make it through South Sudan had parted, and slowly, I began to see the real beauty in the road along the river.

Perhaps because I'd read so much about its history, the name Khartoum evoked in me images of towering minarets, bustling souqs, dusty back streets choked with camels, donkeys and the crumbling remains of a colonialism that had been thrown out with the rubbish. I thought of the great siege, of battlefields and whirling dervishes, of Winston Churchill's last great cavalry charge at the Battle of Omdurman, when the British reclaimed the Sudan in 1898; of shifty-looking Bedouin coming in from the desert to trade in gum Arabic, silks and cotton. But, whilst all of this is there, the reality is that Khartoum is also surprisingly modern, with wide avenues, modern banks and hotels sitting on the lush riverside. After months of walking through the wilderness, this was the first metropolis I'd seen since Kampala – and I entered the city with a sense of relief, even joy, at the prospect of being surrounded by people, cars and a ready supply of food.

Khartoum began its existence as an outpost for the Egyptian army after Sudan had been incorporated into Egypt in 1821. Soon, what was a resupply outpost for soldiers became a centre for other kinds of trade as well, and Khartoum exploded as a thriving community. Here, all the goods of Africa could be transported and traded – and, most infamous of all, Khartoum became one of the hearts of the slave trade in central Africa. Key to this was the river along which I had been walking – for it is in Khartoum that the White Nile merges with its sister river, the Blue Nile.

The Blue Nile first erupts from Lake Tana in the heart of Ethiopia, and has already flowed for 900 miles by the time it reaches Omdurman, the suburb of greater Khartoum that sits on the west bank of the river. This confluence of the two great rivers makes Khartoum unique in Africa, a natural melting pot of peoples and cultures. It also marked the last transformation in the river before the long trek to the delta, and I was eager to see it for myself.

In the Acropole Hotel, I waited for Moez to pick me up. Our task for today was simple: head north, through the city, to the point at which the rivers meet. From there, we would cross into Omdurman on the west bank. There was one more provision we needed before continuing the trek north – from Khartoum, we would enter the edges of the Sahara Desert, and the bicycles we had fought doggedly to roll from the border would no longer suffice. From here on in, we were going to need something more stalwart to ferry our packs – and only camels would suffice.

As I waited for Moez, I leafed through a copy of *The Times*, left behind by another guest on his return to the UK. On the front page, not for the first time, events in Sudan had made world news. Beneath a damning headline lay the story of Meriam Ibrahim, a twenty-seven-year-old Sudanese woman who also happened to be a doctor. After marrying a Christian Sudanese man, educated in the USA, she had been accused of adultery and apostasy – the formal renunciation of religion – and sentenced, first to the lash for adultery, and then to death for the crime of abandoning Islam. The fact that her Muslim father had abandoned her as a child and she had grown up a Christian under the faith of her mother was apparently deemed irrelevant by the judge. The international community, incensed at this disregard for basic human rights, was pushing for Ibrahim to be pardoned – but, so far, Sudan had remained silent.

Lost in the article, I didn't see Moez appear at my side.

'Have you seen this?' I asked.

Moez nodded, grimly. 'Bashir will not listen, Lev. It is not the way.'

Omar al-Bashir had been the President of Sudan since 1989, rising to power at the head of a military coup, and had then been elected three times in succession, each time in elections under international scrutiny for corruption. Bashir's record on human rights had always been in question, but never more so than in 2009, when he ordered a systematic campaign of pillage, rape and mass murder against the citizens of Darfur in the west of Sudan. The crisis in Darfur led to Bashir being the very first incumbent president of any nation on Earth to be indicted by the International Criminal Court – but, partly due to the unwillingness of other African states, the warrant for his arrest has never been executed.

I flung the newspaper down, eager to think of better things.

'It has always been the way in Sudan,' said Moez as we stepped, blinking, into the blinding light. 'We fought a war with the South because they are Christians. We fight little wars every day, because we are Muslims and Christians trying to live together.'

Together we crossed the city, through concrete skyscrapers and gaudy hotels, past university buildings and boutique shops, through crowds of men in smart designer gear and sunglasses, women in loose-fitting hijabs and skinny jeans. It all seemed so surreal. After the wooden huts and mud shacks, even the traffic lights and pedestrian crossings seemed absurd. At last, we reached a leafy park nestled between the two rivers – the White Nile surging by on my left, the Blue closing in on my right. A rickety-looking Ferris wheel rose out of the bushes of the Blue Nile riverbank, its deadly carriages containing young couples. A miniature roller coaster, equally lethal, twirled alongside the White. All around, families and couples were having picnics as the fierce sun shone down.

Up ahead, where the park tapered to a point as the two rivers met, security guards manned a barrier. Reaching out a hand to stop me, Moez uttered, 'Stay here,' and strode ahead to shake hands with one of the moustachioed guards. After a few minutes, he returned. 'It's okay. We can go through and film the river – but we have to be quick. If you see anyone wearing a suit, hide the camera and smile.'

'Moez, isn't this just a family amusement park?'

Moez shot me a look and, without another word, I followed him through the barrier.

The path ran through entangled bushes, down to a headland overlooking the river. Standing at its pinnacle, where the White Nile rose from the south and the Blue Nile from the east, we could see fishermen arrayed along the grassy bank, their rods projecting out into the flow. At the point where the two waterways converged, the liquid was slow, the brown water gently lapping against a muddy shore. The fishermen ignored us as we ventured to the bank to dip our hands and symbolically wash our faces. This was a special moment, and in an instant, I felt as if I was back at the beginning, stooping down to drink from the headwaters with Boston in the Nyungwe Forest. Moez must have done this a hundred times already, but he took to the ritual with such obvious relish that I liked him all the more.

'I am Nubian,' he said. 'We're the people of the Nile. We wouldn't exist without it.'

'It looks so . . . ordinary,' I admitted. 'The water from one river's just the same as the next.' I lifted my camera to take pictures of the confluence, and the vast sprawl of Omdurman on the opposite bank.

'It's different in the rainy season. The Blue Nile is usually much clearer than the White. The White Nile should really be called the Brown Nile, but it doesn't have the same ring to it.'

One of the fishermen laid out a rug on the grass and stood with his hands upturned. Facing the east, the Qiblah – the direction of the Kaaba in Mecca – he began to pray. Closing his eyes, he began to recite verses from the Koran. It was a mystical vision and suddenly I felt very humble to be in his presence. It seemed that the world around this man no longer mattered. The city, the fairground, the sudden plop as a fish jumped to evade a fisherman's line, the history of a city born out of slavery and destruction, even the constant surging of the Nile – all of this was nothing compared to the thought of this man's God. To him, this special place was just a piece of dirt on which to prostrate himself. I was watching him, transfixed, when suddenly Moez grabbed me by the arm.

'Move!' he said. 'Let's go. *Now.*'

There was something in the tone of his voice that made me obey. Watched by the inquisitive eyes of the fishermen, I took after him up the bank.

'What's wrong?'

'Put the camera inside your shirt . . .'

I fumbled to hide it away.

'Now smile and look back cross the water.'

At the top of the bank, Moez pointed and grinned, beginning to talk loudly about the beauty of the water and the greenery of Tuti Island, the three miles of citrus orchard, vegetable farms and arable land that sits in the middle of the river and provides Khartoum with so much of its fresh food.

I barely noticed a speedboat in the distant water of the Blue Nile slow down and then speed up. After it had passed, Moez stopped his oration and whispered as we hurried back along the path.

'It's security. They were watching us.'

'Moez, they barely glanced at us. They hardly slowed down at all . . .'

'They *saw*.'

'Who gives a damn if they did? What were we doing?'

'Lev, you don't understand. They are everywhere. They watch *everything*. They don't like foreigners at all – especially English ones with cameras. Do you know how many times I've been arrested, for no reason at all? I've been with tourists who've had their cameras smashed in front of their faces. I had a security agent try to stab me with a bayonet in the Nuba mountains . . .'

The Nuba mountains lay in the south, close to the border with South Sudan. 'That's different, surely? Moez, this is *Khartoum*, not some half-forgotten backwater . . .'

'You'd be a fool to think so. You'll find the people of Sudan welcoming and friendly – but the government is another matter. I don't need any trouble, Lev. They'll close my business and lock me up. They're already following me for my other activities . . .'

At last, we had reached the fairground. The rollercoaster tumbled by on my left, children in the front seats screaming in hedonistic abandon.

'What do you mean . . . other activities?'

'I'll tell you later . . .'

We hustled across the fairground. Every time I thought Moez was mad, things twisted in the corner of my vision – and everything looked suspicious. Every man in black shoes became a spy. The slightest look in my direction made me imagine secret policemen. Sideways glances, women in burqas, even teenage boys – they all seemed out of the ordinary now.

'Before we go for the camels, we should get *jellabiyas*,' Moez said. 'We'll look less like tourists. With your beard, you'll pass for Sudanese – or at least an Arab . . .'

I stopped dead. 'Moez, is there something you're not telling me?'

At the edge of the fairground, Moez relented. When he looked me in the eyes, I saw a man who was scared.

'I'm Vice President of the Nubian Front,' he said. 'And Secretary of the Anti-Dams Coalition. We . . .' At first, he did not have the words. 'We campaign against the dams they build along the river. You have heard of the Aswan High Dam? In 1964, they submerged the entire Nile valley south of Aswan in Egypt for 450km – it wiped out the Nubian heartland, even here in Sudan. It was the biggest forced migration in history – 50,000 of my fellow Nubians had to leave their homes or else be drowned.' He paused. 'I can't tell you how many times the security have tried to take me away – but I've always managed to talk my way out of it. I don't want to take any risks, Lev. The only reason I'm helping you with this expedition is because I think it's good for Sudan. I'm a patriot. I love this country more than the government that gives it a bad reputation. I want to show the world that it's a beautiful place, full of beautiful people, not just the government and its terrors – and you, Lev, you can help do that. But I need you to understand: I'm risking everything here, so, please, just do as you're told.'

Not once, in the weeks we had spent together, had I heard Moez speak like this. Without another word, I nodded in assent.

Moez smiled and put his hand on my shoulder. 'And while we're at it,' he said, 'you can double my pay . . .'

THE GREAT BEND

Eastern Sahara, Sudan, May 2014

'Ships of the desert,' said Moez. 'That's what we call them. Somali beasts aside, Sudanese camels are the best in the world.'

Moez and I arrived at Omdurman's Souq al-Muwelih after midday, when the sun was at its zenith and most sane people stayed in the relative cool of their huts. The souq wasn't so much a market as a vast expanse of sand, with a small collection of shacks where local Sudanese men lounged on string beds drinking *chai*. We'd already passed the goat market, but here the scene was less frantic. Hundreds of camels stood around, chewing the scrub like cows. Gathered in groups, with the females clinging together and the males tied up in clots of four or five, they didn't seem to mind the heat at all. In front of us, one of the males tried to stand but, finding his legs tethered together, all he could do was hop comically about in search of tufts of grass poking out of the sand. I could have watched him carousing all day.

From the midst of the camels there appeared a man in a long white shirt and blue waistcoat, his head wrapped loosely in a turban.

'This must be Bala,' I said, and we made our way to meet him.

I had first heard of Bala from the great explorer Michael Asher, whose home I had visited in Kenya just before my expedition began. A noted desert explorer, Michael had spent three years living with a nomadic tribe in Sudan, becoming as familiar as any man on earth with the deserts I was about to traverse. His advice had been invaluable: camels were a necessity, but a bad camel was worth less than no camel at all.

'Whatever you do,' he had said, 'don't get a *Sharaat*.'

'What's that?'

'It's a runner. They'll try and sell you one, but tell them no. If a camel does a runner with all your water in the desert, you'll be dead in a day. And look serious when you're buying – look like you know what you're doing. Otherwise, they'll sell you something old and feckless. Check their teeth – you can tell their age by the teeth. You want a male, four to eight years old. Anything under and it'll be too weak and inexperienced. Older and it won't be up to the journey. You need a strong camel – so ask to see it stand up and get back down. If it trembles at the knees, don't go near it. You want one that's up to carrying two, even three, hundred kilos. You'll probably need two just for the food and water . . .'

Asher had had other advice: the Sudanese, he promised, were an honest people and, for the most part, wouldn't intentionally rip a buyer off. 'They'll probably presume you've bought camels before. I mean, who in their right mind goes into a camel market in Sudan who knows nothing about camels?' He winked at me, gleefully. 'Look, there's a man I know, name of Bala. He joined me on several jaunts across the Sahara. Give him a call when you get there. Mention my name . . .'

'*Salaam Alaikum*,' I said respectfully as Bala approached.

'You are Asher's friend?' he asked, without any apparent emotion.

'Yes.'

'Come for *chai*.'

Bala, the overseer for a market where many different traders brought their camels, led us to one of the huts and clicked his fingers at an Ethiopian serving girl. Everything about Bala had an air of authority: he swaggered as he walked, his pockets bulged with cash and he kept having to shake the gold watch around his wrist back into position. Carefully, he laid three phones out on the carpet in front of me. I guessed it was his way of showing how important he was.

'You've come at a bad time for camels,' he said, slurping sugary tea. I had to wait a moment for Moez to translate: Bala's English was even worse than my Arabic. 'Saturday is market day and we sell all the best camels before lunch.'

'Well, there seem to be a lot of camels out there,' I said. 'You must have one for sale?'

'They've all been sold already. It's mostly females left. And you can't ride a female. They're for breeding only. What you need is a strong male, aged four . . .'

'. . . to eight,' I interrupted. 'I know. I need one with strong legs, one with experience of the desert. And what I do not want is a *Sharaat* . . .'

Bala simply stared, trying to work out where I had got this information.

'Where are you travelling?'

'North,' I replied. 'I'm following the Nile to the border with Egypt. It's going to take sixty days.'

His ears pricked up as he nodded. 'A wonderful journey! I used to follow that road as a boy, long before we had trucks. They've ruined the old ways . . .' He paused. 'Come then! We shall find you your camel. But, for that journey, you will need three camels, not one . . .'

'Three?' I said, slightly stunned at the prospect of becoming owner to three of the behemoths standing outside.

'You'll need an extra one for water. You'll be crossing the Bayuda Desert, won't you?'

The Bayuda Desert was technically the most south-east corner of the unending Sahara. From Khartoum, the Nile goes north, before making a great loop westward. The Bayuda sits inside this loop, empty and parched.

'I won't need water. I'm following the Nile all the way, around the great bend.'

Bala only laughed. 'You can try, but you won't get near the Meroe Dam! You'll be arrested or shot on site. You'll have to do a detour through the desert for a week at least . . .'

I glared at Moez.

'It's true.' He shrugged. 'They built the dam in 2009. Our people opposed it, but it's the most important piece of strategic land in the country.'

'Strategic how?'

'It's to do with water, who controls it, who can use it . . . And the dams are under constant threat from the peoples they displaced to build them. We won't get near it, Lev. They'll think we're saboteurs and shoot us. We'll have to give it – how do you say? – a wide berth . . .'

'Yes,' Bala interrupted, 'so you'll need to carry six drums of water. That's 120 litres at least . . .'

We returned to the baking souq. One group of females, perhaps forty strong, were all hopping in unison as a new buyer herded them towards a truck. The flat-bed didn't look like it could possibly take them all, but a pair of Bedouin wranglers somehow managed to shout, whip and shove half of them aboard. The beasts were clearly unimpressed but, after lots of grumbling, they got on and twenty larger-than-life camels were driven off into a haze of dust.

We meandered through the males. Most, Bala insisted, had already been sold, but here and there some sellers remained with their beasts. At last, stopping every few yards to take a phone call and strike some other deal, Bala led us to a corner where a pair of large, white dromedaries – the Arabian camel, with only one hump – were standing.

'They look strong,' said Moez, patting the closest on the thigh.

Remembering Asher's words, I walked around the first animal, carefully inspecting every cut and graze. It was a handsome beast – and the scars were nothing out of the ordinary. If Asher was right, its long front teeth meant that it was aged five or six – perfect for an expedition.

'Can you make it sit down?' I asked the owner, who was standing nearby.

The man proceeded to make the strangest sound I have ever heard, a cross between a snake's hiss and a gargle. After four or five times, the camel seemed to understand. In an inimitably awkward way, the camel first sank to its front knees and then rocked back until, after some groaning, it was finally down. I was relieved to see that the legs didn't tremble.

Without another word, the owner leapt onto the camel's back and the animal got back to its feet, almost jumping in a display of surprising agility. With the man now on top, the pair trotted around in a large circle. The man smiled, clearly enjoying showing off his riding prowess.

'Well?' said Bala.

If Bala had been born in England, he would no doubt have been an excellent used-car salesman; I decided to remain impassive, unimpressed.

'Let's see some more . . .'

Three hours later, sun-burnished and tired, I stood at the edge of the souq, staring at three camels – and with a wallet that felt considerably lighter. The first, brown and smaller than the other two, had a quiet serenity about him, but there was a sparkle in his eyes that intimated a definite sense of mischief. I had decided to call him Gordon, after General Charles Gordon, the British officer who had masterminded the year-long defence of Khartoum when it was besieged in 1884 – only to be killed two days before reinforcements arrived. The other two camels, both white, were much grumpier, snorting and snarling the entire time.

'We'll call those two Burton and Speke,' I told Moez. 'Let's hope they don't go after each other like those two explorers did . . .'

In his hut, the negotiations complete, Bala appeared happy with his deal: all three camels sold for the princely sum of 23,000 Sudanese pounds. 'Of course,' he added, 'you'll be needing saddles as well . . .' He smiled as we handed over yet more money. I only hoped I'd be able to sell them again when we reached the border, and somehow recoup some of my losses.

'You know,' said Bala as we returned to the camels, 'it isn't going to be easy. Your man, does he know camels?'

Moez was a tour guide, not a camel man. We watched the way the handlers skilfully threaded ropes through holes in the camels' noses, how they fed them *sorghum* – a grass rich with nutrients – and massaged their necks to ensure it went down the right hole; how they picked ticks from their eyelids and arseholes. I was under no illusion that I knew what I was doing, and Bala seemed to have sensed it.

'I'd love to go with you,' he said, 'but I'm just too busy.'

I did not need to be a prophet to know what was coming next. I simply waited and watched Bala's face light up.

'But I know some men who will. How would you like me to make an introduction? It will cost you, of course . . .'

Two days later, we left Khartoum in our wake.

The battlefield at Kerreri lies only eleven kilometres north of Omdurman. This desolate wasteland on the very edge of the Sahara is the spot where Lord Kitchener's army waged the five-hour Battle of Omdurman in 1898 – and, in claiming victory, restored colonial rule to the Sudan. Somewhere amongst these acacia bushes and gravel ridges, a young subaltern named Winston Churchill took part in the last cavalry charge in British military history – all a part of Kitchener's campaign to avenge the death of General Gordon and destroy the Mahdist forces who had, thirteen years earlier, captured Khartoum.

General Gordon had originally been commissioned by the British Prime Minister, William Gladstone, to go to Sudan and organise the evacuation of all the Egyptian garrisons there. Since the Anglo-Egyptian war in 1882, Egypt had been a British protectorate in all but name – and, because Egypt had claim to the Sudan, this region also fell under British protection. But, in 1883, a charismatic Muslim leader named Muhammad Ahmad led an uprising against Egyptian rule. Styling himself the Mahdi, the prophesied redeemer of the Islamic world, he had quickly gained a devoted following and threatened the major cities of the Sudan. At last, the British came to a decision: instead of rushing to Sudan's defence, they would organise the evacuation of all the garrisons there, effectively abandoning

Sudan to self-government, and permitting the existence of a Mahdist state. General Gordon was dispatched to organise the evacuation. Yet, on his arrival at Khartoum, Gordon made a startling decision. Rather than do as his prime minister had commanded, he set about organising the city for defence against the Mahdists. Before long, Khartoum was under siege, with Gordon administering the defence.

It quickly became apparent that the siege would not be broken without the help of British soldiers from outside the city, help that the British parliament was reluctant to provide. It took an entire year before infantry were dispatched to relieve the city – and when they arrived it was too late. Khartoum had fallen two days before, and General Gordon had been slain.

It was to be thirteen years before Britain commissioned Kitchener to come and smash the Mahdist forces on the ground on which we now stood. I gazed out over the ancient land. Despite being the stage for such colourful heroism, these days the battlefield looked forlorn, a waste-ground mostly fenced off as part of a Sudanese military barracks. On top of one of the jebels, or mountains, armoured cars and tanks were covered with camouflage netting. Radio masts poked out of the hills and soldiers could be seen patrolling the compounds near to the road.

At my side, Moez began to pick his way across the battlefield. Behind him, Gordon, Speke and Burton seemed oblivious to it all. The other two men who made up our party were Awad and Ahmad – both camel handlers of some renow – who had joined us at Bala's behest, and a not inconsiderable pay packet. Awad was the younger man, but even he looked about seventy. Ahmad, or so Awad insisted, was at least a hundred years old – and, from the look of him, it was easy to believe.

Bala had introduced us to them on the eve of our leaving Khartoum, insisting they were the best camel handlers in all of the Sudan. Bedouin by birth, Ahmad had magnificent whiskers that made him look like an Indian pirate, while Awad took great pleasure in making obscene noises, bursting into raucous laughter whenever one of the camels broke wind. Neither of them had had an education, except for the rearing of camels. 'I milked my first camel at the age of three!' Awad had declared when I first met him. Neither of them could write and the only thing they could read were the distance markers on the roadside stones. 'We learned it,' Ahmad said with a grin, 'by playing cards with the blacks at an alcohol den . . .'

Under Awad and Ahmad's direction, the camels made swift work of the desert ground, and we quickly found a rhythm, covering almost 40km each day. As the river cut its course north, the land around us grew more flat and featureless, but the monotony of the landscape had a different quality now that Ahmad and Awad were here. In between long bouts of silence, Ahmad's voice would sometimes flurry up in song. For hours, he'd sing, keeping a perfect harmony with the sound of the camels' footsteps – and, every time Gordon grew bad-tempered, Ahmad's songs soothed him. For an old man, he had a beautiful, delicate voice. I only wondered what he was singing about.

'Camels and women, mostly,' said Moez, trying to control his laughter. 'This one's a play on words. You see, we call a woman's private parts '*jamal*' – it means camel. So he's joking about how he wants to screw his camel . . .'

I looked over my shoulder, to see the glint in Ahmad's eye.

For days, we followed the river north, seeing vestiges of the colonial era along the way – not least the old British railway line that followed the course of the river. A relic from the late 19th century, this had been a feat of engineering like no other – connecting Khartoum with Cairo in the far north, and allowing British troops to be deployed into central Africa with alarming speed. Now, modern Chinese bullet trains ply the same routes, and the network is being expanded to reach into Ethiopia and Chad. There's talk of South Sudan, too, but I suspect that may be several years away.

In the remote villages we passed, there was often nowhere to stay, so instead, we'd camp on the village outskirts, making our beds out of blankets underneath the stars. On the fifth night, Awad and Ahmad tethered the camels to some nearby bushes so that they could eat, and set about making a fire. Somehow, even in the middle of a desert, these two rogues could always find enough wood. Soon, sweet *chai* was simmering over the flames. As night hardened, Awad and Ahmad settled down to prayer. Like good Muslims, they prayed five times every day – although, somehow, Awad always seemed to finish his prayers first, and be back drinking coffee long before Ahmad was done.

'My grandfather was an Imam,' said Ahmad to his cousin, when he was finally finished. 'I have to set an example to you, you heathen . . .'

I lay back, to look at the stars plastered across the blackness above. Ahmad and Awad had begun to bicker like boisterous teenagers again, but I barely heard them.

'What is it, Lev?' asked Moez.

'Do you know what today was?'

Moez hazarded a guess. 'Your . . . birthday again?'

'No,' I said. 'Today was the day I passed half-way.' I stood, to take in the sounds and smells of the desert at night. A warm wind gusted sand and grit about my feet. 'Today, we passed the middle of the Nile. Do you know what it means?'

Moez shrugged.

'It means,' I said, 'that I'm on my way home.'

'But, Lev, there are still more than two thousand miles to walk . . .'

I knew it, but in that moment those two thousand miles didn't seem so far. Every step I took from this night on was part of the countdown. After five long months, the expedition's end seemed a real, tangible thing.

There was just the small matter of the Sahara Desert to contend with first.

Three days later, we had passed through Shendi, a sprawling town where traditional trade routes across the desert used to converge, and pushed north into land that was unmistakeably the Sahara. The town itself seemed strangely modern, and as we travelled through its outskirts, our procession of camels and ancient handlers – grimed in dirt, Awad and Ahmad looked like extras from *Lawrence of Arabia* – garnered strange looks from drivers waiting at the intersections. To the north, what had once been scrubland was transforming into a sea of gold and russet sand. The undulations of dunes marked the horizon. This was the desert as I had imagined it: a parched ocean under an unforgiving sun.

We had been following the river as closely as possible. Here it began its great sweep west, the Bayuda Desert separated from the rest of the Sahara only by the curve in the river. An hour north of Shendi, however, Moez brought the procession to a halt. 'Come,' he said. 'There's something every traveller passing this way has to see . . .'

At Moez's direction, we left the river behind, blazing a trail across the sand. After a few hard miles, enormous dunes of golden sand, piled up against a backdrop of sandstone mountains, marked the horizon. It was already midday and the sand underfoot was incredibly hot, especially as the dunes got deeper and the sand poured in over my boots. Moez, who was wearing only sandals, gritted his teeth admirably. 'This way!' he said, with childish glee. Fuelled by a new-found burst of energy, he steered us towards a steep wall of sand. The dunes grew steeper as we began the ascent. Above, there was an obvious ridge, beyond which the only thing we could see were craggy mountains off to the east.

Behind me, the camels were grunting in disgust at the steepening slope, snorting as the hot sand inveigled its way into their hoofs. Ahmad began one of his lilting melodies again, and I heard Gordon calm down.

At last, Moez and I reached the summit of the dune – and I looked down on one of the most amazing sights I have ever seen.

In the desert below us, scarcely a hundred yards away, a collection of crumbling pyramids and burial chambers protruded from the sand, their brown bricks a sharp contrast to the endless yellow sand. These, Moez told me, were the famous Pyramids of Meroe, the last vestiges of the ancient city that once straddled the river here: Meroe, the capital of the Nubian Kingdom of Kush for hundreds of years.

The Egyptians were not the only ones to build pyramids to honour their dead and here, before us, was the evidence of a culture every bit as advanced as Ancient Egypt. There were three great clusters of pyramids in what had once been the city of Meroe, totalling more than a hundred in all. What we were looking at was the Southern Cemetery, where nine pyramids housed the remains of Nubian Kings and Queens. Beyond these, another half-kilometre away, lay the real treasure. On a ridge of rock, now swamped in sand dunes, another line of pyramids could be seen – forty-one, according to Moez, all made from the same brown volcanic stone. As we made our way towards them, Awad and Ahmad huffing behind, they seemed like headless giants gazing out over the desert. Their decapitations were the work of Giuseppe Ferlini, an Italian who had come here in 1834 in search of treasure. Using dynamite and local hired help, he proceeded to smash the tops off many of the buildings. Spurred on by finding gold jewellery hidden in the apex of his first target, his destructive rampage forever ruined Meroe.

'These were your people then, Moez?'

Moez beamed, proud of being Nubian himself. 'Meroe was a mighty place,' he began. 'A place of real industry. The city was famous for iron. We'd trade metal to India and China, long before you whites even knew those places existed. And gold . . . Nubia always had its gold. Meroe controlled the Nile valley for a thousand kilometres all around. The whole of Africa came here to trade. We had writing, too. When you were just barbarians, Meroe had its own alphabet and scholars.'

'So what happened?'

'Meroe lasted for a thousand years, until 400AD, but nobody really knows what happened here. Some people think it was the rise of other city states in the Sudan. They started competing for trade, and trade was all Meroe had. But the Nubians went on. There were Nubian kingdoms in Sudan and Egypt long after Meroe disappeared . . .'

For a moment, I lost myself, trying to imagine that ancient time – and how civilisations some of us have barely heard about once played such a big part in the world. What I was looking at, now, was the heartland of a civilisation all but wiped out of history – except, of course, for in its descendants: Moez, and the thousands like him. Because Nubia was once at the heart of the world, and the Romans considered it the gateway to all of Africa's treasures.

The Roman Emperor Nero is usually remembered for his despotic rule, murdering his mother, persecuting the first Christians – and, of course, allowing Rome to burn. What is less well known is that he spent much of his reign, from 54–68AD, promoting trade, exploration, and the arts. Egypt had been a part of the Roman Empire since the death of Cleopatra in 30BC, becoming an important centre of produce and trade. To the south, where we now stood, lay the Kingdom of Kush, accessible by the great River Nile, whose headwaters rose in some mythical south. It was the Nubians of Kush who were seen as the keepers of the Nile, guarding all the wealth of inland Africa. Rome knew this well, and often sent armies to raid Nubia and pillage the land of its gold, iron and slaves. In retaliation, the Nubians would often attack the towns of upper Egypt. Nubia and Rome, it seems, both considered themselves the natural inheritors of Egyptian civilisation, and were prepared to go to war over such matters.

It was Nero, though, who saw the value in Africa and, by negotiating a problematic peace with the Nubians, was able to indulge his other passion: exploration. Nero was clearly fascinated by the Nile and especially the mystery surrounding its source – so much so that he ordered a party of Praetorian soldiers under the command of a tribune and two centurions to go and look for it. No Europeans had ever ventured this far south before and it was a bold expedition. Not only did they travel further than any Roman had ever gone – crossing, as I was about to (in the opposite direction), a vast chunk of the Sahara Desert – they also came face to face with their recent enemies, the Nubians. What they encountered must have been a pleasant surprise – for, after following the Nile through the Kushitic Kingdom for the best part of a thousand miles, they came across the splendid capital of Meroe, over whose remnants I now looked. Far from being barbaric savages, as some Romans believed, they found the Nubians rich and developed. Meroe had a flourishing metal-working industry, and its pottery was famous throughout the ancient world. The Nubians also dealt in slaves, 'exotic' animals, and textiles made from cotton – a sure indicator that agriculture and industry were then more widespread across the Nile than they are now.

'They must have been awed by these pyramids, too,' I said to Moez, who – despite having been here a hundred times before – was still agog.

Awad and Ahmad had finally caught up, dragging Gordon, Speke and Burton with them. In spite of the magic all around, neither of them seemed to be interested in the ancient structures.

'Do they even know what these are?' I asked.

Moez asked them, but Ahmad only muttered back: 'Piles of stones.'

'Don't they care?'

'It's not that they don't care – they just don't have a concept of it. Time, history, tradition . . . They don't have reverence for anything other than God.'

Telling Ahmad and Awad to stay with the camels, Moez and I ventured closer to the north cemetery. Pyramids rose out of the crust on either side of us and, as the sun began to fall, they cast long shadows, giving the scene a surreal appearance. These were nothing like the Pyramids of Egypt, thronged by tourists day and night. The Pyramids of Meroe were smaller, and nowhere could we see any signs of human habitation. Dwarfed by the ancient monoliths, Moez pointed out the hieroglyphs etched into the walls: dog-headed gods and the sign of Anubis; depictions of eagles, rams and crocodiles. He pointed to later inscriptions, too, names carelessly carved into the rock: W. Matthews RE and R.A. Trowbridge, 1898 – a clear sign that the English soldier of the Victorian era cared but little for the antiquities the colonies.

'They seem so small, compared to Egypt.'

'They are smaller,' said Moez, 'but not as small as you think. Most of these pyramids are buried under the sand. The desert's so much deeper than it was when Meroe was at its height. It would take an army of men to excavate these pyramids and find out what was truly inside. But, one day, we'll know . . .'

As the sun began to set, I felt like I wanted to be alone, and tramped off as Moez and the others returned to set up camp in the shadow of the tallest pyramid. Awad and Ahmad were befuddled at the thought of camping here, but I wanted nothing more than to see the dawn break over these magnificent structures. Alone, I climbed to the ridge, letting the last rays of sunlight warm my face as they disappeared into the desert beyond the mighty Nile. Suddenly, I felt very small. The realisation was finally dawning on me that the footprints I was trailing across Africa were ephemeral, transitory things – that, whatever I could accomplish with this expedition, it could never last as long as these symbols of civilisation before me. Here I was, on the threshold of the ancient world, where human beings have left a tangible reminder of their existence in the form of great tombs pointing to the heavens – a dedication, as it were, to the gods, of their own achievements and sacrifices. It was a humbling feeling.

Only days ago, I had been buoyed by the thought of passing the half-way mark and beginning the long road home – but now another thought drew me in. Tomorrow, I would begin my journey into the Nile of antiquity, a Nile whose history and people have been recorded in a way that, further south, was not the case. This was the cradle of civilisation, a place where empires had risen and fallen millennia before there was even such a thing as England.

It must have been here, in the shadows of these pyramids, that the little band of Romans, having come from the north on the adventure of a lifetime, prepared for the next leg of their expedition, into the vast swamps of the Sudd. Though one dissenting Italian historian, Giovanni Vantini, believes they made it through to the glittering expanse of Lake Victoria, it is more widely believed that the Sudd defeated them, just as it defeated me. I think I now knew how they must have felt. They, too, had watched the sun set across the Nile from the ridge on which I sat – only, for them, they were departing from the known world, into the unknown. I was going the opposite way – back into the known; both into the past but, also, the future.

THE SANDS OF TIME

Bayuda Desert, Sudan, May – June 2014

The town of Atbarah, home to more than a hundred thousand people, straddled the river two days north of the Pyramids of Meroe. A grey, industrial town, Atbarah was brought to life by only two things: the seasonal confluence of the Nile and the River Atbarah, the Nile's most northerly tributary; and the two men who tumbled out of a taxi on the highway running into town.

We had been tramping for more than forty kilometres under unrelenting sun. Caked in dirt, eyes to the ground, all I heard was the revving of an engine and a screeching of tyres. It was the camels who spooked first. Loping nervously to the side of the dusty highway, they craned to look back. Too late, I did the same. A taxi overtook us in a cloud of sand and slowed to a stop just ahead.

Out of the door tumbled Will Charlton. As I had known he would, he was here to keep his promise.

'And look who I found,' said Will as the second door opened.

Another figure staggered into the dust, all teeth and smiles. In a second, I was being smothered in its arms.

'Ash!' I began. 'What the . . .'

Ash Bhardwaj was as old a friend as Will – I'd known both of them since university. Ash enjoyed the finer things in life – a modern-day dandy roaming the coffee shops of East London in tweed jackets and skinny jeans, I'd often thought of him as an Indian Oscar Wilde. When I'd left the army, Ash had invited me to help him run a luxury ski lodge in Switzerland – and, on the day I turned up in Verbier to join him, I'd discovered him standing outside the chalet wearing nothing but a bath robe and flat cap. 'Brandy?' he'd bellowed, with the biggest grin I'd ever seen. 'It's 9am!' I'd said, but Ash had only rolled his eyes in disgust. 'I know. We're behind schedule.' I still don't remember the rest of the month.

By the time Ash had released me from his bear hug, Will had reached into his pack and produced a small gift. When he opened his hand, a single pack of condoms was sitting in his palm. 'Emergency water carriers,' he declared. 'That's the only use they'll get out here. Well, you did say you wanted some company crossing the desert, didn't you?'

I'd lived with Will at university in Nottingham years before and we'd travelled the world together ever since we'd both joined the army. Will had become a doctor and, when he wasn't on operations with his unit, or on exercise in some far-flung part of the world, he was always on the lookout for another adventure, so it was hardly surprising that he'd used up his annual-leave allowance to come and keep me company.

'Can't have you crossing the Sahara on your own!' he said with his usual dark humour. 'You need me here in case you pile in . . .'

At a canteen in Atbarah, I introduced Will and Ash to Moez. Awad and Ahmad were content to camp outside the town, but we decided to make the best of what Atbarah had to offer before the long desert crossing would begin. Atbarah is a major centre for railway manufacture in the Sudan, and has the air of an industrial town – but it served the best chicken and liver I had tasted in weeks. As we ate, Moez got to explaining the way ahead.

'The river bends west, but then it reaches the Meroe Dam, and the reservoir behind it. We have to avoid it at all costs.'

'Why?' asked Ash. Ash was a travel writer, with a knack for getting ridiculous assignments, and the urge to quiz Moez a little further was instinctive. 'I thought we had to stick to the river. Aren't those the rules of your expedition, Lev?'

'They are, but . . .'

'Listen,' said Moez, 'it isn't that simple. The Meroe Dam's only five years old, but they've been talking of damming the river here, at the fourth cataract, for decades.' The Nile traditionally has six cataracts – places where the river is noticeably more shallow, broken by rocks and giving rise to white-water rapids – between Khartoum and Aswan in Egypt. 'It's the most powerful dam in the country, and also the most destructive. Almost fifty thousand people were displaced to build it – that's as many as the High Dam in Egypt.' Moez's face was tightening in anger at what the government had done. 'Nobody in the government listened to those people. They'd rather not have had the electricity than be forced from their homes . . .'

I could tell he was about to say something he'd later regret, so I decided to interject. 'The importance of that dam to Sudan can't be overestimated. It practically doubled the amount of power in Sudan. And that means . . .'

Finally, Ash understood: 'You mean there'll be army there?'

'Everywhere,' said Moez, calmer at last. 'It's a prime piece of national infrastructure, so it's guarded to the hilt. If we try and go near it, they'll think we're spies or foreign agents. Saboteurs. They'll shoot us on sight.'

'So what's the plan?' asked Will, skewering another piece of liver with his fork.

I produced a crumpled map and spread it out before us. 'We're going to leave the river, and cut across the Bayuda Desert instead. We'll follow one of the old camel-caravan routes, and bypass the dam altogether. There won't be soldiers out in the desert. Anyway, I figure, dressed as we are, we'll pass for roving Bedouin. Speaking of which . . .' It was time for me to produce my own welcome gift for Will and Ash: two new *jellabiyas* in perfect white. 'We have turbans, too,' I said grinning.

Will and Ash took theirs and spent an age trying to wrap them around their heads.

'And your camel handlers out there,' Ash began, 'they know where we're going?'

Bala had said they knew the Bayuda like the backs of their hands, that they had made the crossing many times before, droving camels along the old caravan routes. 'I trust them,' I said – because I did. Awad and Ahmad seemed a step out of time with modern Sudan, but above all else, they knew the ways of the desert. 'Boys,' I said, 'you can't back out on me now . . .'

North of Atbarah, the Nile was flanked by farms of verdant green. Along its banks, a procession of pylons marched down from the Meroe Dam, taking electricity to the masses of Khartoum. For a day, we walked through plantations of cotton and sorghum, orchards of date palm – but, on the edges of the farmland, the bleak, lunar plain stretched out for as far as the eye could see.

The Bayuda is a vast volcanic desert, over one hundred thousand square kilometres of open plain, jagged mountains, sand dunes and black volcanoes. This eastern extension of the Sahara was formed several million years ago by the Earth's crust pushing up, spewing out lava and diverting the Nile on a three-hundred-mile detour. For the last few thousand years, the Bayuda has formed an inconvenient barrier to those travelling along the Nile, whether it be adventurous Romans in search of its source, or entrepreneurial Nubians extending the trade of their city states. For all those travellers, as for me, the choice was stark: stick to the river and add hundreds of miles to your journey, or risk a perilous desert crossing. Many preferred to take the shortcut – and, over time, a caravan route was established. Much later, the Bedouin Arabs dug a series of wells along the way, features that still exist and that have saved hundreds of lives across the generations. When General Gordon was besieged in Khartoum and the British sent troops to relieve him, they hedged their bets by sending one column of troops by boat up the Nile, and establishing the elite 'Camel Corps' to charge across the Bayuda and reach Khartoum fastest. It was the fact that this new camel cavalry had to spend ten days re-watering their beasts at one of the Bedouin wells that meant they arrived at Khartoum two days late to save poor Gordon. Nevertheless, the British used the same tactic thirteen years later, when Kitchener was sent to reconquer Khartoum, with the two columns rendezvousing outside Omdurman for the final confrontation. The rest of that is, as we know, history.

The village of Kadabas was to be our last stop before entering the desert. Forced away from the riverbank by irrigation ditches and pipelines, we returned to the desert road, marching north with the pylons through miles of acacia scrub. By fall of night, we had reached Kadabas, one of a succession of adobe villages along the road. Stark and lonely, it must have been too trivial to be tapped into the electricity flowing down the wires, because not a single light shone among the shacks, except an eerie green glow from the minaret that rose from the mosque.

In the village, an old man emerged from his hut to greet us. 'You must be Pakistani Dhawas?' he asked.

Stumped, I looked at Moez. 'Teachers,' he began. 'They're quite common in these parts. Some preach jihad but they're mostly harmless.' Then he turned to the stranger. 'Not teachers. Explorers. These men are walking the Nile.'

'Of course,' the old man said, as if it was the most natural thing in the world. 'But first, you must stay in our village.'

I began to tell Will and Ash how hospitable the villagers had been in every part of Sudan, all the way from the border, to Khartoum and beyond – but the man continued to chatter, and Moez continued to translate.

'No, not only tonight,' the man went on. 'For always. We will feed you. A house will be provided at no cost to yourselves. Please, come this way . . .'

As the man returned to the huts, beckoning us to follow, Ash muttered, 'Do you think this is a good idea?' I only shrugged and tramped after the old man. 'We need to stay somewhere, Ash. One last night before you sleep under the stars for a week.' I hesitated. 'Or you could always stay out here with the camels . . .'

Eventually, resisting the overtures of the old man to forever make this our home, we made camp behind one of the adobe huts. As the old man from the village brought us food, insisting we share what he had, Will produced a stack of old Russian maps he had somehow procured. What we were looking at were out-dated charts of the interior of the Nile's great bend. At a scale of one to five-hundred-thousand, they showed all the trails marked between the contours, and small blue dots scattered across the sand.

'The Bedouin wells?' Ash asked, tracing the blue dots with his finger.

We could only assume that was the case; none of us had the faintest grasp of the Russian language.

'What if they're not?' Ash went on. 'What then?'

'We've got water,' I said. 'Enough for six litres each a day. The crossing should take eight days. If it's any longer, well . . .' I paused. 'Awad and Ahmad travel this way all the time. They know the desert like the backs of their hands. That's why they're coming with me. The camel trader Bala promised it.'

'Oh well,' said Ash, 'if he *promised* it . . .'

'Do you know,' Moez began, 'if we make this crossing, we'll be the first to cross the Bayuda by foot at the height of summer. That would be a miraculous thing.'

'You see, Lev,' Will chipped in, 'there might be a world-first for you in this expedition after all . . .'

'Wait a minute,' said Ash. '*Why* has nobody done it before?'

The thought had dawned on me too.

'Oh,' said Moez, 'the Bedouin know the desert too well to risk such a thing . . .'

Long into the night, we sat staring into the blackness over the desert. Only when our fire had finally flickered out did we turn in ourselves. I barely slept that night, lost in thoughts of the desert to come.

In the morning, Awad and Ahmad were waiting for us on the outskirts of Kadabas; Gordon, Speke and Burton already saddled and laden down with the packs and jerry cans we would be dragging into the desert as supplies. On the outskirts of the village, we said our goodbyes to the old man, who still insisted we return. As the village gradually dwindled and disappeared behind us, masked by a mirage of heat and knolls of sand, the sun was flooding the desert with a golden sheen. This land we were walking into looked solemn and quiet, as alien to man as the stars above. We hesitated before going on. It is only natural, I suppose, to hesitate on the threshold of stepping into the unknown. So, on the edge of the desert, three white men stood in nervous anticipation, unused to the emptiness of the horizon. Moez, Nubian to his core, and Awad and Ahmad, Bedouin through and through, strode off without a second thought.

'Come on, *Ingleez*!' shouted Awad, from his saddle atop Burton. 'You'll be blacker than a *Beja* if you stand around in the sun all day. Get walking!'

'Gentlemen,' said Ash, 'we're about to walk across a small, but not insignificant, chunk of the Sahara Desert. We don't know where the wells are, we've only got enough food for eight days, and there is a bloody great volcano in the way. Do we really know what we're doing?'

Will looked at Ash, and then at me. I guessed it was my turn to do the comforting: 'It's fine, mate. We've both been to Afghanistan. It's . . . the same sort of thing.' Even I could tell I didn't sound sure. To save my blushes, I pointed after Gordon, the spare camel, who was loping over a sandy hillock, tied by a length of rope to the back of Speke's saddle. 'And, look, if you get tired, you can always ride him . . .'

'I may well do that . . .'

'Same for you, Will.' I grinned, and waited for him to bite.

'Fuck off!' he said, as I had known he would; and together, we strode off into the West.

*

'Ancient Bedouin tomb,' said Moez, crouching at a series of unnatural mounds, where stones had been placed in a circle and still pierced the sand. Awad had tipped his turban respectfully at them as we had passed, but the camels didn't seem to have any compunction about munching on the bits of thorn scrub growing from the graves.

We had been walking through the punishing heat for eight hours and, though the day was getting old, the sun was just as fierce. Pausing to rest in the tiny shade of an acacia tree, I drank greedily from my canteen, only to realise that I had, long ago, drunk my day's fill. According to our thermometer, it had been 56 degrees in the sun, and almost 50 in the shade. 'We'll have to be cannier tomorrow,' I said.

'Wouldn't it be better to walk at night?' asked Ash.

From up on Burton's back, Ahmad snorted. 'The camels would break their legs. No,' he went on, Moez translating, 'we should walk early, from six till eleven. Then again from four until sunset.'

Will grimaced. 'Only mad dogs and Englishmen go out in the midday sun . . .'

'We can still cover 40km a day,' said Ahmad and, singing to his camel, continued to walk.

We tramped on. Now that the day was fading to dusk, the edge was coming off the heat. The dunes, soft underfoot, gave way with each step; no amount of walking, not even the two thousand miles since the source of the river, could prepare a body for how difficult it was to walk here. Every time the sand touched my feet, my body glistened with new sweat. I seemed to be losing as much water in perspiration as I was drinking.

'You know,' said Moez, 'it's hard to imagine now, but once, only a few thousand years ago, this was all lush and fertile savannah – and before that, a swamp, or maybe even a vast lake, long before the desert started to form. It isn't just your footsteps in the sand that fade away – it's the land itself, changing all the time. This was where the agricultural revolution happened. It was here people started farming for the very first time. There were cattle cults that looked after huge herds, all grazing on rich grasses for as far as the eye can see. Now – only this . . .'

By fall of the first night, we had covered 40km, but drunk twice as much water as we had planned. Our bodies hungered for it. Making camp beside an outcrop of jagged sandstone, we broke open the army ration packs Will had brought along and refuelled. On the edge of camp, Ahmad and Awad began their prayers, then sang to the camels as they fed them sorghum and massaged their necks to aid the digestion.

We ate in silence, so drained by the day that even idle conversation seemed too much. The only sound to disturb the silence of the desert was Ahmad's song, then the chatter as he and Awad began to play a kind of backgammon using nothing but lines in the sand and camel droppings.

'Are you listening to this, Lev?'

Moez inclined his head towards the camel handlers, but they were speaking in Arabic, so quickly that I could not perceive a word.

'What is it?'

'They're saying . . .' He smiled nervously. 'They're saying they've never been to this part of the Bayuda . . .'

I almost choked on my words. 'What? But Bala said . . .'

'Yes, yes, I know – but it seems they always go the same way, along an old caravan route some way south of here. It's the same way General Gordon took between Metemma and Korti.'

I moved closer to Moez eager that Will and Ash would not hear. 'But what about the wells?' I asked, in disbelief. 'We drank more water than we rationed today. It's hotter than we thought . . .'

'They only know Jakdul,' Moez explained, 'and the wells south of the volcanic plateau. Up here, well, they can guess, but . . .'

I was about to launch into some tirade when I felt movement on my shoulder; Ash, sensing something was wrong, had joined us.

'Did I hear that right? Awad and Ahmad have never been this way? They don't even know where the wells are?' Aghast, he turned over his shoulder. 'Are you listening to this, Will?'

Always one to get stuck into a bit of controversy, Will left his ration pack and strode over. 'What's going on? Wait, let me guess . . . Lev is lost?'

'Worse!' spat Ash. 'The camel guides haven't a clue where they're going.'

Will's face changed; where once he had been keen to poke fun, now he looked sombre. 'That's . . . not good, Lev,' he said, in earnest. 'Are we being incredibly arrogant here? Three men who've never crossed deserts before, and two guides who don't know the way . . .'

It was Will's concern that, finally, made me pause. Will was usually game for any ridiculous idea; if he was questioning the sanity of a project, there had to be a good reason. I stared into the blackness of the desert, where the light of a million stars lit only rolling dunes and outcrops of thorn. The prospect of not finding a well out here was unthinkable. The old adage of 'three days without water, three weeks without food' didn't apply in a land as inhospitable as this. In the heat we had walked through today, we wouldn't last twelve hours without water; we'd be as dead as the shrivelled donkey carcasses we'd seen outside Kadabas before the day was through.

'Look,' I said, half to convince myself, 'it'll be okay. We have enough water for three, maybe four days – that should get us almost half way. And, if the worst happens, well, the river's never more than

40km away. That's only a day's walk. If things get low, that's what we do – we head for the river.'

'Yes,' said Moez, with a hint of cynicism, 'and hope the soldiers from the dam don't notice when we drop our heads to drink.'

Though Will seemed pacified, the look on Ash's face had only hardened. He stared at me, mortified. 'I don't really have a choice, do I?' he said. 'Lev, I'm just going to have to trust that you won't kill me . . .'

As Will and Ash settled back down, I stared at Awad and Ahmad. In the starlight, they looked particularly roguish, spreading out their camp. Neither one of them seemed the least bit perturbed; perhaps there was a lesson to learn from that.

'They must be confident they'll find a well,' I said, reassured by their calmness.

'No.' Moez grinned. 'They're just confident they can be the first to jump on a camel and get to the river . . .'

'But, Moez, there are only three camels.'

'And six of us.' He grinned. 'Let's hope it doesn't come to that, right?'

We were up with the dawn but, by 6.30am, the temperature was already 28 degrees, and quickly getting worse. By the time we had covered our first three kilometres, it was inching towards 40; then it exploded, past 40, 45 and 50. When we broke for water, Moez pressed the thermometer to the sand and recorded a high of 62.

It was our second day and we had already used almost half of our water.

We made a midday camp, stretching the tarpaulin over thorny acacia for shade, and resigned ourselves to waiting out the worst of the day's heat – but by the time the camp was established and we were closing our eyes, desperate to conserve what energy we had, the camels began to grow skittish. When I looked round, Moez was stripping off his turban and rebinding it around his face. That was the first signal that something bad was coming; the second was the wall of brown hardening on the horizon.

I turned to Will and Ash. '*Haboob*,' I said. 'Look, do what Moez does, and try not to panic. We just have to wait it out.'

The brown line on the horizon seemed small, but what we were seeing was only the first wave of a tide of dust and sand rampaging our way. I had seen *haboobs* before, but only from the comfort of a camp along the roadside, where adobe walls could shelter us from the onslaught. What we were looking at was none other than a land tsunami – a vicious maelstrom that tore up everything in its path, gathering up sand, earth, grit, and moulding it into a single, unstoppable wave. In the time it had taken me to explain it to Will and Ash, the line had already darkened. As it grew closer, it seemed to swell, more and more distinct from the desert floor. Now it was a vast phalanx of filth, stark against the clear blue sky.

The wind was already picking up. Unwrapping my turban, I bound it around my mouth, covering my nostrils. This, I knew, would be the only way to breathe once the storm arrived. Moez had unearthed pairs of sand goggles and was handing them round – but, no sooner had I donned them than the first dust devils, tiny whirling dervishes of grit, hurtled into the camp, like heralds of the storm. Awad and Ahmad rushed to rope the camels together, while Will, Ash and I gathered our packs.

Sudden sprays of grit arced up from the floor, slicing across my face. As I turned away and cowered, the dust devil flurried up from the ground, clawing at the tarpaulin strung in the acacia. There was already sand inside my goggles, sand inside my turban, riming my lips.

I waited for the barrage to die down, and then looked up. The roiling wall that had seemed so many miles away was now almost upon us, bearing down. The desert was being plunged into premature night, as the storm blocked out the sun.

'How long is this going to last?' cried Ash.

I stole a look at Ahmad and Awad. As ever, they seemed completely unperturbed, finding a way to stake the camels down. Yet again, it was their calmness that gave me confidence.

'Try and get some rest,' I said. 'It's going to be a long one.'

In that same moment, the wall of dust cascaded over us, drawing a veil between me, Will and Ash. All around, the world was a frenzy of yellow and brown. I could see no more than a few paces in every direction, locked into a raging bubble in the middle of the storm. Now, with my eyes burning, my throat rasping, there was nothing to do but wait.

By the time the *haboob* had passed, the day was old. In the relative cool of evening, we walked west, until darkness returned. In camp that night, we took inventory of our supplies: enough food to last all the way across the Bayuda; water for only another two days. Perhaps we could make it for three if we rationed it, but the memory of Matt Power still lived with me, and the thought of rationing water in this heat did not fill me with confidence. There were at least six days between here and the end of the desert. Somehow – whether Awad and Ahmad could lead us there or not – we would have to find a well.

The next day felt hotter than the last, even though the thermometer showed the same temperature. It was the burgeoning fear that made it feel so much more intense. Every time I lifted the water to my lips, every time I saw Will or Ash sate themselves, the thought blossomed in the back of my head: that was another gulp, another sip, closer to our supplies running dry.

And still, all around, only the same featureless land.

By mid-afternoon, the sky was darkening again. In an instant, the wind picked up. Instinctively, we reached for our turbans, anticipating the worst. Behind sand goggles, I shied from the raking wind. For twenty minutes, the dust devil lashed at us – but when, at last, it subsided, what remained were not clouds of dust. They were simply clouds. Swollen, grey reefs hung over the desert, giving this barren landscape an even more ethereal appearance. Moments later, the temperature plummeted; a soothing cool breeze floated down from the north. Moez and I exchanged a curious look. Awad and Ahmad looked to the sky and smiled.

A great crash tore the silence apart, and sheet lightning lit up our surrounds. Thunder reverberated in the vaults above, rolling over distant mountaintops. On the horizon, the sky was black. 'It's rain,' said Moez, 'and it's coming this way . . .'

Torrents of water were drenching the parched horizon, sweeping inexorably towards us. We watched in wonder. It was Ash who felt it first: a cold, fat globule of rain fell from the shifting clouds, to land on his upturned hand. Here, in the middle of the Sahara, we let the rain wash over us and opened up our mouths to the skies.

Fifteen minutes later, as suddenly as it had come, the rain was gone. The sun, fierce as ever, reappeared from behind retreating clouds, bathing the desert in its merciless light. Wondering if this had been a strange mirage, we tramped on – but there was no illusion in how those brief rains had transformed the desert. Flash floods demarked the depressions where ancient waterways used to flow, the dry riverbeds given a brief, second chance at life. Water gushed along tiny tributaries. The acacia bushes, normally so brown, had in an instant become green. Flowers sprouted and shoots opened on bushes and desert melon. Lizards lapped up droplets from rocky outcrops and – as if out of nowhere – a plethora of rabbits had appeared.

The camels, fluttering their eyelashes, drank from puddles and grazed on the sudden flourishes of green. And, for a time, there was more spring to our steps, more buoyancy as we followed the trail into the west.

Only hours later, the water had all been sucked into the greedy sands. Gone were the fledgling rivers, back the ancient riverbeds. Gone, the flocks of rabbits come up to gorge on the new greenery; back the cracked feeling in the back of my throat, and nervous looks at the jerry cans hanging from Burton's saddle. For a brief moment, we had danced in the rain of a Saharan thunderstorm – but, like everything in this inhospitable land, it had only been the gods of the desert taunting us with the promise of water.

Thirst is a terrible thing. It destroys you from the inside out.

Throughout the next day, I watched our supplies dwindling. When you have water, you take it for granted – but when you don't, not only does it ruin your body; it ruins your mind, planting ugly thoughts, poisoning every corner of your being. To begin with, you try to comprehend what it might be like to die of thirst. That's when the panic sets in. Your mouth gets dry, your tongue refuses to move, your gums grow numb. Your lips, already cracked and peeling, stick together, sealing your words within. In silence, you look at your companions – old friends, new friends, trusted guides – and begin to wonder if they feel the same. I found myself jealously watching the water bottle in Moez's hand. Was he as desperate as me? Did he have more water? Was Ash keeping some of his secretly hidden away, a salve against the end? Was Will? Would any of them share with me if

I was dry, if I begged them? Would *I* do the same for them? Such are the thoughts that were taking root in me as, by the end of our fourth day, we drank down to our last few litres.

It is a myth that camels can go weeks without water. In the heat of the Sahara, they can barely survive more than four days. We'd watered Burton, Speke and Gordon well before embarking, and watered them every evening since – but, tonight, there was nothing for our camel friends. What little we had left had to sustain us humans until we could find a well.

'We need those camels,' said Ash as we ate rations beneath the brilliant silver light of the moon. 'They're carrying everything. Food, medical kit, all the technical gear. Without them, we're shafted.'

As I did every time nerves threatened to overwhelm me, I looked to Awad and Ahmad – but even they seemed subdued tonight. There was no gleam in their eyes, no ribald joke or song. 'If we don't find a well tomorrow,' I said, 'that's it. Soldiers or no soldiers, we have to head for the river.'

In silence, our column of men marched across the desert.

I paused, lifting my canteen to my lips, thought better of it, and hung it at my side again. Moments later, Ash and Will had caught up. They were staring, bewildered, at Moez, who – as ever, walked contentedly to our rear.

'How does he do it?' Will asked.

'The man's a machine,' muttered Ash.

As he passed, Moez only smiled, looking at the burnt-lobster faces around him. I had not seen Moez take a drink in long hours and – in contrast to Will and Ash – not a bead of sweat glistened on his face.

Awad and Ahmad had re-joined the procession, along with the camels, an hour before. Late last night, Will had pored over his Russian maps and, highlighting a blue dot not far from where we camped, had sent the Bedouin out in search of a well. But when they returned, their faces told the story: there was no water here; if there had ever been a well at all, it had long been dry and subsumed by the sand.

'They don't seem to give a shit,' said Will. Perversely, he seemed to be relishing the thought of a close call with death.

'We'd better not die, Wood,' said Ash.

I wanted to tell him we wouldn't, but I had seen death already on this voyage.

By midday, the sand dunes had ebbed away and we marched across a plain of grey and black. Jagged black stone stretched out before us, capturing the heat of the sun and searing the soles of our shoes. In the distance, a line of gleaming purple mountains marked the heart of the desert. These, Moez told us, were the volcanoes of the Bayuda. Innumerable peaks rose up, shimmering in the haze. All in all, there were ninety volcanoes of differing sizes across the plateau, fifteen rising taller than the rest to claw at the sky.

'Are we going to get burnt to death, too?' asked Ash.

'They're dormant,' said Moez. 'In fact . . .'

'In fact, what?'

I stopped dead. The same thing had occurred to me as to Moez. 'If we head straight for the highest peak, there ought to be a gorge down into the volcano itself.'

'And?' said Ash.

'It's our best chance at finding natural water.'

The mountains, in their enormity, took an age to reach, the wavering heat obscuring their true size and range. One mile turned into two, then three into four, and it was not until twenty miles of silence had passed that we stood in their shadows. Even Awad and Ahmad had ceased to sing today.

Behind a sheer cliff of black basalt, a small trail wound into a narrow gully. We snaked along its length, emerging again onto the plain west of the volcanoes.

I stared into the distance. At first, all I saw was the same unyielding black and grey, the plateau extending into the west. Then, my eyes lit on a passage in the rock another mile away, a place where the volcanic mounds rose up, and a ravine was the only way through.

At the other end of the passage, there was green.

'There!' I shouted out, with the last of my remaining energy.

'You're not bloody wrong,' said Will, climbing to a gravel mound to see for himself.

'Trees!' screamed Moez.

'Water?' asked Ash, in utter disbelief.

Awad rode level with Will and, high up on Burton, stared into the distant tree-line.

'*Moya,*' he said, with sheer relief. 'Water.'

With renewed vigour, we made for the cleft in the rock, emerging onto a small cluster of acacia bushes clinging to the base of the pitch-black mountainside. Pillars of rock rose like ancient monoliths out of the scree and there, to my utter disbelief, stood two boys.

By the looks of them they were Arab, Bedouin like Awad and Ahmad, dressed in simple *jellabiyas* with beads around their necks. At our sudden appearance, they started, exchanging a panicked look. The first tightened his hold around the rope by which they were leading a diminutive donkey. It took me a moment to realise what I was seeing in their eyes. It wasn't quite fear, and it wasn't quite shock; they were bewildered, staring at a collection of rough, sand-blasted vagabonds who seemed to have stepped straight out of some desert past.

Ahmad was the first to speak. From up on Burton, he cried out, 'You, lads! We are Bedouin of the Hawawir tribe. We come in peace. Now tell us . . .' He leaned forward, half mischievous, half menacing: 'Is there a well near?'

In silence, the boys exchanged a look, their faces transforming from nervous horror to relief. The first lifted his hand and pointed towards a crevice, only a few hundred metres to our west. Raising his whip in thanks, Ahmad reined Burton around and took off.

Summoning what vestiges of energy we had left, we hurried into the valley. For the first time in a hundred miles, the desert plain opened up with trees and bushes, tall and green, growing thicker and more verdant with every step. Between the trees stood crudely constructed stone corrals, seasonal pens for whatever nomadic herders used this route through the desert. We rounded the corrals, dropped into a crevice between the rocks – and there, surrounded by stones carved in intricate design, stood the well. A rope trailed out of its open mouth, a single bucket beckoning us to come and drink our fill.

Ash and Moez hurtled forward. The camels, too, must have smelt water – for suddenly there was no stopping them as they charged towards it. Dumping our bags under the shade of an acacia, Will and I dragged the jerry cans to the lip of the well. My entire body was telling me to dive into its sweet depths and never come up again, but Moez, Awad and Ahmad were already praying and we waited for them to finish.

After that: we drank, and drank, and drank.

For the first time that day, I felt human, my tongue no longer numb and shrivelled. Just a few seconds was all it took for the water to touch every corner of my body. I was alive again.

'Well done, Wood.' Ash winked, finishing his second litre. 'I never doubted you.'

Alongside us, Awad was digging a small pit, laying a tarpaulin inside and filling it with water for the camels to drink their fill. Burton, Speke and Gordon – in that order – hustled each other to the pit and I watched as the water brought life back to their eyes.

Once I had regained my senses, I turned to the well. Here we were, miles and miles away from the Nile, in the middle of the desert – and yet, somehow, someone, hundreds of years ago, had known to dig here and provide water for the generations to come. We, very simply, owed them our lives.

'But where does it come from?' I asked, turning to Moez.

'I don't know,' he replied. 'Let me ask.' Turning to Ahmad, he posed the question in Arabic. Ahmad smiled, busy smoking one of his cigarettes in triumph; and when he replied, I did not need a translator to understand the answer:

'Allah.'

For three days, we followed the trails west. Though our water had been replenished, by the final day, our food was running low; with all ration packs spent, we kept hunger at bay with dried dates and tins of pineapple. The sight of the distant Nile was like a mirage, appearing on the horizon as a ribbon of emerald green. The mountain of Jebel Barkal rose from the plain and, in its shadow, stood the remnants of yet more pyramids, like the ones we had seen at Meroe. As we drew close, heading into the agricultural land flanking the Nile, the head of a sandstone cobra could just be seen poking out from the cliff – the crown on the head of the old god Amun, sculpted from the rock two-and-a-half-thousand years ago.

The farmland bounding the Nile was a surreal place of sorghum fields and irrigation channels. We saw people tending to their crops. We trudged along paths between undulating waves of grain, and no longer did the air taste of sand and grit; no longer did we keep our eyes half shut against the reflected glare of the sun.

We had not yet reached the banks of the river when a farmer hailed us from his field. Waving for us to slow down, he careened through the grain to catch us.

'You!' he cried, in disbelief. 'Where have you come from?'

'We came across the desert,' said Moez, wearied.

The farmer tried to take this in, gazing back east, as if he could see the enormity of the expanse. Shaking his head, he began to laugh. 'No, no one could do that . . .' He paused. 'Where are these from?' he asked, gesturing at Will, Ash and myself. 'Pakistan?'

'No,' said Moez, 'they're from England.'

Something close to realisation settled across the farmer's face. He nodded, sagely. 'England? Like the English who were here before?'

At first, I thought he meant other travellers, but of course, he was referring to the British administration that had ruled Sudan until 1956. It had been fifty-eight years since Sudan had gained independence, but he spoke about it as if was yesterday.

'Yes,' said Moez, solemnly.

'Well,' the farmer went on, 'that's different. Of course I believe you, now. The English can do anything, my friend, even cross the desert.' Earnestly, he looked to me. 'Please, sir,' he began, 'tell your Queen she must return. The Sudan has gone to ruin since you left . . .'

Sometime later, we reached the bank of the Nile. Here the river, continuing its bend around the Bayuda, swung south-west, before curling north again.

'What did he mean, that man?' I asked.

'It is not an uncommon thing to hear. Since Sudan gained independence, there have been thirty-nine years of civil wars. That's less than twenty years of peace. And . . .'

What Moez wasn't saying was that even those years of peace had hardly been peaceful. Sudan may have been famous for its hospitality, but I hadn't forgotten the story of the woman condemned to death for converting from Islam, nor Moez's own stories of thousands of Nubian people continually being displaced by a government extending its infrastructure and power. This was a world in which a strict code of hospitality sat side by side with daily human-rights' abuse.

'Don't get used to it, Lev,' said Will as we tramped, one final mile, down the river. 'It isn't every day you'll hear an African begging for the British to come back . . .'

The town of Karima stretched out in front of us, surrounded on all sides by date plantations. Through the trees ran a single railway track – still plied by Sudanese trains, but yet another relic left behind by the British. I realised, then, that we had been seeing it everywhere, the stamp the British had left on this land – and not only in the railways and roads, the decaying barracks buildings or the brass plaques in the towns that harked back to the English companies who had once worked here: SHEFFIELD STEEL, STOKE-ON-TRENT CERAMIC, WATERWORKS OF BIRMINGHAM. We were seeing it in the hearts and minds of the people as well, the memories of those old enough to have been there then, and the stories handed down to those who had not.

Old British tractors rotted in fields and old British steam engines lay overgrown with weeds. By the Nile old English water pumps formed a rusting metal memorial to a bygone age. It had been the Golden Age for Sudan. In spite of defeat at the hands of Kitchener, the Sudan had become a breadbasket for North Africa, producing wheat and a seemingly endless supply of cotton for a needy Empire. Here the Nile looked verdant, especially after three hundred miles of barren desert. I'd fallen in love with the river once more, and with, I hoped, only a fortnight of walking to reach the Egyptian border, I was doubly excited.

Still sand-blasted and bedraggled, we followed the tracks into town. It was time for another snatch at civilisation before we followed the river onwards.

THE LAND OF GOLD

Nubia, Sudan, June 2014

'We Nubians love the river,' said Moez. 'We are not like those Bedouin. Nubians are the truest people of the Nile. Those Bedouin are Arabs, only ever at home in the desert.'

We made camp at the edge of the river, close to the village of Korti. Since Karima, we had followed the river on its curve south, past the ruins of the Ancient Nubian city of Napata and tonight we were to rest here too – for this was to be Will and Ash's last night.

We watched Awad and Ahmad tramp away, muttering darkly, with the camels. 'Leave them.' Moez grinned. 'Those Bedouin can't bear to be near the river at night. Do you know what a Bedouin hates worse than the thought of dying of thirst in the desert?' He shook his head, laughing. 'A mosquito. They can't bear the insects down by the water . . .'

In Korti, a local man had offered us the use of his house for the night – but, tonight, more than ever, we wanted to be close to the river. As we broke open ration packs and listened to the water's constant flow, the man reappeared out of the darkness, carrying in each arm string beds, a package of dates, fresh water and *chai*.

'If you dishonour me by not being my guests, you must, at least, have my beds!' he declared, before retreating into the night.

Will, Ash and I looked at each other, still bewildered. The strangest thing was, this wasn't even the most extreme hospitality we had seen since leaving the desert two days before. In one dusty little shanty, where we had stopped to buy soda and water the camels, a shopkeeper – within ten minutes of discovering I was English – had offered to give me some land, build me a house, and find me a wife. One man actually threatened to divorce his wife if we refused to stay for lunch, and I swear that a Sudanese host would rather die than drink before a guest. The fact that virtually every household sees it as their duty to provide a ceramic urn full of water for passing travellers is testament to the national pride in revering guests.

'Why do the people here treat foreigners so well?' I asked, turning to Moez.

'Oh,' he said, half dismissive, 'I'm sure it would be the same in your country.'

I wondered what the folk in my home town would do if a group of Sudanese came tramping down the street, and politely declined to answer.

In the morning, Will and Ash disappeared the same way they had come: in a cloud of dust and a taxi, taking them all the way back to Khartoum. It was bittersweet to see them go, but the river beckoned – and, with the Egyptian border only three weeks to our north, it did not seem so long until I would see them again.

After they had gone, we continued our trek along the bend in the Nile, walking through the date plantations and – after our sojourn in the desert – refusing to let the river out of sight. After another two days the Nile turned north again, plunging straight into the enormity of the Nubian desert, itself part of the Sahara. Two more, and we had reached the town of Dongola, the capital of Sudan's Northern State and the scene of one of Kitchener's most notable victories against the Mahdists in 1896.

North of Dongola, the Nile truly collided with the desert. Here, agriculture no longer flourished on its banks; sand dunes tumbled straight into the water, forming sheer cliffs of gold – a stark contrast to the glittering, clear blue waters. The Nile had a clarity here like never before: this was a scene straight out of *The Arabian Nights*, the crystal blue broken only by an occasional palm tree growing on the banks.

Two days north, Moez bent down and plucked something from the sand. When he handed it to me, I saw what looked like a long, twisted tube of rock.

'What is it?'

'Coral,' said Moez, smiling like a wise old professor. I recalled the various pieces of stone that had decorated his office back in Khartoum. 'Proof, Lev, that the Sahara was not always a sea of sand. What you're holding, there, is two hundred million years old.'

Further along the sandbank, Ahmad and Awad trailing behind with complete uninterest, Moez pointed out more of the stuff – some thin, some thick, some gnarled like the branches of a tree, some full of holes. In the middle of the coral field, he bent down again and picked something else up. Holding it at eye level, he asked, 'Well, Lev? What do you think this one is?'

Undoubtedly, it was a piece of wood; I could even see the grain and bark on the outside. Yet, when he put it into my hand, it was hot to the touch. I couldn't quite believe the sensation. Wood doesn't get that hot. What I was holding could only be stone.

'Petrified driftwood,' said Moez, rather too smugly. 'Once there was a sea here, and then there was forest . . .'

What we were walking through, I realised, was nothing less than the history of the world – not just the history of Sudan or its peoples, the Ancient Nubians, or even the prehistoric people who had come before. Everywhere we looked, there were reminders of how recent mankind's appearance on this planet has been – and of how the earth has been transformed and transformed again across its lifetime. The further north we went, the more artefacts we collected: more fragments of petrified wood and coral, small balls of lava that harked back to the region's violent, volcanic past. Between them – a jumble of different time periods, all thrown together – lay shards of pottery. 'Three thousand years old,' said Moez as he picked up, then flung away, a beautifully painted piece of Nubian art. 'Two thousand,' he said, kicking the remains of a bowl. '*Egyptian*,' he said, with mock disgust.

Then, he paused. 'Ah! *This* is more like it . . .' Bending over, he scooped up a rough square of pottery, black on one side and dyed red on the other. 'This is from the Deffufas at Kerma,' he said. 'Five thousand years old.'

Kerma was one of the earliest Sudanese states, emerging almost five thousand years ago. What Moez was holding was a fragment of that distant, unknowable past. The historian in me screamed out to touch it.

'This belongs in a museum,' I said, in disbelief.

But Moez simply tossed it back to the sand, where it lay among yet more piles of relics. 'There's loads of it!' He grinned. 'Tell the British Museum they can come and get some if they want it.'

A short walk upriver lay the site of the ancient city of Kerma itself, millennia older than Old Dongola. Surrounding the bare ruins lay petrified gazelle bones, Palaeolithic hand tools made from flint, and yet more mountains of pottery. Moez barely flinched as we passed it all. At last, north of the ruin, his eyes sought out an old camel track leading into the dunes, and he beckoned me to follow. There was new light in his eyes, giddy at being in tour-guide mode once again. 'Let me show you something, Lev. I haven't brought anyone here – only some scientists who came five years ago . . .'

Along the trail, the desert was pocked with large boulders. According to Moez, these rocks had once been underwater mountains, eroded over millions of years until they had gained the appearance of giant, polished marbles. Moez picked his way between the piles until, over the top of a procession of steep dunes, we stood in the shadow of one boulder as big as a car.

'Can you make it out?' he asked.

I stared at the sandstone but, at first, could see nothing. Then, gradually, it came alive. Lines scratched into the surface began to join together and, though I questioned my sanity, soon I began to pick out the giant picture of an elephant.

'But . . .'

'Wait,' said Moez. 'There's more.'

We walked a circuit through the boulder field. All around were more rock carvings: a lion, larger than life; an unmistakeable giraffe; horses, antelopes, and stick figures of men bearing spears.

'Six, maybe seven thousand years old,' said Moez.

Behind us had been proof that the Sahara Desert was once the bottom of an ocean. Now, all around us, was proof that it was once a vast, lush savannah, home to primitive man and big game. In the last few days, we seemed to have tramped from one aeon to the next, covering not only a hundred miles but a million years. We had watched the sea recede, the forests flourish, primitive man living in hunter-gatherer tribes, then civilisations – like the Ancient Nubians – rising and falling. All of it leaving its mark on the land.

'It's even more than that,' said Moez. 'Think about it, Lev. It's simple. All this – what would we call it, climate change? – is how civilisation started.'

'What do you mean?'

'Imagine when there were forests here, and savannah, and all these hunter tribes lived independently, foraging the land, just living for the day. Then imagine how the forests start to wither and the savannah dries up and, five thousand years ago, all of this turns into desert. The game dies away, or migrates, and the only place left for those tribesmen to go is to the big river they all know, the one that goes north. The Nile valley was the only place left with water, or any greenery at all . . .'

I began to understand what Moez was saying. 'So, suddenly, all those disparate tribes have to live in the same thin strip of land. They have to start relying on the same resources, coming into contact with each other daily. They have to start living in *communities*.'

'And stop fighting,' said Moez. 'And, after they've hunted all the big animals into local extinction, they have to start farming, too. Farming *together*. Which means the first villages grow up, and then the first towns and, eventually, cities themselves. That, Lev, is how Ancient Egypt was born – and it was the same down here, for the Nubians like me.'

For the longest time, we stayed staring at the etchings on the rock, before making the trudge back to the river. Where the sandstone cliffs tumbled into the water, Awad and Ahmad were waiting. Rolling their eyes at what they thought our indulgent foray into the desert, they reined the camels around and, again, we set off along the river.

'Mr Lev . . .' said Ahmad, with the air of a pirate, as we sat down to our lunch of fried goat's liver and refried beans. We were on the outskirts of a village called Sorry, named because the English governor who had once ruled here had barely understood Arabic – so, when passing travellers asked him for directions, it was all he could say. 'We would like to renegotiate our contract.'

My eyes flitted between Ahmad and Moez, who was doing his usual best at keeping a straight face while he translated this wily Bedouin's words.

'You see,' Ahmad went on, 'we are quite tired of riding now. We would like to go home.'

'Home?' I said. 'But there are more than four hundred kilometres until we reach Lake Nasser . . .'

Beside me, Moez coughed. 'Lake Nubia,' he corrected.

Four hundred kilometres north, the mighty Nile entered the third largest man-made lake in the world. Between 1958 and 1971, the Egyptian government had dedicated themselves to damming the River Nile at their southern city of Aswan – providing electricity for great swathes of North Africa, and creating an enormous reservoir in the process. The reservoir now straddles the border between Egypt and Sudan – called Nasser in the north, and Lake Nubia in the south. It was at the town of Wadi Halfa, sitting on the lake, that I planned to cross the border.

In English, so that they would not understand, I asked Moez, 'What do they want?'

'Money, of course. What else do these Arabs want?'

We had seen so much hospitality on the Sudanese part of our trek that, for a few weeks, I had forgotten the sullen malcontents who had sometimes accompanied me in Uganda and further south. Boston would not have been surprised by Awad and Ahmad's sudden request; I supposed I should not have been either.

'They've worked hard,' I said. 'They've been invaluable. Business is business. I respect that. Why don't you ask them what they want?'

Moez chattered with them in Arabic, his face growing more confused. When he was finally done, he reverted to English and said, 'It isn't money, Lev. It's Ramadan.'

'Ramadan?'

'Ramadan begins on the 28th June,' said Awad, as Moez translated. 'We want to be done by the 25th, so we can go to our families.'

'I have to tend my goats,' said Ahmad.

'And my wives will never let me hear the end of it if I don't get back.'

I didn't need to check my diary to know that 25 June was only ten days away. The spectre of Ramadan had been looming over me as well; I still didn't have the requisite permits to cross the border into Egypt, and if I turned up in Wadi Halfa at the start of the month of Ramadan, there was a big chance I'd have to wait until it was over.

'It's impossible,' I said to Moez. 'It's like doing a marathon, every day, for ten days straight – and in this temperature as well . . .' I did not like to say the other thing that would hinder us: the Sudanese had been so hospitable that we had already lost endless afternoons accepting water and *chai* and food from the overly friendly villagers we met – unable to refuse their overtures for fear of dishonouring them.

'I don't think we have a choice, Lev. These men are going home . . .'

We set off in earnest the next morning, pounding along the highway close to the river. The water was beautiful here. We'd reached the Nile's third cataract, the river pouring gloriously over boulders to form crests of perfect white. Sai Island sat in the rapids, with crocodiles basking on its banks – and, all along the riverbank, stood beautiful, colourful Nubian villages with their unique walled vaults, dome roofs and brightly painted gates: pink, green and blue formed a stark contrast to the yellow desert around.

Our task was simple but punishing: six kilometres an hour, eight hours a day, missing out only the sun's most vicious hours. The further north we came, the fewer habitations we passed. The land grew wilder, the cliffs increasingly jagged – every day, the same as the last. By the time we came within a hundred miles of Wadi Halfa, Moez began to know people in the few settlements on whose outskirts we camped. In Wadi Halfa itself, his brother Mazar waited for us, eagerly working on the papers that would get us over the border.

'Wait until you see it!' he kept exclaiming. 'Halfa is green and beautiful, and full of wonderful Nubians . . .'

Three days away from our destination, we left the river's immediate bank and joined the main highway, ten kilometres inland. In our dash to the border, we gazed on the great Nile from afar, its glistening waters obscured by a fringe of verdant palms.

On 24 June, we stopped to rest by the roadside. As the camel boys brewed *chai*, a lorry ground to a halt and a friendly face bawled out: 'What are you doing walking? Has your car broken down?' We had heard as much all day, everyone eager to stop and ferry us to the border – and everyone unable to comprehend that walking was what we'd set out to do. I was finding it hard to believe myself. My feet were swollen so badly that my boots barely fit, blisters were forming beneath my calloused skin, Moez was limping – and even Ahmad and Awad had begun to complain about saddle sores.

'There are still fifty kilometres to go,' I said, kneading my feet. 'What do you think?'

'They're going home tomorrow,' Moez replied, shrugging.

We forced ourselves on: ten kilometres, twenty, then thirty and more. By the time evening loomed, a great expanse of blue glimmered on the horizon. 'Lake Nasser,' I whispered – before quickly correcting myself: 'Lake *Nubia* . . .'

Just two miles distant lay Wadi Halfa. There has been a settlement at Wadi Halfa for millennia. Once an Egyptian outpost, and an important stop-off for armies heading into the Sudan, it is now the end of the railway from Khartoum, the gateway to Egypt. Before we had reached the outskirts of town, a crowd had gathered underneath the sign that welcomed visitors. A throng of men in military and police uniforms were waiting and, in the middle of them, the town governor, mayor and several journalists stood with none other than Moez's brother, Mazar, and their mother. It had been years since I had last seen Mazar. Between them, they held a hand-painted banner aloft. In block capitals, the banner proclaimed: 'WALKING THE NILE'.

Bewildered – and not a little numb from the pain still searing through my feet – we entered the crowd. In a second, Moez's mother had thrown her arms around him. Mazar reached out and pumped my hand, before embracing me himself.

'Well done!' he said with a dry smile. 'You dragged my brother home. He's usually too busy to come and visit . . .'

'We didn't get it, Lev. The authorities shut down on us.'

We had spent the night in Moez's family home, in the centre of the dusty town, with Awad and Ahmad camping outside with the camels. Now, we stood on the roadside, watching them disappear into the south – two old pirates who I'd miss enormously.

I turned to Mazar, who looked chagrined. 'What do you mean?'

'You don't have permission to walk over the border. They wouldn't agree to it. No foreigner's ever walked from Sudan into Egypt. It just isn't done. Not even the Sudanese do it. We're forbidden from doing anything more than taking the ferry from here, all the way up to Aswan.'

Aswan lay 375km across the border, at the very head of the lake, deep inside Egypt. The Wadi Halfa ferry famously carried passengers all the way, but that had never been my intent. I cursed, inwardly. There is nothing more problematic in Africa than a border crossing.

'Normally,' I said, 'I'd try and sneak across at night, or . . . pay somebody off. Only, I risked a sneaky crossing three years ago – when I was driving the ambulances to Malawi. I ended up in an Egyptian jail. They deported me after that.'

'Things are different in Egypt now, Lev. You do things by the book, or not at all.'

Mazar was right. Since the last time I had been to Egypt, the country had been transformed by the revolutions of 2011 and 2013, both of which had removed presidents from power. The nation I was about to enter was not one I knew, nor one I understood – not yet. The consequences of appearing to be a risk to national security by making an illegal border crossing didn't bear thinking about.

'What are the options?'

Moez said, 'It's Ramadan in two days . . . but there's a boat that leaves tomorrow afternoon. After that, nobody knows when the next one will go. There may not be another one until after Eid, and that's more than a month.'

'So it's take the ferry, or sit it out, and hope something changes . . .'

'You're welcome to stay, Lev.'

I knew I was; I had been welcome to stay in almost every village we had passed on the way north. But Egypt was right there, so close I could almost touch it – the final country on my way back home.

I wandered out into the dusty street, turning in the direction of the lake. The border was tantalisingly near. I wanted to put my feet on

Egyptian soil, wanted to know I was walking the final furlong, wanted to leave the contradictions of Sudan for something altogether different.

My mind was made up. If the ferry was the only way I could cross, I would take the ferry to Aswan, then find a way to negotiate the security pitfalls, backtrack to the border and continue the walk from there.

'Moez,' I said at last, 'I'm going to need a ticket for that ferry.'

THE MOTHER OF THE WORLD

Upper Egypt, July 2014

The ferry horn blared out across the water. From the gaggle of passengers on deck, I looked down and saw Moez disappearing off the gangplank, down into the tussling crowd on the dock. Soon, his *jellabiya* and turban had disappeared among a thousand others. I watched as his noble face and eagle nose turned with a smile, and knew he was happy to have completed his mission, to have shown the best of his land to a foreigner. As the ferry drew away, across the glittering water, this proud man – who it still seemed I had never truly got to know, even after two months' companionship – evaporated out of my life as quietly and mysteriously as he had entered it.

The ferry sailed north, across the waters of Lake Nubia. Then, without any declaration, we crossed the invisible line between Sudan and Egypt. The crystal waters underneath us had become Lake Nasser, and stretched north for more than five hundred kilometres. At their head sat the ancient city of Aswan, once a frontier post for Ancient Egypt, guardian to the southern kingdoms and inland Africa;

now, a modern metropolis guardian only to the High Dam. It was to be almost a day before we reached it – and every one of those hours was to be an ordeal.

The deck was baking beneath the sun, but the place was so packed that I had no hope of getting below, even if I had wanted to brave the passengers, packed in like cattle, who sweltered underneath. Shoved into a corner, next to a spit bucket, I shared the space with hundreds of *jellabiya*-wearing Sudanese who spread themselves across the deck like a carpet of flesh, moving only to pray or piss. Occasionally, people tried to pick their way to the communal cookhouse inside the belly of the boat – but I decided to avoid it at all costs; the stench was unbearable and the meals, served on metal trays, put me in mind of some prison cafeteria: endless beans and sickly *chai*.

For long hours, my entire being was focused on moving myself and my packs into the ever-shifting shade. Occasionally, I found myself by the balustrades and gazed out across the glistening waters of aquamarine. On both sides the desert rolled past, seemingly unchanged by the passing of the hours: red mountains to the right, rolling orange sands to the left – and, on the shore, an infinite number of bays, creeks and valleys. As I stared, through the shimmering heat haze, a new form of terror started to touch me – this was a desolate no-man's-land, famous only for being an area into which foreigners, and even most Egyptians, could not venture. For the first time, I was glad to be on this packed boat, this tiny piece of hell floating up the lake with the current. *I'm glad I'm not walking around this*, I thought, bitterly. *To hell with the rules of this broken expedition.*

Twenty-two hours later, Aswan came into view. On the banks of the lake stood military radio masts and radar domes, vast barracks and endless barbed wire fences. It all seemed an ominous welcome into my final country. Beyond stood the prized possession itself, the reason for all the protection: the Aswan High Dam, the biggest in the world. The sheer grey wall emerged out of the sparkling lake like an enormous sculpture, its very presence inspiring awe. Perhaps, I thought, there was something about Egypt that led Egyptians to build big – after all, it was the predecessors who had built the Great Pyramids, still hundreds of miles to my north.

Two miles wide and almost a mile thick, the Aswan High Dam represents the biggest man-made influence imposed on the Nile in all history. To many it is a symbol of man's dominance over nature – to others, like Moez, a mark of utter arrogance. To me it represented my final hurdle, and beyond it lay the final stretch of my journey.

I had lost a day to the lake and, as the ferry disgorged its manifold passengers, I fought my way through the throng to disembark.

No sooner had I begun to wend my way through the crowds on shore than two customs officials ordered me to one side. With my head hanging low, I followed them. I already knew how this was going to go. I'd been anticipating arriving in Egypt with utter relief, but I was under no illusion that this was going to be easy. Fifty years of dictatorship had turned this country into a virtual police state – and the two revolutions that had upturned the country in the last three years had only made matters worse. I had travelled in Egypt twice before, in the days before the revolutions, and even then I had spent a good deal of time either under arrest or being followed by the secret service.

'American?' demanded an official in a leather jacket and dark Ray-Bans.

'English,' I corrected him.

He simply sneered: 'This way.'

The soldier led me along a murky corridor of the customs building, away from the queues of Sudanese travellers. Inside a large side office, another man – this one in the uniform of a major – considered me from behind his dark sunglasses, smoking a cigarette. On his desk, amid haphazard piles of paper, stood an Egyptian flag. Behind him hung a stained photograph of the country's current ruler, President Sisi. A former military commander, Sisi had become president only a month earlier, while I was trekking through the deserts of Sudan. It had been Sisi who had announced the deposition of Egypt's former president, Mohammed Morsi, after the uprisings of 2013 – when millions of protestors took to the streets to demand that the increasingly authoritarian and Islamist government step down.

'Where have you come from?' asked the man behind the desk.

'Well, the ferry comes from Sudan . . .' I told him my story, presenting a copy of Sudan's *Tribune* newspaper, its front page showing Moez and myself on the long trek into Khartoum.

The major didn't look at all impressed. In one long drag, he finished his cigarette. 'Where is your permission?'

I had faced this question countless times before. In Uganda, I had fought it with officiousness of my own; in Sudan, with humility and respect. Here, I would have to play the hapless tourist if I wanted to find a way through.

Soon, more men were arriving – some border police in uniform, others agents with no uniforms at all. It began to feel as if they had scented blood – everybody wanted a piece of the action.

'Name!' barked the first.

'What is in this bag?' demanded the second.

'Destination!' declared a third.

The questions came thick and fast: first, my satellite phone singled me out as a spy; then, my cameras as a foreign provocateur. It was only as the major unearthed an envelope from my day pack that a distinct calmness settled over the room. There was no doubting the reason why: in that envelope was all the cash I had been given in exchange for the three camels in Wadi Halfa, the morning before I set off. I had been hoping to change it into Egyptian pounds in Aswan.

I saw the glint of greed in the major's eyes as he slid the envelope into his pocket. 'They're worthless here. You can't change them outside . . .'

One of the other soldiers, a weasely bald man, interjected: 'I'm afraid we'll have to confiscate all your machines as well. This camera, these medicines, this knife . . .'

My heart plummeted. I could understand their taking the machete – even though it galled me to lose the one piece of kit I'd relied on for so long in the jungle. But the prospect of losing all my photographs filled me with dread. As the man began collecting everything into a pile, I could see the greed in his eyes. These, my precious belongings, were going to make nice presents for his family.

I needed to change tack. My hapless-tourist act wasn't working.

'You're not taking them!' I stood up, slamming my passport in front of the major. 'You. *Sir.* What is your name?'

The major peered over his glasses, startled.

'What is your name?' I repeated, louder and with more force. 'I am here working directly for the Ministry of Tourism. I am a good friend of . . .' I racked my brain for a name, something Moez had told me about Aswan. The name I came up with was apparently the only person who could get me the permits to walk around Lake Nasser. '. . . General Mostafa Yousry! I am here writing a book for the good of the Egyptian people.'

Across the room, ten pairs of eyes stared at me. When none of them spoke, I continued my barrage.

'I want every one of your names! *Right now*.' Taking a pen out of my pocket, I helped myself to a piece of paper from the desk and shoved it in front of the major. 'If I'm not treated with some respect, I'll have the lot of you sacked. I've been sitting here being interrogated for two hours. I demand to be released.'

The bald man forced a grin. 'Sit down, friend. We are not interrogating you – we're just doing our jobs . . .'

He might have been grinning but, in his eyes, I could see disappointment. This man's bluff had been called, and he was backing down; now his family wouldn't get my cameras, memory cards and satellite phone after all.

'If what you're saying is true,' the major began, 'you'll be happy to show us your photographs.'

A sudden thought struck me: the camera the major was picking up was loaded with the pictures I'd taken of the Aswan High Dam as we came into port. Taking pictures of strategic assets was not a good idea in a country like Egypt. I reached out to snatch it back, my mind scrambling for something to say.

'Fine! You can see everything. I've nothing to hide. Let me show you . . .'

Quickly, I flicked through the pictures and opened them again at the start of the memory card. Here, rather than pictures of the Aswan High Dam, were endless images of camels, lizards and the sand dunes of the Nubian Desert. I was back to being a hapless tourist – if I couldn't fight my way out of this, I would have to bore them into letting me go.

'So this is Gordon,' I said. 'He's eight years old. You can tell by his teeth.' I held the picture still for a good ten seconds before clicking to the right. 'And this is a goose. You'll notice it's a male from its size, rather than the black colouring around the tops of the wings – which is actually identical in both sexes. Did you know they can fly over five thousand miles as part of their migration? And . . . you see the boulders in the desert? Formed from millions of years of freeze–thaw conditions that create an onion skin effect on the granite . . .'

I could see his eyes rolling back in his head.

'Okay, enough!' He forced a smile again. 'You may take your things.'

Careful not to show my relief, I packed up my bag and stormed out of the office. Outside, once I was clear of customs, I stopped to take breath. Aswan stretched out before me, my first stop on the final leg of this voyage. Before setting off, I checked my bag: camera, memory cards, satellite phone, all still intact. The only thing missing was the envelope of cash. That was still hidden in the major's back pocket.

You win some, you lose some, I thought, relieved to have finally broken through.

But this wasn't the last time I would get ripped off in Egypt – and five hundred Sudanese pounds was the least of it.

'For you, I'll do a special price,' said the man at the end of the telephone. 'Thirty-four thousand dollars.'

My jaw hit the ground.

The man on the line was called Tarek El-Mahdy. I'd been put in touch with him by Moez, and his words came back to me now: 'He's probably one of the few men in that country you can trust. But that said, he's Egyptian, Lev – he'll want cash, and lots of it.'

With over three million kilometres of off-road travel under his belt, Tarek was the go-to man in Egypt. He ran a tourism outfit called Dabuka, taking wealthy clients on 4×4 safaris into the desert. Many of his punters were rich Americans and Princes from the Gulf, and he knew how to get things done. What I needed were the security clearances to leave Aswan and all the support the security would need, transport, food and safe accomodation, to continue the expedition – and it seemed they didn't come cheap.

'Anything is possible,' he said in broken English, 'but it takes money. And it'll take at least twenty-one days to get the necessary permissions. Whatever you do, Lev, don't try and leave Aswan. Believe me when I tell you – you are under house arrest. Well, I mean, *hotel* arrest . . .' He laughed at his own joke.

After escaping the border police, I had checked into the Mövenpick Hotel on Elephantine Island, a small island in the middle of the Nile, so named because of the elephantine boulders that form its banks – and because, long ago, it used to be an ivory trading station. The hotel looked like an airport control tower, a hideous incursion into the otherwise spectacular setting. I had been here for less than two days, but already I could feel the eyes of the Egyptian authorities on me. As I took a felucca across the river, I'd noticed I was being followed – and, as I checked in, the same man sat in the hotel lobby, pretending to read a newspaper as he kept his eyes on me. The next day, when I tried to leave the hotel, the manager himself asked me to join him for lunch. It was an odd request, but it wasn't until he began a barrage of probing questions over the first course that I realised he was, in fact, a government agent, tasked to write a report on my movements. What Tarek was saying made me anxious: the prospect of not moving for three weeks made me want to be sick. This was the last place I wanted to be stuck.

'How do you get to thirty-four thousand?' I asked.

'Well, you'll need an escort and a guide. Turbo will be perfect for that.'

'Who's Turbo?'

'He's a great desert guide and driver. You'll love him. He's brilliant with cars.'

He bloody better be for that price, I thought.

'Then there's all your food and water. No alcoholic drinks included! And the vehicle. You'll need a support vehicle, plus fuel, taxes – and, of course, money.'

'Fine, I get that but I've never had a support vehicle before. I've never had a driver . . .'

'Well, this is Egypt. You must do things the official way.'

'But thirty-four thousand . . .'

He cut me off. 'Well, it's up to you. No negotiation. I'm half-German, not some trinket seller in the market. You can stay in Aswan if you like, but I can guarantee you'll never leave.'

He was right, of course. Since the last revolution, which saw another general take charge, Egypt had grown bored of its brief democracy and reverted to being a police state, only this one seemed more controlling, even more paranoid, than the last. Tourists, Moez had told me, are officially not allowed to wander outside of certain 'permitted zones' – those being Aswan, Luxor, Cairo, Alexandria, and the Red Sea resorts. No independent travel was allowed outside those areas without special permission and a security escort.

I listened intently to this mystery fixer on the end of the phone. I had battled my way through many things on this expedition, but agreeing to this – all because of Egypt's totalitarian regime – was not what I'd expected.

Wearily, I mumbled my assent and hung up. That sort of money would not only break the bank, but it would max out my credit, bring a tear to the eye of my sponsors and bring into question the entire ethics of the expedition. But if I didn't pay then the past seven months of walking, and several years of planning, would be a complete waste of time. There'd be no film, no book, and no money to give to the charities I'd wanted to support. In effect, it was pay or give up.

The next day, I decided to upgrade to the Old Cataract Hotel. If I was going to spend three weeks under virtual house arrest, it may as well be somewhere nice.

Three weeks later, I was going stir crazy.

I'd been trying to stay sane by sessions in the gym, swimming in the pool, and keeping abreast of the ever-changing political upheavals in the country I was now in. Now I sat on the terrace at the Old Cataract Hotel: waiting, just waiting. I hadn't heard anything from Tarik, or Turbo, in more than a week, and I was beginning to wonder where all of my money had gone. Waiters in quaint black waistcoats and red fezzes scuttled along the opulent corridors and, outside, the fierce sun scorched the banks of the Nile. The hotel pool was still and the sun loungers glistened, unused. On the terrace, breakfast tables sat empty – yet all the places had been laid, in the vain hope that somebody would take a seat. Hamed, the chef, appeared forlornly out of the kitchen to see if there was anyone to cook for.

'Mr Wood,' he said with a forged smile. 'Just you again?'

'Just me, I'm afraid.'

It had been the same ever since I'd arrived. The tourists didn't come to Egypt any more. Egypt has had a history of violence against tourists before, mostly perpetrated by Islamic fundamentalists – during the 1990s, a spate of attacks saw trains blown up, foreigners kidnapped and shot, all culminating in the 1997 Luxor Massacre, in which fifty-seven German and Japanese tourists were disembowelled on the steps of the Hatshepsut Temple of the Valley of the Kings – but, until recently, things had been good. Aswan and Luxor were money-making machines. Feluccas and cruise ships filled every inch of the Egyptian Nile. It was the Arab Spring that had changed all that. In March 2011, the Egyptians took to the streets and forced President Mubarak into leaving office. Chaos reigned supreme, even despite Egypt having its first-ever democratic elections. Somehow, the Muslim Brotherhood – an organisation founded to resist British colonialism, and given to fundamentalism – came to power with the clumsy Mohammed Morsi at its head. Tourists stayed away and, for two years, there were shifts in power, political defections and more protests. In 2013, a second revolution occurred. Some prefer to call it a coup, as the former army commander Abdel Fattah el-Sisi ousted Morsi in what was effectively a military overthrow of an elected government. But the arrival of Sisi and the arrest of anyone with Muslim Brotherhood credentials had done little to instil confidence in the beleaguered tourist industry. Just four years ago, there had been hundreds of boats serving tourists out on the Nile, but now they were all mothballed, moored up, four or five abreast, on the banks of the river with only skeleton crews to keep them afloat. Shops were boarded up or left empty; now nobody sold trinkets and you'd struggle to find a plastic pyramid even if you wanted one. Tour guides fluent in ten languages were sweeping the streets or driving taxis, or otherwise sat idle in the coffee shops lamenting the good old days. As far as I could tell, all of them seemed to regret the revolution – the first one, at least – and blamed it on the ignorance of youth.

I came to from my daydream to see a man standing in the hotel lobby, dressed in a pair of surfer's shorts, a trendy T-shirt and flip-flops.

'Mahmoud Ezzeldin at your service!' he declared. Then, when I only looked at him oddly, he said, 'Mr Wood? It is me – Turbo!'

I rubbed my eyes. The man I'd been waiting for, all this time, was the most unlikely Egyptian I'd ever encountered. Thirty years old, with fiery red hair and a hybrid American-English accent, he looked more like a tourist than I did.

'We're set,' he announced, striding over to grasp my hand. 'Everything's in order, chap. You ready to rock Lake Nasser?'

The truth was I wasn't at all. Perhaps it was the three weeks of enforced indolence, or perhaps it was the memory of how bleak and inhospitable it had looked from the deck of the ferry, but I'd almost hoped I wouldn't get permission to walk around the lake and could just continue my journey north from Aswan. The last place I wanted to go, after Sudan, was back into the desert – and backwards, at that. But it seemed Turbo, and his boss Tarik, had secured permission.

'Thirty-four grand didn't go to waste, then?'

Turbo smiled. 'Nope! It's all good.' I knew what that smile meant: it had taken every penny to pay my minders, guides and expenses; and he had had to move heaven and earth to get the police, army, security service, Ministries of Information, Tourism, Antiquities and Borders on side. Wearily, I stood up.

'That's the spirit, Mr Wood. We leave this afternoon!'

It took four hours, rattling along the lonely desert highway in a 4×4, to reach the border, stopping only to present our papers to bewildered policemen at isolated checkpoints. As we followed the lake's western bank, the bleak desert stretching out on our right, I decided it was time to get to know Turbo. Once this journey began there were still a thousand miles between me and the delta, and I didn't want to walk them in silence.

'I have to ask. Why do they call you Turbo?'

'I like cars,' he said, plainly. 'Especially classic cars. I organise rallies in the desert and meetings for classic car owners. Oh,' he added, 'and people think I'm a bit hyperactive.'

Whoever those people were, they weren't wrong. We drove on, Turbo bouncing behind the wheel – and I found my mind straying. Was Turbo a government agent, reporting on me like the hotel manager had done? There was only one way to find out. I decided to ask.

'Me?' he balked. 'An agent of this corrupt, Third World government? You must be joking! I can't stand them. Police, army, politicians – it's one big racket here. No, Mr Wood, I'm a Bedouin. We don't do *jobs*.' He flashed me a smile. 'What, never seen a ginger Bedouin before? I was an architect for a while, but I couldn't stand the thought of sitting in offices or wearing a hard hat. I'd much rather be out in the desert. Look . . .' And here he slowed the car to a crawl, the blue waters glittering outside. 'I know you don't want me tagging along, but it's the only way, trust me. Nobody has ever walked around Lake Nasser – foreigner or Egyptian. You should feel privileged. You can't imagine the bullshit I've had to go through to get the permission. You see, these government officials are so stupid, they don't realise how ridiculous it is to prevent tourists exploring. Anyway, you'll barely see me. I'll keep a good distance and just meet you at a prearranged rendezvous where we can camp . . .'

'You mean – you're not walking?'

'*Walking*?' Turbo laughed. 'Why walk when I have a car? I'll go on ahead, warn you about police checkpoints, book you into guesthouses. I'll carry the supplies. I even have a cool box for soft drinks. Feel, there, under your seat . . .'

I reached down, and produced an ice cold can of soda, sparkling with frost.

'It doesn't feel . . . right,' I admitted. 'It isn't in the spirit of the expedition.'

'These government officials don't care about that! And it won't only be me, Lev. There'll be police escorts, when the police can be bothered. I'll have to taxi a soldier or two. Look, don't sweat it, because you don't have a choice. And, besides, how is it any different from using a troop of poor camels to carry your gear?'

I was stumped for an answer. I supposed it wasn't.

'I'll never be more than a few miles away,' Turbo said. 'That is, unless you want me to roll alongside you, as you walk?'

'I think I'll manage.'

'Then it's settled!' Turbo beamed, and brought the car to a halt.

We had reached the Sudanese border, directly opposite the shore where Wadi Halfa sat. As I climbed out, into the implacable sun, I muttered, 'It all seems rather ridiculous, Turbo.'

Already, he was swinging the car around to go back the way we had come. 'Welcome to Egypt,' he said drily, and disappeared into the north.

It was to take a week to reach the northernmost point of the lake and return to Aswan. On the first day, I passed the famed temples of Abu Simbel. Devoid of a single tourist, they looked all the more glorious, the great stone faces of ancient pharaohs gazing out over water and sand. Over three thousand years ago, the temples had been hewn from a mountainside by Pharaoh Ramesses II as a lasting monument to his Queen Nefertari – but, like everything in Egypt, they had been victims of the will of the government and the damming of the river. When the Aswan High Dam was built, submerging the desert to create the great lake – and driving tens of thousands of Nubians out of their homeland – the temples had been painstakingly moved to where they now stood, watching me tramp silently by.

Occasionally, I could see the tracks of cars out in the desert, the only sign that the shoreline wasn't entirely uninhabited – but, as I navigated the cliffs, beaches and bays of the lake, I began to see a profusion of other life that was entirely unexpected. Fifty years ago, when this land was plundered to make the great lake, all kinds of life had been wiped out – but, across the generations, it had slowly returned. The Nubians might never come back to this part of their homeland, but trees and bushes had sprung from the desert beaches, small forests had grown up, and at night I could hear the scuttling of rattlesnakes and vipers, the rustling of rats and foxes. When I woke the first morning, to the glistening splendour of the lake and the pink hue of the desert, I could see the tracks of wolves who had come padding through my camp as I slept.

'There's talk of hyena, too,' said Turbo, shaking his head. Lake Nasser was to be the only part of my Egyptian odyssey where the authorities would allow me to camp, and Turbo had joined me – only, like the Bedouin in Sudan, he refused to sleep too close to the water. 'Because of the crocodiles,' he said. 'Big bastards. And scorpions. It's the little ones you have to watch for. The small yellow fuckers can really ruin your day.'

'That's why the government doesn't let tourists down here, is it? Because of the wildlife?'

'Ha! The *real* reason the government doesn't want people down here is because of the smuggling.'

'Smuggling?'

'It's prime smuggling territory, coming over the border from Sudan.'

'So, people don't come here because the smugglers are dangerous?'

'You've got it wrong, Lev. The government doesn't *want* the smuggling to stop. It's worth too much money to not let it happen. Look around you – all of this could be prime farmland. Instead, it's wasted, so that the smugglers can bring in camels, guns and drugs from Africa . . .'

'What do you mean, Africa? We're *in* Africa . . .'

'No, I mean *Africa* – the Africa over there. Egypt isn't really Africa. We're almost civilised here – not quite, but almost.' He paused, changed tack. 'Did you see the car tracks out in the desert?'

I remembered seeing them in the sand north of Abu Simbel.

'That's the smugglers,' Turbo confirmed. 'Usually Bedouin. Tribesmen from the Sinai or the coast, they do deals with their mates in Sudan and bring all sorts of shit this way. All the guns in Palestine, where do you think they come from? Hashish – yep, that too. And gold – there's plenty of that in Sudan. Antiques from Kush, diamonds from South Africa.' He paused. Where once he had been enjoying telling his tale, now he seemed solemn. 'Those smugglers don't mess around. If they see anyone, they'll kill them, throw the body to the crocodiles and change the plates on their car. They can't afford to stop the supply route, so if you see anyone in a 4×4 that's not mine . . . well, hide.'

At that moment, Turbo stood up, poured the dregs of his morning coffee into the sand, and moved towards the car. Climbing back in, he waved goodbye, choked up the engine, and left me in a cloud of sand and dust.

Throughout the next days, I took Turbo's advice, keeping to the creeks and gullies, out of sight and out of mind. The walking was hard but it was much cooler here, and at least I was close to the water so – unlike in the Bayuda – I'd never run out. Sometimes I saw more car tracks in the sand, but for several days the only people I saw were illegal fishermen across the water, or the distant glow of a campfire at night. Turbo was never far away, and always on the end of the satellite phone, but this was the first time in the trek I'd felt truly alone: no Boston, nor Moez, nor any porters constantly chirping in my ear.

On the fifth day, mindful of Turbo's advice, I crested a sand dune and, for the first time since setting out, the stark landscape was broken by human habitation. About a mile away, at the bottom of a valley, completely isolated from the main body of the lake and accessible only by a small channel, sat what looked like a farm. Even at this distance I could see the glint of a tin roof, and the shapes of disused tractors rotting in the scrub.

For a long time, I stopped and stared. There was no way around the valley, not without making a twenty-mile detour to circumnavigate the channel. I was not sure my legs or feet could take that – but, more importantly, I was not sure the permissions allowed it. I dreaded to think what it might mean if my government overseers discovered I had gone off-piste.

But, all the while, Turbo's words were in the back of my head: *This is a place for smugglers, Lev. If they see you, they'll kill you. The supply lanes are too important.*

I proceeded carefully, keeping low amongst the boulders on the banks of the lake, and following natural *wadis* – dry, ancient riverbeds – to get as close to the farm as I could without being seen. With the sun beating down, I stopped to catch my breath where a fishing boat was tied up among the reeds. In its meagre shelter, a thought hit me: perhaps I could steal the boat and avoid the house completely, by rowing through the lake until the coast was clear? For a moment the temptation was too much – but then I imagined being caught in the act, and consequences that didn't bear thinking about. No – I would have to do as I'd done so many times before: put my life in the hands of a complete stranger.

The farmhouse sat on the other side of the channel. Cautiously, I waded through the water, my boots sinking deep into the mud as I cast stones into the deeper parts to scare away whatever crocodiles lurked there. On the far bank, a few camels grazed, unperturbed by the stranger clambering out of the creek, and fish plopped around in the shadows.

No sooner had I set foot on the bank than there was sudden movement up ahead: the unmistakeable noise of a human being treading on gravel. I took one step, one step more – and there, between the parting bushes, stood a man in a white vest, a shotgun in the crook of his arm.

I froze. The man stared at me. In that moment, I imagined a hundred different possibilities – but all of them boiled down to this: I was a trespasser, a stranger in a strange land, hundreds of miles from the nearest village, staring down the barrel of a gun.

A voice flurried up, somewhere beyond the gunman. 'Lev!'

At first, I hardly recognised my own name. Then, as the man stepped aside, all my terror evaporated. Behind the man stood Turbo, waving cheerily.

'Where have you been?' he asked. 'I thought you'd have reached here hours ago . . .'

Turbo was standing outside the tiny farmhouse, happily drinking a glass of *chai*. Deeply relieved, I pushed through the reeds and clasped the eccentric red-head by the hand.

'This is my friend, Osama,' he said, patting the gun-toting man cheerily on the back.

'Like *Bin Laden*!' he said with a wicked grin and a wink.

I didn't know what to say.

'Don't worry,' said Turbo, 'he's harmless. He's just a local hunter.'

'I grow crops out here, do some fishing,' the man named Osama explained, as he offered me *chai*, his gun now over his shoulder. 'Sometimes I shoot crocodiles, too,' he added, as nonchalantly as if he was talking about his morning commute.

'For fun?'

'No,' Osama replied. 'For handbags. And because one ate my father's leg.' He pointed to the side wall of the shack, against which was propped an enormous skin, hardened by salt. Next to it was a massive skull, shiny and white, bleached by the sun. 'Would you like to see my pigeons?' he asked, with the enthusiasm of a child wanting to show off his new toy.

I looked sidelong at Turbo, who only shrugged. 'Sure,' I said.

Inside the house, a stark room containing only a bed and a single chair, was a single bookshelf – on which a family of pigeons had nested. 'Baby pigeons!' Osama announced. 'Nobody gets to see baby pigeons . . .'

'Is he mad?' I whispered at Turbo.

'Not really,' said Turbo. 'He just likes the solitude. But he won't get it tonight.'

'Why not?'

'This, Lev . . . this is your guesthouse!'

'Sorry there are no spare rooms,' said Osama, seemingly coming back to life. 'You'll have to sleep on the trailer.'

Outside, a flat-topped wooden cart sat under a tree. 'It's okay,' I said, not wishing to offend the madman's hospitality. 'I don't mind sleeping on the floor . . .'

Osama only gave one of his cryptic smiles. 'You don't want to do that.'

'Why not?'

Quickly, he snatched up a stick from his veranda and hooked up a shirt left drying on one of the boulders just outside. Something fell from the collar onto the sand – and, with the speed of an Olympic javelin, Osama speared a rogue scorpion right through its back. As he held up the gruesome creature, it wriggled in the throes of death. With his forefinger and thumb, he pulled off the tail and threw it into the bushes.

'Too many monsters.' He grinned and walked away, presumably to feed his pigeons the remains.

It was the end of the month of Ramadan, and the feast of Eid Al-Fitr was upon the town of Kom Ombo.

Two days after a fitful night at Osama's farm, we had reached Aswan – but I had already had my fill of the city and didn't plan on staying long. Lingering only to ditch all my camping gear and all my other redundant pieces of kit, I crammed everything into an old British Army issue desert satchel and set off. I was about to embark on a different kind of journey. The path from Aswan to Alexandria would be a thousand miles of roads, towns and cities; it was no longer snakes and scorpions I'd have to watch out for – it was internal politics and secret police.

By the end of the second day, I had come fifty kilometres along the river, to find that Turbo had already booked me into a guesthouse at the town of Kom Ombo. Famous for its great temple, dedicated to the crocodile god Sobek – protector of ancient men from the powers of the Nile – Kom Ombo was originally the ancient city of Nubt, a 'City of Gold', and it was as a centre of trade into Nubia that it had originally made its name.

In the morning, I woke to find Turbo standing over my bed. A squint at the clock on the wall told me it was not yet 5am, and outside Kom Ombo was still smothered in darkness. Usually, we tried to be on the road by 7, but today was special. It was formally the end of the month when Muslims around the world fasted. Turbo was bouncing energetically from wall to wall. It was time, he told me, for us to eat.

Blearily, I got out of bed. Naturally, I hadn't been fasting throughout Ramadan – and neither had Turbo. It wasn't until this very moment that I'd even considered he might have been Muslim, let alone one who prayed.

'It doesn't apply if you're *ala safar* – a traveller,' he said smiling.

The police escorts who had trailed us up the road from Aswan had taken advantage of this particular loophole too – sneaking a crafty cigarette or sweet *chai* whenever they could. I supposed Turbo was not so different from those Christians back home who only went to Church for weddings and Christmas – all he wanted to do was make an effort.

'Come on,' he said, 'let's go and join in morning prayers . . .'

How could I resist?

In Kom Ombo, the local sheikh welcomed us warmly as we followed crowds of men into the open courtyard of the town mosque. About half the men wore traditional *jellabiyas*, and the other half Western dress – just jeans and T-shirts. Turbo was very much in the latter camp. Around us were young men and old men, many proudly wearing a dark bruise on their foreheads from striking their heads on the floor of the mosque during prayer. 'It's called the *alamit el salah*,' Turbo whispered. 'The mark of prayer. Or, if you prefer it, a *raisin* . . .'

By the mixture of dresses, beards and raisins, there seemed to be a widespread representation of the Islamic faith here: the devout, strict adherents, as well as the more casual, pragmatic types like Turbo. Among the men, I saw several Salafists – these men, in strict traditional dress, were standing together, but somehow apart from the rest.

'They follow the *wahhabi* doctrine,' explained Turbo. 'It comes from Saudi Arabia. There never used to be any here. My mum used to say that, in the '60s and '70s, no women ever wore the veil – and anyone with a beard would have been considered barmy. But it's different now. Lots of poor Egyptians went to find work in Saudi when I was a kid, back in the '80s and '90s. When they came back, they looked like relics from the Middle Ages. That's what Salafism is – they think the oldest form of Islam must be the purest. Now all the women look like . . . bloody ninjas.'

I looked at the men he was pointing out. You could spot the Salafists by their long black beards and the absence of a moustache.

'They look like Abraham Lincoln.' Turbo chuckled. 'Look, you hang out over there, at the back. It's about to begin . . .'

At Turbo's instruction, I retreated to the back of the mosque, while he took up a spot on the front line. By the time all the men had entered, the mosque was crammed with two hundred devotees. Most had brought their own personal prayer mats, and they congregated in straight lines ten deep. At the front of the room, the Imam began the prayers – or *salat* – with a rhythmic recital of the *raka'ah*, in which the worshippers joined together in saying the *Takbir*. 'Allahu Akbar!' they cried. *God is Great!* As one, the crowd bent down on their hands and knees and fell to the floor, first kneeling and then pressing their foreheads to the ground. Even the old men seemed flexible enough to perform the operation with grace. The whole process was repeated countless times, interspersed with chanting from the Imam and repetitions from the congregation. It was such a mesmerising scene that I quickly lost track of time. In that moment, I deeply admired and respected the sense of purpose and community that Islam creates. Even Turbo – or, rather, Mahmoud – who was as Western a man as you could meet, seemed utterly devoted for this one moment in time.

The final prayer was uttered and the roar of 'Amen!' flooded across the courtyard. Everywhere, faces broke into smiles – and I could sense the eagerness with which everyone was looking forward to breaking the fast. Turbo turned to me, and slowly he opened his mouth to call me near.

Then all hell broke loose.

In a second, everything changed. No sooner had the last 'Amen' faded away, than two armed policemen thundered through the gates, thrusting anyone who stood in their way to one side. From the back of the mosque, I started; the policemen were heading directly for Turbo. I cried out to warn him – but, too late, they barrelled him aside, grabbing the man who had been standing behind him. Turbo twirled around, bewildered, while cries of protest went up across the mosque. The second cop desperately tried to pacify the baying crowd while the first dragged the arrested man towards the gates. On my tiptoes, I tried to see what was going on – but all I could see was Turbo waving his arms.

'Lev, let's get out of here!' he screamed. 'Fast!'

I didn't need to be told twice. Shouldering my way through the protestors, I reached Turbo in the middle of the throng. 'What's happening?'

'Muslim Brotherhood,' he whispered. 'Quick, before the mob turns on us . . .'

'Why would the mob . . .?'

But, before I could finish my question, Turbo had already dragged me to the gate.

Outside, he turned to me and asked, 'That man – did you see him?'

'Not really. I just saw the police grab him. Who was he?'

Turbo shook his head as we hurried away from the gates. 'Well, I was a bit suspicious. He had a black bag. Nobody brings a bag to the mosque.'

'What was in it?'

'I don't know. Perhaps it was a bomb, or some guns. He must have been Muslim Brotherhood, Lev. Some of the other people were saying they didn't know who he was, that he wasn't from here . . .'

By now, more and more men were pouring into the mosque to find out what the commotion was. Turbo and I raced the other way, stopping only when we were clear of the place and hiding behind a house.

'What were the crowd saying?' I asked.

'It was mixed – that's why it was so dangerous. Some of them were with the police, telling them to round up more Brotherhood supporters, grassing up their neighbours . . . but some of them were actually on his side, trying to drive the police away.'

'Why would they do that?' I asked, confused.

'There's still a lot of support for the Brotherhood. Don't forget, after the first revolution, in 2011, Egypt basically elected the Brotherhood to government. Morsi was one of their key leaders. So there are plenty of people who sympathise – people you wouldn't expect it from either. School teachers, farmers, taxi drivers – I know plenty of people who voted for Morsi. They're normal people, but there's such a divide in this country, it runs through every village.' Turbo paused, if only to catch his breath. 'It's lucky we escaped, Lev. Some of the men in the crowd were blaming us. They thought we're the reason the police were there.'

'But . . . why?'

'Well, the police have been following us since Aswan, right? They thought we'd led them to the mosque. They were going to lynch us.'

'Wouldn't the police have stopped that?'

But Turbo only laughed. 'What power do you think the police have here? That's why they waited until the end of prayers – they just wanted to do a quick smash-and-grab. Lev, the one thing you need to know about Egypt, the one thing we learned from the revolutions, is . . . it doesn't take long for things to get out of hand here. Every man has a gun hidden away in his home. Honour killings, revenge killings, tribal violence – if you so much as look at their wives, some of these men will disembowel you. The police rarely interfere. There are whole districts they don't dare enter.'

'A bit like London, then,' I said – but underneath, I wasn't in a jocular mood. We'd only just begun this journey into upper Egypt's rural heart, and already I was discovering the dark side of this blighted country.

THE LONG ROAD HOME

Lower Egypt, August 2014

'Won't they ever go away?' I asked.

'Never.' Turbo grinned, rolling in the car alongside me. 'Do you still need to ask?'

We'd been on the road for a week since Kom Ombo, and were finally nearing the city of Luxor. Wearily, I looked over my shoulder – and, sure enough, Turbo's wasn't the only car tracking me. A jeep packed full of uniformed police officers was trundling just behind, at barely three miles an hour. As they'd done every step of the way, the coppers looked on in utter disbelief. 'Are you sure you won't jump in?' one of them crowed, for what must have been the tenth time today. 'Much quicker this way!'

From a different window, another chirped in, 'We tell nobody . . . Don't worry!'

'Ever get tempted?' asked Turbo.

I tried to shut out the policemen's guffaws. The truth was, I'd been tempted on more than one occasion – especially on these long stretches of agricultural road, which seemed to be communal dumping grounds for all kinds of dead animals. Yesterday, the stench of death had been unbearable as I'd slowly walked past the carcasses of rotting camels, buffalo, donkeys, dogs and cats. Flies had swarmed me – the only pedestrian for dozens of miles – and, just when I thought I was out of range, another mountain of carcasses would appear and I'd begin the rigmarole all over again. The police didn't seem to care; they simply wound up their windows, turned on their air-conditioning and shook their heads – not at the carcasses, but at my stupidity for walking among them.

'Not far now,' said Turbo.

I wanted to make Luxor by nightfall, because, if I didn't, I'd have to jump in the car with Turbo and drive back to whichever the last small town was and book into a guesthouse there. My journey through Egypt had begun at the centre of a labyrinth of bureaucracy, and from there it had only got worse. According to the rules imposed by the Egyptian authorities, I was not allowed to camp beyond the shores of Lake Nasser – so I was always ferried backward or forward, to a town where the police could put me under a twenty-four-hour guard. Sometimes we'd sleep on an empty Nile cruiser, watched over by the maritime police who'd circle my watery abode in a blow-up dinghy like an episode from some abysmal spy movie. I had to walk to a prearranged schedule, and never deviate from the route Turbo had submitted back in Aswan. The expedition had become a circus act, a kind of Orwellian charade, and I was the dancing monkey, performing for the pleasure of the Egyptian Ministry of Tourism. Every time we entered a new governorate, I'd have to go through the same theatrics of drinking tea with the governor and being presented with a plastic plaque in front of a government-approved journalist. My every move was being watched, my every word recorded, my every action noted.

*

It was with the police crowing in my ear, and in a constant mood of paranoia, that I arrived in Luxor. Modern Luxor has grown up on the site of the ancient city of Thebes, and its ruined temples, monuments and tombs once drew hordes of tourists from all over the world – but, as I woke on my first morning in the government-approved hotel, the city seemed eerily still: like everywhere in Egypt, there was barely a tourist in sight.

In the morning, Turbo and I crossed the town to the deserted Temple of Luxor. The Nile runs directly alongside the ruins, and was key to its creation – the Ancient Egyptians brought its massive stones downriver by barge from the quarry at Aswan – and to walk along the banks of the modern corniche is to live and breathe the historical wonder that this outdoor museum evokes. Our footsteps echoed spookily as we came into the temple's main chamber, watched from on high by the faces of gods and a colossus depicting Thebes' ancient ruler, Ramesses II. The temples at Luxor had been built as long ago as 1400BC, and slowly excavated across the 19th and 20th centuries. At some time in their history, these vaults had been places of worship for Ancient Egyptians, a centre of the Greek administration and a fortress for the Roman legionnaires that manned this southerly outpost; now they were as hollow and untouched as in the days before they were rediscovered.

'Here he is,' said Turbo. 'Ibrahim?'

There was only one other man at the temple. Ibrahim was a tour guide from Cairo, who now had to travel far and wide to find any business at all. An ebullient, round-faced man in his mid-thirties, with thick-rimmed glasses and a slightly balding head, he'd agreed to show me around the temples while Turbo, who'd seen it all before, lounged by the riverside.

Ibrahim was a member of the Egyptian minority: a Coptic Christian.

Meeting him here was a stark reminder that Egypt was not entirely an Islamic country – and never had been. According to Biblical tradition, it was into Egypt that Joseph and Mary had fled with the baby Jesus, after King Herod had commanded the death of all first-born male infants. By the middle of the 1st century, the Coptic Orthodox Church had been born. For six centuries, Christianity prospered here – and it wasn't until the Islamic conquest of Egypt, beginning in 639AD, that the faith had been forced into the country's borderlands. Ever since, Christians have been persecuted, taxed more heavily to undermine the Church's foundations, and generally driven underground. Nowadays, only ten per cent of people belong to the Coptic Church – but, in a country as big as Egypt, that's still a sizeable population.

'Mr Wood,' Ibrahim said, as we walked through the inner chamber. 'What do you think?'

'I think I may be the luckiest person on Earth. Who else gets to see the Temple of Luxor without a hundred other people bustling around?'

For a fleeting moment, Ibrahim was visibly upset. 'What's lucky for you is not lucky for us. It wasn't like this in the good old days. Mubarak was a good man . . .' His voice had faded to a whisper. 'Look at this,' he said, pointing at one of the intricately decorated inner walls. 'It breaks the heart to see what some of these Muslims have done to the temple. They did this last year, when that clown Morsi came to power . . .'

I followed Ibrahim's gaze. Four-thousand-year-old hieroglyphs adorned the walls, but across the top of them somebody had scrawled writing in Arabic – graffiti left by the mob when the revolution had spiralled out of control.

I looked around the hall. Some of the statues had been disfigured, decapitated or worse. 'Was that the Muslim protestors, too?'

'Well,' Ibrahim admitted, 'that was actually Christians. But it was 1500 years ago – they didn't know any better. Today people have the internet, they have education – but they still use religion as a justification to deface our history.'

Ibrahim seemed to be typical of the tour guides of Egypt – he spoke a plethora of languages, held a master's degree in ancient history, was married to a European woman, and generally hated the anarchy that had resulted from the so-called 'Arab Spring'. 'At least we had stability in those days. Everybody had a job, the money was amazing . . . but now look! We had almost two years of mob rule. I only hope this latest guy can bring back order.'

'Sisi?'

'He has such a tough road ahead of him . . .' Against his will, Ibrahim had started to shed tears. Beneath the colossus, he stopped to dry his eyes. 'At least he's clamping down on the Brotherhood. He's arrested most of them and threatened them with the death sentence. It's the only justice these killers will understand.'

I remembered vividly the policemen rampaging into the mosque to drag away the member of the Brotherhood. Ibrahim's was a view held by many – but there were still plenty of fanatics. However the fissures had formed in Egyptian society, it seemed clear that they were not ones that could be easily healed.

We walked on. As he regained his composure, Ibrahim pointed out yet more graffiti – this time from Ancient Greeks, Arab invaders, Italian and French explorers, Egyptologists, and soldiers from the 18th and 19th centuries. One was from a mercenary in Napoleon's army, another the signature of a senior British diplomat from 1820. 'This is Greek,' he said, pointed to something scratched on a pillar, 'and this belongs to . . . Alexander the Great.'

Inside the priest's sanctum stood a vast stone shrine, into which had been carved – in ancient hieroglyphs – the name of *Alexandros*. 'He stood in this exact spot,' said Ibrahim, once again welling up. 'Doesn't it make you feel humble?'

I couldn't help but agree. Four thousand years of name-carving, artwork, defacing and tit-for-tat scribbling showed that the human condition – the endless desire to leave one's mark on the world – hadn't changed across the aeons. I'd seen the same at the Pyramids of Meroe.

'And now for the *pièce de résistance*,' said Ibrahim, now back to his bouncing, enthusiastic self. He led me around the side of the shrine to where human and godlike figures were carved in a beautiful example of late era pre-Ptolemaic art. 'This is Min, the god of fertility.' I could see why. The figure of a man stood proud, pointing rudely at Alexander's signature. 'Look how big he is!' grinned Ibrahim. 'It's the biggest member I've ever seen. They say if you wish for good luck and children and point at it, your wishes will be fulfilled. I used to bring the Japanese ladies here, it makes them blush . . .'

Outside, we made our way to the riverside and rejoined Turbo.

'Are you ready to hit the road, Lev?'

I wasn't sure that I was. At least in Luxor there were moments – a precious few, but there were still some – when I didn't feel the police crowing at my shoulder, and didn't have to dance for the ministries as I made my way north. My legs were aching, my feet seemed to have permanently changed shape from the months of endless walking, and the frustration of being scrutinised every step of the way was adding a new dimension to the pain. Even so, Cairo was our next big stop – and, after that, it was only a short hike to the Rashid and the Mediterranean Sea. I took a deep breath, thanked Ibrahim for his counsel, and told him we'd see him further north, in his home city of Cairo.

One last push and I would almost be home.

*

Eighteen days, I cursed to myself, ignoring the police over one shoulder, thinking of Turbo somewhere up ahead. Eighteen days to cover the six-hundred and sixty-six kilometres between here and Cairo. I had to be crazy to even attempt it – but those were the rules set down by the Ministry of Tourism, and the expedition would be ruined if I failed.

Miserably, I continued into the north.

Thirty-four thousand dollars, Turbo had told me, only afforded me forty-five days of 'supervision'. Leaving aside the fact that being heckled by a group of bored, invidious policemen hardly counted as 'supervision', this left me with less than three weeks to reach Cairo. It was not going to be easy. It wasn't that I'd never covered thirty-seven kilometres a day before – Boston and I had done it regularly, pushing up through Rwanda, Tanzania and Uganda. But that was before my body was broken. Somehow, I hadn't accounted for the idea that my body might start to rebel along the way. It was, I supposed, the same trick an athlete's mind plays on his body at the three quarter point of a race – as I approached the finishing line, I was hitting 'the wall'. Each morning, I woke in agony, unable to even walk to breakfast. This morning, it had taken an hour of unbearable pain, hobbling slowly along, before I could convince my brain to stop sending pain receptors to my legs and just get on with the job at hand – and, all the while, I could hear the policemen barracking me from their car, tempting me to climb in.

Late in the afternoon, on the outskirts of a small riverside town, I caught up with Turbo. As he had every day of this interminable march, he handed me a can of soda, filled with sugars to restore my electrolytes, and a handful of painkillers. I hated it, but I was on a steady diet of them now – a chunky dose of paracetamol and ibuprofen with every meal of refried beans and boiled egg. We had reached the stretches of Middle Egypt, where people seemed to live as their forefathers had done for generations – men in shades of white tilling the land along the Nile, still working their fields with buffalo-drawn ploughs, while women in black flitted between the shadows of half-obscured gardens.

'Are you okay, Lev?'

He asked it every time and, like every time, I didn't answer. With the end of the journey in sight, somehow it seemed further away than ever; perhaps that was why I was at my wits' end. I'd lost a lot of weight on this journey, my stomach had shrunk so that only one or two small meals a day seemed enough – and, though I tried to find small moments of beauty every day, it had become a constant battle. With the eyes of the policemen on my back, and the insanity of jumping into a car each night to be forcibly ferried to the nearest guesthouse, I was tired of living in this government-controlled farce.

'I miss it, Turbo.'

'Miss what?'

'What it was like much further upriver. The serendipity of the walk – of meeting people, *different* people, of expecting the unexpected, of . . . Look, I came here to discover Egypt, but I can't even speak to a local without that lot . . .' I gestured at the policemen still idling somewhere behind '. . . interrupting. I want to get under the skin of Egypt, the *real* Egypt, not just the version the government wants me to see.'

'Wait until Cairo, Lev. Ibrahim will show you the real Cairo.'

'Cairo's still two weeks away.'

'Well, what do you want to know?'

'Take . . . *this*,' I said. On the side of one of the buildings was a familiar piece of graffiti: the stencilled image of a four-fingered hand. I'd seen it often since we left Luxor, and still didn't know what it meant.

'It's the sign that shows solidarity with the victims of Rabaa,' Turbo explained, solemn for the first time.

'Rabaa?'

'The Rabaa Massacre. It's almost a year ago to the day. Wherever you see the four fingers, that's shouting out to the victims. It's a pro-Morsi signal. It's Muslim Brotherhood.'

The Rabaa Massacre had occurred on 14 August 2013, in one of Cairo's major squares. For six weeks, protestors in support of President Morsi, who had been ousted from office at the start of July, occupied the square – and, when talks had failed to move them on, the army intervened. At least 638 people were killed that day – though the Muslim Brotherhood put the figure at more than 2,600. Of all the swirling information and misinformation there is about the massacre, all sides agree on one thing: this was the most deadly day in Egypt since the revolution of 2011 that had first brought Morsi to power.

'I've seen other graffiti, too . . . *CC. Donkey. Pig.*'

'That's anti-Sisi graffiti. Sisi, CC, get it? All of Egypt's the same, Lev – half of them wanted Morsi, half of them didn't. Half of us want Sisi, half of us don't. It's the same up and down the Nile – no one side ever wins the day, and that's why we've had two revolutions . . .'

He was right. Later that day, as we tramped on, I saw Egyptian flags flying from the houses of one village, pictures of the incumbent leader plastered on every wall – while, in the next, the four-fingered hand was daubed onto the sides of houses. The pattern of support and dissent seemed to alternate with every mile.

It was late when I came to the outskirts of a village called Al-Kush. For the first time in what felt like days, my police minders were leaving me alone; some time ago, they had cruised past, up the road, eager to turn in early for the night. As I came between the first houses, a collection of tall, roughly made mud-brick structures, a gaggle of men appeared between two buildings and darted away from the road. Moments later, a burst of automatic gunfire penetrated the silence from only a few hundred metres away. Instinctively, I scurried for the safety of the nearest wall. Using it for cover, I waited for the gunfire to die away and looked up, desperate to know what was going on. An old woman looked on from a nearby garden, seemingly unperturbed by the fracas, her suspicion reserved solely for this strange man hunkered down behind the garden wall.

In that moment, a car came screeching down the street, heading straight for me. Adrenaline hit me, I prepared to take flight – but it was only Turbo, hanging half out of the 4×4 as it ground to a halt.

'Did you hear that?' I yelled, as he tumbled onto the road.

'Hear what?'

'The gunfire . . .'

'I just saw a load of guys with guns running into the fields. They looked like Muslim Brotherhood, so I thought I'd come back and check on you . . .'

'Where are those police, the only time you need them?'

But Turbo only gave a crumpled grin. 'I'm glad they're not here. It's probably the police those Brothers are shooting at.' He paused. 'Either that, or a really wild wedding. Well, you did say you wanted to get under Egypt's skin, didn't you, Lev?'

Battered and bruised I might have been, but on 20 August 2014, almost nine months since I tasted the Nile's first waters in the Nyungwe forest, I stumbled into the smoggy suburbs of Africa's biggest city. After endless days tramping north through traditional villages, corn fields and tall date palms, it was surreal to see the skyscrapers of Cairo hanging in the skyline. This was a city of twenty million people, a true metropolis, and I was walking into it a broken man.

As Turbo ferried me into the centre, through the affluent western suburb of Zamalek, all I could see through the windows were plush hotels, fancy restaurants and upscale yacht clubs. Turbo gestured at the unveiled Egyptian girls shopping for designer handbags in the boutique stores and, at once, I was reminded of Paris or Rome. Somehow, in only a moment, I'd been sucked out of my voyage and unceremoniously dumped back into the modern world. The idea that I was close to Europe, close to home, welled up inside me. Digital billboards shone down, electric taxicabs whizzed by – and, by the time Turbo left me at the hotel, I could quite imagine the end of the expedition; only a few short days of walking were left between here and the coast.

In the morning, rested but not healed, I was met by Ibrahim in the hotel lobby. As he had been at Luxor, he was eager to show me around his home city. Cairo is one of the oldest cities in Africa, its modern-day incarnation founded in 969AD on the site of a settlement much older yet, that of Ancient Memphis. This was the city from which the tourists who once flocked to Egypt would set out to see the magnificent Pyramids of Giza, or the Great Sphinx itself – but it was a very different side of Cairo that Ibrahim wanted to show me. As we set out into this 'city of a thousand minarets', he turned to me and said, 'I'm taking you to see a side of Cairo most tourists won't ever hear of.' He paused. 'Lev, I'm taking you to Al Zabaleen – *Garbage City.*'

Leaving the centre of Cairo, Ibrahim led me to the hilly suburb of Mokattam. Unlike the heart of Cairo, with its gleaming skyscrapers, ornate Islamic minarets and digital billboards as bright and garish as Piccadilly Circus or Time Square, Mokattam was a sprawling shanty town. Yet, Ibrahim had another way of describing it. 'This is Cairo's Christian ghetto,' he said. 'There are thirty thousand Coptics living here.'

'The word *Copt* means *Egyptian*,' Ibrahim explained as he led me into the shanty's winding roads. 'It was an Ancient Egyptian word for the temple at Memphis, Het-Ka-Ptah, the "place of the soul of the creator God" – but it got bastardised by the Ancient Greeks into *Aigyptos*. Hence, Copt. And, of course, until the Arabs invaded, Egypt had been Christian for three hundred years. Mary and Joseph took the baby Jesus on a grand tour of the Nile. I bet you didn't know that! They probably saw Memphis and the Pyramids, Alexandria . . .'

We walked on, deeper into the shanties.

'In Egypt, the Christians have to stick together – for protection. With all the violence against us in the last sixty years, Christians from all across Upper and Middle Egypt have come to places like this to live together. Not that it's stopped the violence. Last year alone, eighty-five churches were burnt down by Muslim gangs, and all because we didn't support that terrorist Morsi. So . . . now look what terrible conditions these garbage-collectors are forced to live in. Me, I'm lucky – I have a little money – but these people, they have nothing.'

The reason Ibrahim had called this Garbage City quickly became clear. As we ventured deeper into the shanties, I could see the streets marked by piles and piles of rubbish. Men were flitting between the heaps, sifting through the detritus and taking barrows of it back to their houses. Children as young as three were joining them, picking up bottles and bottle-tops and collecting them in different piles. Old women were bent double, sorting out cardboard into small bales.

'What are they doing?' I asked.

'They're doing what they must to survive, Lev. These people are recycling. The whole community takes part. Plastic in one bag, metal in another. It's how the Coptic Christians keep going. The government pays them one dollar for every twenty kilograms of sifted plastic. Cardboard's even less.'

'It's a shame nobody thinks about the organic waste, too,' I said, holding my breath against the stench.

'It didn't used to be so filthy here. The Christians used to keep pigs here. They'd keep the streets clean of all the waste, just by eating it away. But then the government came along and told them they all had to be killed. Swine flu, they said, but the real reason . . .? Well, because the Muslim neighbours complained. So now Cairo is filthy again – and all because they won't let Christians keep pigs. Now, all the shit just gets thrown into the Nile. Your beautiful Nile, Lev. These people are killing it for their religion.'

We stood in silence for some time, watching the locals work.

'Come on,' said Ibrahim, threatening to shed another tear. 'There's someone I'd like you to meet.'

Taking my hand, Ibrahim led me through more narrow streets where barefoot children stood in the doorways, waving as we passed. Coptic priests sauntered like bearded angels through the shadows and religious icons hung from ropes slung across the streets. In the sprawl, donkey carts, driven by small boys, delivered yet more rubbish for the locals to sift through.

After some time we stopped before the face of a half-finished apartment block, and Ibrahim led me up a forbidding set of stairs, loose wires dangling down like dead spiders' legs. On the second floor, we arrived at a wooden door, already hanging open.

'Yasser?' yelled my guide – and, at once, a man approached from the shadows within. Barefoot, in old grey trousers and a sleeveless vest, he had one of the saddest faces I'd ever seen. He extended his hand in embarrassed welcome. 'Come in,' he said, staring at the ground as he spoke.

'*Shaay?*' he asked, unable to look me in the eyes.

'Thank you,' I replied, and he shuffled away to make it.

When he returned, I sat on a low sofa, on which were arranged a collection of brightly coloured stuffed toys. The living room was tiny, barely enough space for the sofa and a small table – and it was only when Yasser opened the curtains, allowing daylight to spill in, that I understood the reason for his shyness. He was hideously disfigured.

As he turned to us, I couldn't help but look at the scars across his face. Several of his fingers were missing, and for the first time I realised he had been walking with a pronounced limp. Nobody said a word, as if daring me to ask. I turned, instead, to Ibrahim.

'You wanted to understand the Copts,' he said. 'Well, here's a Copt. Ask him anything you want. Ask him why he is the way he is. He won't mind.'

In the window, Yasser stood with shards of light across his ruptured features. On the wall behind him was a large poster depicting the Last Supper. Sensing my reluctance to ask, he began to speak. 'It was a Tuesday,' he said, softly. 'The 8th of March 2011. I was driving back from my work as a garbage collector. It was late, almost midnight, when they stopped me in the road. A gang of men, all of them Muslims, all of them with big beards, even though they were young. They can't have been more than twenty-two, twenty-three. One of them asked if I was a Christian or Muslim.' He paused, the memory so painful to bear. 'I couldn't lie. I told them I was Christian.'

Yasser faltered, turned away from me and stared out of the window. Raising a stumpy hand, he wiped away a tear. As he began to shake, Ibrahim went to his shoulder, whispering some words of consolation into his ear. Whatever he said, it seemed to give Yasser strength. He left the window and came to sit beside me.

'I didn't know at the time what had happened. There had been fighting between the Muslims and the Copts, after our boys made a protest against the Muslims burning our churches. That was when the

Muslims started to attack our areas. They dragged me out of my car and set it on fire. Then they beat me – first with sticks, then with a metal pole. Then . . . they took a sword and tried to cut off my head.' He drew a half-finger across a perfect line that ran across his face, from ear to ear, just below his eyes. 'After that, I was on the ground – but that didn't stop them.' Slowly, Yasser began to undress, revealing the full horror of his torture. Across his back were the wounds where he'd been stabbed and whipped with wire and chains. On his legs were the slashes the Muslim boys had made with their sword, and in his groin and shoulders were yet more stab wounds. They'd even torn the skin off his buttocks, trampled his kneecaps, cracked his skull in three places with the pommel of the sword. 'After they were done, they rolled me up in a sack and dumped me in a skip. They thought I was dead. They were putting me out with the rubbish, saying we Christians are nothing but filth.' Yasser paused, choking up. 'But I was rescued. A man came and saw the sack was wriggling. It was me inside, covered in blood, my brains hanging out in the bin. That man took me to hospital. It was two weeks before I woke.'

Yasser was visibly shaking now, but I didn't have a thing to say.

'I haven't told anyone the full story,' he admitted. 'Not even my wife and children know what really happened. I haven't been able to work since. I don't like leaving the house any more.'

The only words I had were pathetic, useless things: 'I'm sorry . . .' I said.

'It is God's will,' Yasser breathed. 'I must forgive them. They know not what they do.' At this, he wiped away another tear, leaving me uncertain whether he believed it or not. 'I hope God will forgive them, too,' he said as Ibrahim and I readied to leave him in the dark recess of his bedsit. 'But that,' he said, finally, 'is none of my business.'

*

Despite being one of the most infuriating, bureaucratic and frustrating countries to walk across that I had ever encountered, I couldn't help but feel in awe of the welcome I received at the Pyramids of Giza. The night before I was due to leave the city I'd been summoned by the Minister of Antiquities, Mr Mamdouh Eldamaty, who said he'd got a little something for me.

I won't even attempt to describe the last remaining ancient wonder of the world, except to say that the pyramids here are the most inspiring human structures on earth. You can imagine my surprise then when I turned up at dusk, just as the enormous yellow tombs were being lit up for the evening sound and light show. 'Straighten your collar,' said Ibrahim with a beaming grin. That afternoon he'd insisted on taking me shopping to buy a jacket and some smart shoes, but it was all part of the surprise. I couldn't have expected what I found.

Beyond the new wall that divides the rickety city of Giza from the boundaries of the desert, a walkway led past the ticket office to an open space right in front of the Sphinx itself. There must have been well over a hundred chairs placed facing the looming giant, and every one of them was filled.

There were journalists, well-wishers, film crews, soldiers as well as the ambassadors of all the countries I'd walked through, the British Ambassador John Casson, the governor of Giza and of course the ministers of tourism and antiquities, and all of them stood to welcome me and bade me sit at the front with the glowing pyramids against a starry desert night behind me.

I was overwhelmed by the incredible support I'd received, not to mention a little embarrassed by all the attention. I knew Egypt wanted to use my expedition as a means to promote tourism and show the world that the country is safe, and, well, good on them. I hope that the tourists do come back – Lord knows the Egyptians need them. So for all the theatrics and political platitudes, I was truly humbled to have been received by so many rather important people in the same spot that Napoleon and Alexander had once stood gazing up at one of the most magnificent human creations on the planet.

The ambassador, governor and ministers all gave short speeches in praise of my little stroll and made gifts of more plaques to add to my luggage-allowance-burgeoning collection but it was the words of Ibrahim that meant the most to me.

'It isn't the walk that's important, or the politics, or what you show to your people, or even the sense of achievement that you'll get – it's what you learn yourself, deep inside. And I hope you've learned that Egyptians, like people everywhere along this great river will look after you.'

I wanted to say that perhaps they had kept me too safe, but decided it was churlish, and actually he had a point. Whatever people's politics or religion, I had been looked after, here and elsewhere. In Sudan and further South it was the normal people that I had met day to day that had shown me the importance of the kindness of strangers, without which I could never have reached this historic place.

'Not far now, Lev. Are those legs going to make it?'

'They have to,' I said taking one last look behind towards the infamous Tahrir Square, where the headquarters of the ousted President Mubarak still stood as a charred black skeleton, a symbol of a dark past, a revolutionary present and an uncertain future. Ahead, to the north, the Nile unfolded through the suburbs, flanked by industry and progress and beyond it, the delta I had dreamed of for so long. Behind me my police escort revved their engine as a signal for me to get on with it.

We had lingered in Cairo for four days, but now it was time to leave. On the outskirts of the city, Turbo drove on ahead to check the route and warn army roadblocks of our arrival. It seemed that even with all the right paperwork in place you could never safely assume that the message had been passed on. The police would be on my tail every step of the way but, for the first time, that wasn't at the front of my mind. There were only two hundred kilometres left between me and the port of Rashid, where I would finally meet the sea. I didn't care about blisters or chafing any more; I was about to enter the delta.

The Nile Delta is the epitome of man's mastery over nature. Once a vast swamp, it is now one of the most productive and fertile agricultural regions in the world. As I soon discovered, it is also one of the most densely populated.

North of Cairo, the delta truly begins, the Nile parting into two great channels, each bound for the sea. I had chosen to walk the western channel, meeting Rashid – or as it is more famously known, Rosetta – two hundred kilometres further on, simply because it was longer, and because I wanted to end my journey beside the city of Alexandria, in honour of Alexander the Great, who had spent so many years pondering the secrets of the river. For six days, I tramped through increasing humidity, following the main roads which weave between the two channels. Here, the highways thronged with traffic, the pavements still thick with the carcasses of abandoned animals. Street dogs, the ones that weren't rotting on the pavements, barked viciously as I passed, and, on more than one occasion I was chased by a swarm of angry bees, bent on expelling this foreign intruder from their neighbourhood. My minders trailed me constantly, in a variety of police cars, motorbikes, and tuk-tuks – but, oblivious to them at last, I fixed my thoughts on the sea and continued to walk. All I could think about was the end.

It was 30 August when I finally arrived, dishevelled but elated, at the port of Rashid. Like so many Egyptian towns I'd passed through, Rashid was a hive of narrow medieval lanes and tall mud-brick houses. It was here that the secret to deciphering Egyptian hieroglyphs was first uncovered, because Rashid was once home to the celebrated Rosetta Stone. I stopped for tea at the fortress in which it had once been housed. It hadn't been here for two hundred years though – instead residing in the British Museum ever since it was 'discovered' by a French soldier in 1799, much to the chagrin of the Egyptian authorities – but, for now, I was glad to be here, only a short skip from the end. Men in turbans gazed at me as I relaxed, and I greeted every single one with the most enthusiastic *Salaam* I could muster. When I was restored and took off again, children ran after me as they played. Fishermen, mending their nets in rusty doorways, looked at me curiously. Taxis vied for the roads with donkeys and carts, and market vendors cried out with offers of melons and mobile phones. Like everywhere else in Africa, this was a place where the old world met the new.

I clung to the river, now wider than since the delta began, and filled with fishing boats and nets. Above, there circled my very first seagull. Out on the river, the water was choppy and waves, stirred by the wind, crashed against the rocks below the promenade. Lost in a daydream, I thought back to the start of the expedition. Two hundred and seventy-one days ago, I'd stood with Boston above the tiny trickle in the middle of the Nyungwe Forest. It felt like a lifetime had passed since then. I knelt down and trailed my hand in the river. I could hardly believe that this was the same water that had emerged out of that muddy crevice months before and thousands of miles away.

The police were still watching. I let them. I didn't care.

Ahead, the river widened even further as it made its final push to the sea. I'd imagined I would see it by now – the glittering expanse of the Mediterranean had lingered so long in my imagination – but the horizon was concealed by a concrete wave defence, obscuring all sight of the sea. All I could do was follow the road. Soon, with the town diminishing behind, the road petered out, the palm trees and fields slowly disappearing until only a barren waste-ground stretched out in front of me. Bunkers and barbed-wire trenches pitted the land, as if left over from some long-forgotten war.

I heard the sound of waves: stronger and stronger, crashing against the other side of the flood defences, seemingly growing angrier at my approach. This wasn't how I'd imagined the expedition would end. I'd been dreaming of an idyllic palm-fringed beach – but, instead, I tramped into a militarised no-man's-land. I supposed it would just have to do.

Readying myself for the final walk to the concrete barrage, I looked back over my shoulder. I would walk this last few hundred metres alone, but behind me a growing crowd had started to keep pace: not just Turbo, and not just my police minders; here were other guards in uniform, journalists, generals from the army – even the governor of Beheira province had descended for the expedition's final moments. Like every other governor I'd met, he was dressed in a black suit and shades that made him look like a clichéd movie mafioso. Whatever I was about to achieve by setting foot in the ocean, he wanted to be part of it.

The path narrowed. Now, it was nothing but a thin streak of tarmac leading up to the wave break. That thick line of concrete had become my entire world: the end of the river, the end of a continent – and, for me, the end of a very long walk.

As I approached it, I didn't hear the journalists baying behind. I didn't hear the policemen, nor Turbo shouting his encouragement. The truth was, I was only half here. The rest of me was scattered, back across Africa, back along the river from which I had come. From which, in a sense, all humanity had come. Images were flickering through my head, the faces of all the people who had made this journey so wonderful: of Boston and Amani, meandering in the Nyungwe; of the porters who had abandoned us in the Tanzanian bush; of Moses and the AIDS orphanage in Kasansero; of the absurd reception on the shores of Lake Kyoga. I saw myself tramping with swollen tongue and lips through the heat of the Bayuda, with Moez and Ahmad and Awad lurching behind. I saw the frightened faces of the civilians scattering in Bor, the hordes of refugees making the best of it in their makeshift camps at Minkaman. And there, hanging in my memory, were the faces of Matt Power and Jason Florio, back on that blighted hillside in northern Uganda; the smell of fire and the sound of a dialling tone, as we scrambled to get help.

Lost in those memories, I reached the wave break. Up close, it appeared as a vast pile of concrete boulders. There was only one memory left for me now: the thought of the magical Nile, the river that had ultimately defeated me, like it had so many others. Perhaps, I thought, the river just doesn't want to be conquered. Perhaps it never will.

Standing on top of the wave break, I could finally look out across the Mediterranean Sea. Europe felt close – and, with it, home. Elated to have made it, I stood there for what felt like an age, while the journalists, policemen and other assorted officials thronged behind me. It wasn't until they were all shouting for attention that I realised: my elation had given way to something else. It was real sadness that was touching me now. There was nowhere left to walk. The sea, brooding and black and empty crashed against the pile of concrete below me.

I turned and shook hands with Turbo. 'Well done, Lev, you made it.'

But there was something I still had to do.

'I promised myself a beach, Turbo. So I'm going to find a beach.'

With the rabble of followers trailing behind, I walked west, back along the track and around the bay until, at last, we came across a strip of sand.

'Here's your tropical paradise, Lev,' said Turbo with a mischievous grin.

It was hardly that, I thought, looking across the dismal gravel filled with sun brollies and loungers, but it would have to do. At once, I took off, scrambling down the stones to reach the sand. Several hundred bewildered sunbathers turned to see what the commotion was – but I was already off, running headlong into the gathering waves and plunging into the foaming surf. The water was cold. It hit me like waking from a dream. I took another step, and another, and another – until, at last, I was fully submerged. The walking was done with. The expedition was at an end.

I was gazing into the sun-drenched north, thinking of Europe beyond, when the cheers rang out across the coast. At first, I took them for the cheers of the rabble who'd followed me – and indeed they were. But there was another voice, undercutting all the rest. 'Stop!' somebody was crying. 'Stop!' Between the cries came the shrill blasts of a whistle.

I looked back, at the hundreds of bemused faces staring at me from the beach. Through them all came one man: an Egyptian, in lifeguard's clothing.

'You're outside of the safe zone!' he screamed, waving his hands around like a madman. 'You are not permitted to be here!'

I looked up. It seems I'd been caught out by bureaucracy yet again.

It was a very strange end to a very strange journey.

ACKNOWLEDGEMENTS

Caput Nili Quaerere was an Ancient Roman metaphor that translates into 'to Search for the source of the Nile'. It was applied to anything that was deemed unsolvable, mad or impossible. I think that the same could be said for trying to acknowledge all of the individuals that helped me along the way.

For the outside observer it would be easy to imagine that one man's pedestrian journey is simply a lone walk into the wilderness. Nothing could be further from the truth. There simply isn't enough space here to give personal thanks to all those kind hosts that I met along the Nile who housed me in the villages and fed me, despite in many cases not having enough food for themselves. And of course there is the team, friends and family that supported me behind the scenes, and without whose constant backing I wouldn't have even been able to set off in the first place.

Personal thanks, however, must go, in no particular order, to the following people:

Ndoole Boston , Moez Mahir and Mahmoud 'Turbo' Ezzeldin, who were so much more than guides, they became my eyes and ears into the places I passed through and ultimately friends for life. The team at October Films, especially Adam Bullmore, Matt Robins and Martin Long, who made my dream into a reality, and, of course, Jamie Berry and Neil Bonner, whose directorship and creative genius somehow not just created thousands of hours of footage, but turned that into a watchable television series. Tom McShane, whose leadership and logistics in the field made the expedition as smooth as it could be. He takes amazing photographs, too. There simply wasn't enough space in this book to include all the adventures we had as a team and reluctantly, I had to exclude the many stories we shared, but the reader must be aware that for several weeks along the way, I was joined by these three gentlemen who not only kept me company but kept me sane, too.

I am indebted to Tom Bodkin, whose patience and resolve as a business partner and friend has enabled Secret Compass to grow into the most exciting adventure travel company in the business; Group M and Animal Planet must be thanked for their financial assistance, and Channel 4 – in Particular John Hay – for believing in the project in the first place. For the entire team at Simon & Schuster, especially Abigail Bergstrom. Mike Jones, who gave the book its impetus, and the team at Campbell Bell Communications who provided PR assistance. Thanks also to the several sponsors who gave financial and material support: Chivas Regal whisky, Country Attire, Bremont watches, Berghaus outdoor gear, RailRiders clothing, Know Malaria, Nomad travel and Secret Compass. I must also make mention and thanks to the charities with whom I partnered and chose to support for their reciprocal help along the way: Tusk Trust, Space for Giants, ABF The Soldiers' Charity, and the AMECA trust.

Special thanks indeed must go to those friends who used up valuable leave to visit me and walk for parts of the journey, especially Will Charlton, Ash Bhardwaj, who wrote several articles about the expedition; Jason Florio, who was with me in Uganda for the most tragic episode; John Copeland and Susie Cain. Enormous thanks, too, of course, for those individuals who let me stay on sofas and floors and for those who gave me moral encouragement in the months and years building up to, during, and after the expedition; Sir Ranulph Fiennes, Ed Stafford, Bear Grylls, Michael Asher, Tim Butcher, Shane Winser, David Higgins, Maegan Tillock, Pete Wright, Chris Mahoney, Ibrahim Morgan, Dennis Kakande, Simon Clarke, Kara Blackmore, Charlie Bell, Emma Challinor, Wamale Siraje, Andy Belcher, Michael Woodward, Kate Page, Pete Meredith, Col. Andrew Seguye, Briony Turner, Ruthie Markus, Charlie Mayhew, Mary-Jane Attwood, Midhat and Mazar Mahir, Abdallah Houmouda, the team at the MSSG and the late Alex Coutselous. Thanks to Ceci Alonzo, who was a pillar of support for so long, and of course, Pete and my parents, who never doubted that I'd complete the journey, even when *I* did.

Finally, I thank Rob Dinsdale for his skill in helping me turn a jumble of memories and scribbles into an actual book and, of course, my agents Jo Cantello and Ben Mason for their unwavering drive and mentorship throughout.

INDEX

The furthest source of the Nile in the Nyungwe Forest in Rwanda

Rwanda, land of a thousand hills

The Nyabarongo River cuts a swathe through Rwanda. The source of the Nile remains contested

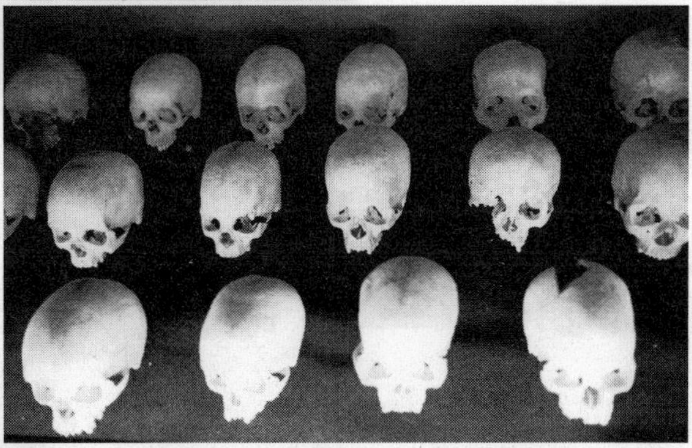

Photographs of the victims of the Rwandan genocide fill the Kigali genocide museum

Gisovu Prison. A million people were killed during a 100 day period in 1994

Children shelter from rain in a Rwandan village. Outside of Kigali the country remains desperately impoverished

Ndoole Boston walked with me as guide and translator from December 2013 until March 2014

With Boston resting in Tanzania

The remains of Christmas lunch
alongside Lake Bisongu in Tanzania

Lake Bisongu in the wild bandit country
of Kagera, north-west Tanzania

Much of the journey was spent
wild camping

The remains of a 6 metre Python killed by villagers on the shores of Lake Victoria after it ate a prized goat

Camping near to villages in Uganda always invited a curious crowd

Water, not always accessible from the Nile due to stagnant swamps, is a precious commodity in rural Uganda. People travel huge distances to find a well

A typical Ugandan village scene

Illegal snares recovered from the Murchison Falls National Park by rangers of the Uganda Wildlife Authority

Poaching is rife across East Africa as human populations extend deeper into animal habitats. Trade in bush meat has brought some species to the verge of extinction

Vast areas of savannah and forest are being cut down and burnt at alarming rates as the demand for charcoal and sugar cane increases

In northern Uganda Kakwa children hunt for bush rat and small antelope with homemade bows

Florence, (later renamed Samuel after a biological oversight) the vervet monkey I rescued on the Victoria Nile, joined the expedition for several days before being taken in by Entebbe Wildlife Centre

Elephants in Murchison Falls National Park. Although populations are recovering here slowly, across Africa the ivory trade means that they are severely endangered and could be extinct in the wild within ten years unless poaching is stopped

Walking through the Murchison Falls National Park, home to Africa's densest populations of hippos and crocodiles

Murchison Falls, named by Samuel Baker in 1864 in his quest for the source of the Nile

Jason Florio and Matt Power, the day before Matt tragically died

Mundari cattle camp near Terekeka on the edge of the Sudd Swamp, South Sudan

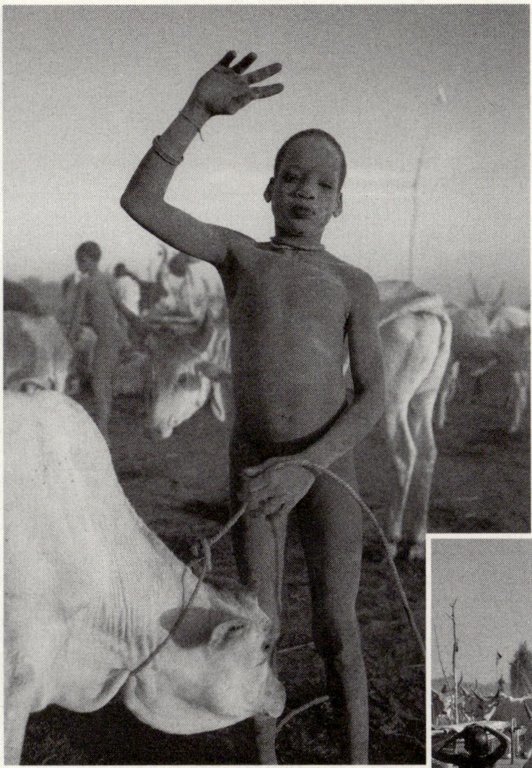

Cattle are the primary source of wealth in South Sudan and are revered and fought over by the main tribal groups

Getting thoroughly defeated in traditional Mundari wrestling

Herdsmen in South Sudan use ash made from burnt cow dung to cover their skin as protection against sun and mosquitoes

Bor town, South Sudan. It was the front line of the civil war for several weeks in early 2014 and much of the town was destroyed in the fighting

One of the SPLA minders escorting me in South Sudan

The bank in Bor had been looted several times as government forces and rebels fought to regain control. The date stamps indicate when the town changed hands

Moez Mahir walked with me across the whole of Sudan

After crossing the Sahara desert

The Bayuda Desert in Sudan where temperatures regularly exceeded 50 degrees

Setting up camp in the shadows of the Pyramids of Meroe, capital of the Kushitic Kingdom

The Pyramids of Meroe, unlike their Egyptian counterparts, don't get many visitors

The tops of the Pyramids were blown off with dynamite after the tomb raider Giuseppe Ferlini came in search of gold in 1834

Awad and Ahmad of the Bedouin Hawawir tribe joined the expedition to look after the camels for 46 days

Camels (left to right) Speke, Gordon and Burton

With Mahmoud 'Turbo' Ezzeldin in Upper Egypt

Walking around Lake Nasser, the formidable reservoir formed after the creation of the Aswan High Dam in 1964, which flooded ancient Nubia and caused the resettlement of over 50,000 people

Moored Nile cruise ships indicate a decimated tourism economy. Only one of the original 300 remained in service in the summer of 2014

Rubbish collectors in El Zabaleen in Cairo, one of the country's Christian enclaves

Nearing the finish at Rashid, surrounded by a military escort and the governor of Beheira

The end. The Mediterranean Sea after walking almost 4,000 miles

N
W
E
S
MEDITERRANEAN SEA
CAIRO
SUEZ
EGYPT
LUXO
ASWA
Nile
SUDAN
Meroë
KHARTOUM
White Nile
Blue
SOUTH SUDAN
JUBA
UGANDA
JINJA
LAKE VICTORIA
RWANDA
KIGALI
NYUNGWE FOREST
BURUNDI
TANZAN

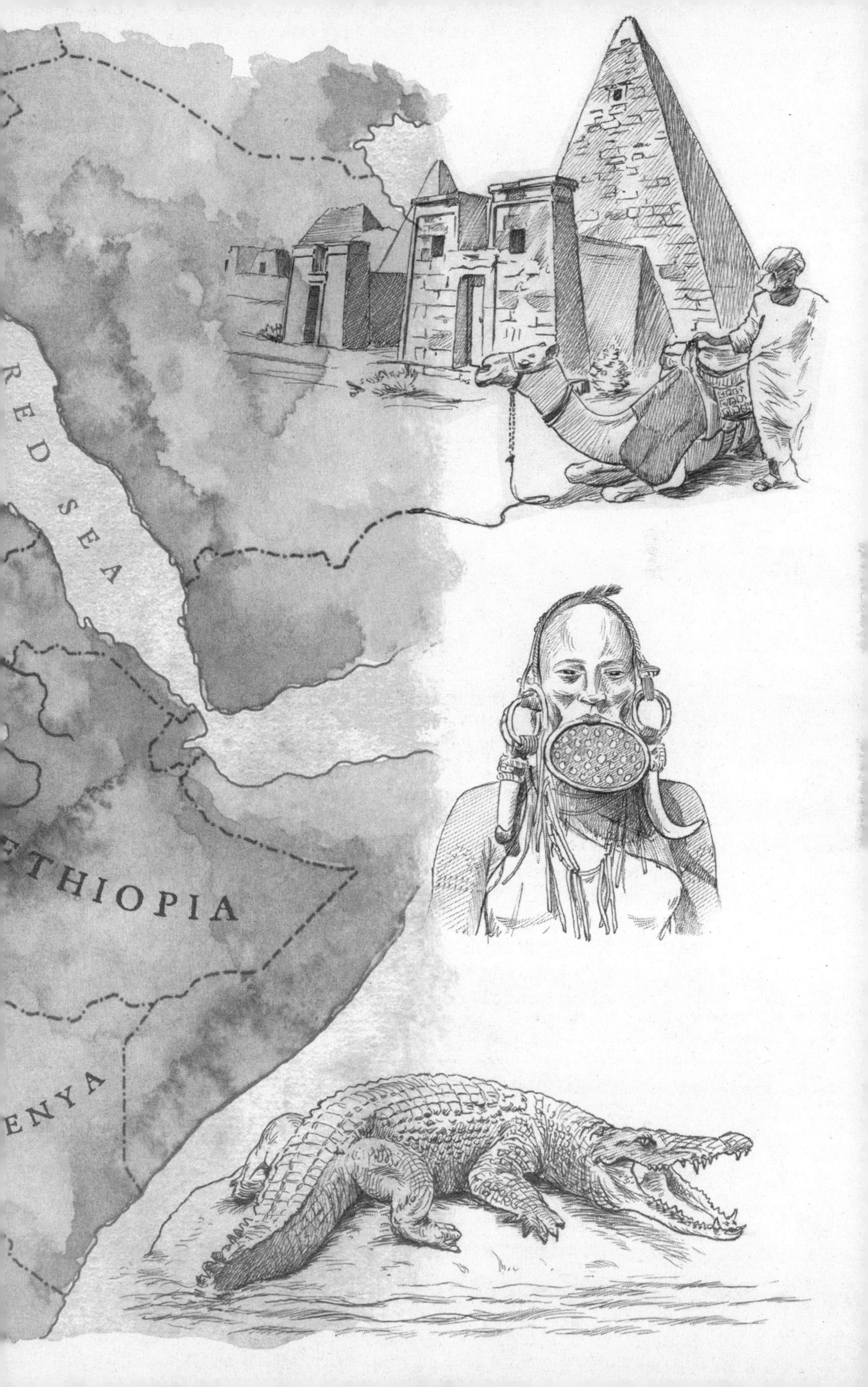
RED SEA
ETHIOPIA
ENYA

ABOUT THE AUTHOR

Levison Wood is a writer and explorer. Having travelled in over 80 countries, he documents the journeys of tribal peoples and minority groups around the world. He served as an officer in the British Army Parachute Regiment, with operational experience in Afghanistan and training missions around the world. His expeditions have taken him from the deserts of North Africa, to the mountains of Central Asia and the jungles of South America. He is a co-founder of Secret Compass, has led pioneering treks across Madagascar and Iraq, and is the first man to attempt to walk the length of the Nile. Levison is a Fellow of the Royal Geographical Society and International Fellow of the Explorers Club. He was born in Staffordshire in 1982 and educated at the University of Nottingham and the Royal Military Academy Sandhurst.